HOW TO WRITE FILM SCREENPLAYS

HOW TO WRITE FILM SCREENPLAYS

ILLUSTRATIONS FOR ASPIRING SCREENPLAY WRITERS AND READERS

NIRMAL KUMAR CHAWDHARY

KANISHKA PUBLISHERS, DISTRIBUTORS
NEW DELHI-110 002

KANISHKA PUBLISHERS, DISTRIBUTORS
4697/5-21A, Ansari Road, Daryaganj
New Delhi -110 002
Phones : 2327 0497, 2328 8285
Fax : 011-2328 8285
E-mail : kanishka_publishing@yahoo.co.in
kanishkabooks@gmail.com

How to Write Film Screenplays:
Illustrations for Aspiring Screenplay Writers and Readers

First Published-2009

Edition-2022

ISBN: 978-81-8457-112-7

PRINTED IN INDIA

Published by Madan Sachdeva for Kanishka Publishers, Distributors, 4697/5-21A, Ansari Road, Daryaganj, New Delhi-110002, Typeset by Sunshine Graphics, Delhi, and Printed at G.S. Printers, Delhi.

"With love to Yogita alias Dolly,
my daughter, and Bhaskar,
my son,
who always encourage
and strengthen
my resolve of creating
new stories

Preface

I had a pleasant experience to go through the stories and the accompanying screenplays, which the author has included in this book to illustrate the skills required for script writing.

With the continued explosion in the number of TV channels in India, the demand for creative multimedia content has increased manifold and this has, inter alia, necessitated large volumes of script writing work.

I hope, the book 'How to write film screenplays' would inspire numerous persons and provide to them practical 'self-help' guidelines for acquiring the skills required to become successful screenplay writer.

Mr. Nirmal Kumar Chawdhary is my colleague and I congratulate him for his brilliant effort. I wish him grand success for his future endeavours of creative writing.

Virendra Gupta, I.F.S
Additional Secretary (ITP & ES)
Ministry of External Affairs
New Delhi
[Former High Commissioner of India in Tanzania
and
Trinidad & Tobago]

Author's Note

Holly-wood and Bollywood filmmakers produce films on the basis of short stories and screenplays for which a story/screenplay writer is required to camp there for close coordination in the matter. Being a Government officer it has not been possible for me to go through the drill. That is why my four stories and their screenplays including the techniques of script writing are given in this book for you to read, enjoy and learn the skills of script writing.

Here I must express my gratitude to Miss Nabenita Deb for her excellent editorial efforts.

I hope my readers will appreciate my next venture, a novel and encourage me to create better works in future.

Nirmal Kumar Chawdhary

Abbreviations

Ext	—	Exterior
Int	—	Interior
O.S	—	Off Screen
V.O	—	Voice Over
1, 2, 3, 4....	—	Scene numbers
Cut to	—	End of a scene
Fade in	—	Opening of a scene
Fade out	—	End of a scene (Portraying a time/period)
Dissolve to	—	End of scene (start and end of a flash back)

Contents

Preface *vii*
Author's Note *ix*
Abbreviations *x*

HOW TO WRITE FILM SCREENPLAYS **1**

1. THE MYSTERIOUS COMBATANT: **12**
This depicts a challenger's powerful drive to save the earth

2. TERMINAL CONDITION: **176**
This depicts a father's resolve to save his son from a fatal disease

3. A BUNCH OF LIES: **265**
The story is set in 2020 AD about the rivalry between Iran and Iraq

4. A MOLTEN MOTIVE: **304**
This depicts hijacking of US Embassy in London

How to Write Film Screenplays

Story

A Brief

Everyone has read or heard some stories at some point of time and has drawn varied level of enjoyment due to the enormous level of emotional attachment with the characters, circumstances and dramas depicted. Stories can be termed as good, bad or worse based on the degree of emotional grip on the readers. Basically, stories contain three stages.

The first stage: Layout of the story with characters, developing situations and background.

The second stage: Building of the story with seemingly insurmountable problems and a compelling desire to solve them.

The third stage: Gradual or sudden crumbling of the hurdles to have the problems resolved to the satisfaction of readers or listeners.

There are some exceptions where stories contain two stages only leaving readers to imagine as to how the problem was finally resolved. A storywriter or storyteller is successful only when he or she is able to create good or bad characters in the garb of living things, non-living things or circumstances and bring up curiosity and maximum sympathy or hatred in favour of its characters in reader's mind.

Screenplay

A Brief

In case a story, however brief it may be, is able to give the entire expanse of a drama in the mind of a reader, this can be adapted to screenplay. A filmmaker can make a bad movie out of a good screenplay but cannot make a good movie out of a bad screenplay.

Good screenplay elicits emotion whereas bad screenplay lacks in making any impact.

- A good screenplay must create a movie in the mind of a reader. While writing a screenplay one has to be alert about the contents and dialogues on the page. Screenplay contains description, dialogue and action. Nothing can be put on a page that cannot be conveyed to an audience. Interior thoughts of a character has to be verbalized by a narrator as (V.O) 'voice over' on the screen to enable audience to hear the inner thoughts of a character, which is, however, not heard by the other characters in the scene. In the screenplay, reader cannot be told anything that an audience cannot watch on screen and hear in the sound track.

- There are **three types of screenplays.** A screenplay (without the description of camera angles) written by a writer and submitted to the film director is called **proposal script.** A film director's blueprint of a film is a screenplay that is improvised with camera angles by the director himself is called **shooting script**. A screenplay, which becomes final print record of the film after postproduction work of editors, composers and others, is called **postproduction script**. A writer has to concentrate on his proposal script only. Other tasks such as writing of shooting script or postproduction script based on the proposal script are the responsibilities of film director/editor, etc.

- While writing a screenplay, the writer should leave the parenthetical directions to the actors on the shoulder of filmmaker. If a writer himself is not the film director, he is not required to write a shooting script having camera directions. He must concentrate on fine-tuning of the description, dialogue and action to maximize the flow of writing.

Given below are some important points, which should be kept in mind while writing a screenplay.

<u>Finding story idea to write a screenplay</u>

(i) Expressing a story idea in a log line (in a single sentence) may not be difficult but creating characters and action is a big deal. An imaginative mind may at once find full-blown blossom of the characters and actions from a log line story idea. There may be a situation when spontaneous creativity may not occur and may take your constant & concerted efforts to chalk out the total expanse of story, its characters and actions. To stimulate imagination for a screenplay, it is necessary to diversify own thinking by observing others and also observe own reaction to a situation that is confronted or read for own brainstorming and creativity.

(ii) When there is no story idea to develop, one is required to find the source for potential story that may be suitable for screenplay.

(iii) **Adaptation:** Adaptation of other fictional forms such as novels, plays or short stories is mostly used for writing a screenplay as they provide an already created plot. Adaptation provides you a story plot and strength to write a screenplay by moulding it the way it is suitable for commercial use. One's own story idea gives freedom to go for its conversion into screenplay. In case of adaptation, one is required to acquire the rights from the original author or publisher to do so. The original story concept can be very old and may not be very attractive, but screenwriter has the liberty to use the concept and devise characters with new look, locations and situations to suit the movie requirements.

(iv) **Contemporary true story:** Contemporary true story can also be a source for screenplay. It is a docudrama, the depiction of an actual event in dramatic form, using actors, actresses and a full screenplay. This should not be confused with a documentary, which is filmed using on-site footage, photographs, interviews, records and so on. An adapted contemporary true story in screenplay means dramatized account of an actual event as it happens. Scripting and filming of an adapted contemporary true story requires acquisition of legal rights to do so.

(v) **Historical Events:** Historical events can also be adapted for dramatization to suit a movie making. Acquisition of legal rights is required for such dramatization of historical events except when all of the principle characters in this dramatization are deceased. In case a single book is a source of the true historical facts, its adaptation would require acquisition of legal rights from the author of that book. The strongest and most effective historical movies are those based on contemporary issues, themes, or plot situations placed in a period context, such as examining the contemporary issues of human rights and morality of war.

(vi) **Headlines:** Story topics from the headlines of newspapers, magazines, TV and radio can also be taken for creating own fictional story concepts. Headlines provide clues for brainstorming of creative imagination to make a total story, its characters and actions, which may eventually form part of a screenplay for dramatization.

(vii) **Personal Experience:** Screenwriter's own experience of an eventful journey, accident, horrible circumstances & dangerous situations can form the basis of a screenplay, which would need forceful brainstorming to make a complete story suitable for dramatization with characters and actions.

Story contents for a screenplay

A successful film necessarily requires the following in its screenplay:

(i) **A hero** : The portrayal of story must have at least one hero, the main character, who holds the story on the screen most of the time. He is a person with whom the audience is deeply involved. The hero can be a man, woman, boy, girl, animal or machine as long as it is the central focus and driving force of the story.

(ii) **Identification:** The audience must identify with the hero by putting himself/herself in the same circumstances emotionally. One must experience emotion through that character. There should be sufficient sympathy and empathy with the hero eliciting emotions from the audience through that character.

(iii) **Motivation:** A writer should be able to portray a specific, visible motivation or objective for the hero to achieve by the end of the story. The writer has to create something that the hero wants to achieve. That objective is in fact the soul of the movie. Whether it is about finding the killer, criminal, treasure, love or about winning a race, unearthing the conspiracy before being mature, successful prevention of disaster, successful disaster management, etc. Objective or motivation is very necessary to create an effective story concept, character development, plot structure and each individual scene.

(iv) **Obstacles:** Obstacles in achieving objective or motivation is also a very necessary content for an effective story concept, character development, plot structure and each individual scene. The hero must undergo a series of serious challenges, hurdles and obstacles in pursuing his motivation. Serious challenges should force the hero to go through a conflict, mental agony, pain and should draw audience to have sympathy with the hero, then the movie would turn out to be superb.

(v) **Courage:** The writer must portray hero's courage to overcome the challenges, hurdles or obstacles that hinders his objective. Hero must exhibit courage, i.e., physical, emotional or both and win the appreciation of the audience. If there is nothing put at stake for a hero or a challenge before him is not convincing enough, the audience will not get emotionally involved. If hero does not exhibit courage to overcome the difficult situation, he cannot gain the recognition of the audience. Writing screenplay and making a movie based on it means involving audience emotionally with the characters of the movie and wining their hearts.

Best story contents for a screenplay

(i) **A high concept:** The term 'high concept' is used in film industry to define a strong screenplay, where the story content alone is sufficient to attract an audience, regardless of casting, reviews or word of mouth. If logline of the story is strong enough to instill curiosity about the story, then it has a high concept, movies like 'Murder of a Mahatma' or 'World War-III', etc.

(ii) **Originality and familiarity:** The story should contain a mix of original and familiar dramas. Finding an exceptionally original story is difficult and its acceptance by a film director or producer is also very difficult as finding a director or producer having courage to risk making a movie on a subject not yet fathomed would be an insurmountable task. Contemporary true stories can be termed as original stories but it does contain familiar themes, situations or circumstances which have already been produced on earlier occasions such as political or crime thrillers, murder mystery, gangster movies, love stories, war movies or family drama with marital discord, child abuse, etc. The original elements of the story should, however, sufficiently be provocative to entice, involve and grab an audience.

(iii) **Subplots:** The original theme alone of the story may be very thin to sustain a full two or two & a half hour movie. A subplot means a second story line of equal importance to the original story concept, providing a second, equally important and visible motivation for the hero or other character of the screenplay. A subplot can be a secondary visible motivation for any of the characters in the screenplay. This story line can be of less importance than the original story concept but runs parallel to it and may or may not involve the hero. Subplots are added to give greater depth, texture, originality and meaning to the plot and theme.

(iv) **Familiarity of setting:** This adds commercial potential if the audience can identify with the setting of the concept, the time and place of the story.

(v) **Film category:** Films can be categorized on the basis of its contents such as 'Action adventure', 'War adventure', 'Patriotic drama', 'Suspense thriller', 'Love story', 'Comedy', 'Drama', 'Musicals', 'Period pieces', 'Biographies', 'Science fiction', Horror films', 'Animation films', 'Cartoon films', etc. Certain category movies make good business in a particular time or period. After Kargil conflict, films like 'Border', ' LOC', ' Lakshya' did good business.

(vi) **Cost:** If a producer is required to spend a big fortune to produce a movie based on a screenplay that chalks out a huge cost, it is likely that the producer would look for another good screenplay that does not force a huge spending. Big special effects, a huge cast, lots of exotic locations, a period or historical settings and inclement weather makes screenplay expensive to film. You may be a lucky screenwriter if a film director accepts your screenplay based on a story of a period or on historical settings, where you have depicted lavish and monumental interiors and exteriors, erection of which would cost big fortune.

There may be a situation when a director is fascinated about a story of a period or on historical setting. But he would like to make a film on this story by spending economically. He would ask you to write a screenplay that conveys the story effectively and makes powerful punch without having shot at the expensive locales or without having shot the lavish and monumental settings. In that scenario, you have to narrate the part of the story either through one of your characters or in the form of 'Voice Over' to avoid expensive shots. In this connection, you may see my screenplay titled 'A Bunch of Lies' in this book where a TV reporter conveys stories in his verbal TV reports.

(vii) **Character growth:** When a hero or any other character of the story frantically tries to find courage that results in greater self-knowledge, maturation or actualisation, the character grows. If the story concept has potential for the hero to become, through the course of the plot, a better, more aware human being, then the artistic potential of the story idea is greater.

(viii) **Theme:** The theme is an idea that an audience can apply to his/her own life, whether or not he/she has been in a similar situation. The theme is not the same as the 'message' of a movie. Theme can be the logline.

(d) Developing a screenplay:

Once a theme, logline or story concept is selected for screenplay, creating and developing the interesting characters becomes the task of the screenwriter. A screenwriter has the responsibility to write individual scenes, characters with descriptions and dialogues that creates emotions and attracts an audience to the movies. The characters are the vehicles for taking audiences on the emotional journey.

(i) **Facets of character:** Facets of character must be described to a certain degree in the screenplay. Any character consists of three basic facts (a) Physical make-ups such as age, sex, appearance and disabilities (b) Personality such as intelligence, emotional make up, etc (c) background, which depicts everything that happened to the character prior to his appearance in the screenplay. While writing facets of a character the screenwriter has either (x) a character in mind based either on reality (if it is true story or adaptation) or on the original concept or (y) to originate a character out of his imagination. If the character is a military man, he should be soft-spoken, tall, well built, strong, tough, good with a gun and a loner. Often, it is found that two different faceted characters, altogether opposite to each other, are put together, resulting in greater depth and originality for the script.

(ii) **Developing a hero:** Hero's motivation drives the plot. Hero is the central focus of the story, he is on the screen most of the time, and with whom audience relates themselves. Hero is the character around whom the entire story revolves, making it essential for screenwriter to keep him the centre of attention, identifiable and original. Facets and qualities that suit the logic and reality of the basic plot should be portrayed for a hero.

(iii) **Developing a character:** Basic concept of the film provides rough outline of a character. Screenwriter has the responsibility to set the facets and qualities for the character. An audience should enjoy encountering a new and original character or a hero, who is not a copy of some other character. Fine-tuning of characters require extensive research of the subject area. If a movie is written about army men or soldiers, the research should be done accordingly. One should talk to army brass or soldiers to get plot ideas, and have closer look of personal traits of soldiers.

(iv) **Creating sympathy or hatred for the characters** : Creating maximum sympathy with the hero and creating great deal of hatred for the villain is the main goal of a screenwriter. By making the hero a victim of unmerited misfortune and villain the perpetrator of inhuman acts, the screenwriter tries to achieve the goal of creating sympathy for hero and hatred for villain. The portrayal of unmerited misfortune can be either a specific accident/circumstances or hero's basic situation at the opening of the screenplay.

(v) **Putting a character in jeopardy:** Screenwriter should put a character in jeopardy, in a threatening and worrisome situation to make an audience concerned /worried about the character, which is an important content for successful screenplay.

(vi) **Make the character likable:** Nice facets of characters make them likable to further the degree of sympathy of the audience. The hero or the character should be a nice person. He can be good-looking and have a smart personality. The character can be funny to please audience or posses good qualities of a good Samaritan. Murderers or criminals have all been made into sympathetic heroes. But these characters must be identified as a good human being first before their negative traits are revealed subsequently.

(vii) **Introduce the character as soon as possible:** The audience wants to see someone on the screen to identify with and root for. It is not considered good where hero does not appear within first ten minutes of the film.

(viii) **Placement of the character in a familiar setting:** The time and place of the character is important as it contribute to greater identification.

(ix) **The superhero:** The heroes of 'Superman', 'Spiderman', 'Indian Zones', 'James Bond' movies are super heroes. Even if there is no real similarity between our own lives and those of the heroes of the stories, audience will identify with them on a fantasy level. It is everyone's desire to imagine that he or she is the super hero and is performing the superhuman deeds of these characters that strengthen our relation with them.

(e) Structure of screenplay:

(i) **Three Acts:** A film story can be divided into three Acts. The objective of Act-1 is to establish the setting, characters, situation and outer motivation for the hero. The objective of Act-2 is to build the hurdles, obstacles, conflicts, suspense, pace, humor, character development and character revelations. The objective of Act-3 is to resolve everything, particularly the outer motivation and conflict for the hero. In film 'Air Force-1', American President's visit to Moscow, his speech, his return to his aircraft, villains' sneaking into the aircraft as media persons form Act-1 whereas hijack of aircraft, isolation of officials in captivity, American President's supposed escape in security pod with parachute, frustration & threats of villain becomes Act-2. Act-3 has the story of President's reappearance in luggage compartment, his efforts to find a mobile phone, his call to white house seeking instructions to empty the fuel tank, President's fight with gunmen, his efforts to deplane his officials from captivity, his fight with villain and throwing him out of the plane and successful air-transfer of President and his family to a rescue aircraft, etc.

(ii) **Individual scenes:** Every scene, event and character in the screenplay must take story's theme forward. Screenwriter should show the audience in his successive scenes as to where the story is leading. His successive scenes should build conflict in Act-2 stage of screenplay and accelerate the pace of the story. Creating very high and very low vibes of the action and humour is ideal for a screenplay. Scenes with less emotional impact, to enable audience to catch breath, may follow the high emotional moments in scenes. Next scenes may have even higher peaks. It should be wave like structure. Efforts should be made to enable audience to guess the next sequence, which may not turn out to be what the audience might think. But the anticipation keeps an audience totally engrossed. If screenwriter is able to surprise the audience and reverse the anticipation, his screenplay is considered superb. In case the audience gets jolt and is kept slightly off balance by reversing the anticipated action with something totally unexpected, his emotional involvement with the movie will increase. His curiosity will be heightened. Curiosity is the key structural device in a crime thriller. The entire film hinges on narrowing down on the murderer or the criminal. By gradually revealing the answers to the questions raised in the scenes instead of providing all the background information causes curiosity and increases the audience's emotional involvement. Apart from hero, other characters can also be put in jeopardy to heighten the emotional involvement in the story. In order to maintain maximum emotional involvement, the story must be logical and believable within its own set of rules. If it is a portrayal of fantasy, anything portrayed, whether a man flying in the sky, becoming invisible, defying death, gravity, etc can be taken as logical & believable. In case a very heavy tragedy is portrayed, some lighter moments of humor or comic relief should also be included so that it remains entertaining for the audience. Screenplay should ideally have an effective opening as well as an effective ending.

Terminology used in a screenplay

(i) **'Fade In'** is a standard opening of a screenplay.

(ii) **Scene number:** If depiction of a location changes, then scene changes on the screen. In a movie, story moves ahead and so the actions of the character, necessitating to number the scene from 1 to bigger number.

(iii) **EXT** (Exterior) or **INT** (Interior) : While writing a scene, screenwriter is required to indicate whether this is an exterior scene, to be shot at an open place under the sky or whether this is an interior scene, to be shot under a roof.

(iv) **5: EXT: Nehru Garden: Day** or **6: EXT: Nehru Garden: Night:** This description conveys scene no-5 and scene no-6, exterior condition, place Nehru Garden and 'Day' shows time having sunlight and 'Night' shows night condition.

(v) **7: INT: Drawing Room: Day** or **8: INT: Drawing Room: Night:** This description conveys scene no-7 and scene no-8, interior condition, place drawing room and 'Day' shows room having lit by light coming in from windows and 'Night' shows room having lit by internal light of the room. If room such as an auditorium does not have windows etc, there is no need to write 'Day' or 'Night'. For Example- **9: INT: School Auditorium.**

(vi) In each scene, after description of the location, character's name and dialogue can be written.

(vii) **(O.S)** stands for 'Off screen' and can be added to a character's name above his/her dialogue if he/she can be heard by the other characters in the movie but is not visible on the screen.

(viii) **(V.O)** stands for 'Voice over'. This is used when audience can hear narrator's sound about the description/background of a character or the inner thoughts of a character, which cannot be heard by other characters in the scene. V.O is used for the inner thoughts of a character or the voice of a narrator and follows the character's name above his/her dialogue.

(ix) **'Cut to'** is used to end a scene.

(x) **'Fade out'** is used to end the story/script. Nevertheless '**Fade out'** can also be used to show end of a particular period or a flashback. '**Dissolve**' can replace '**Fade out'**, in a flashback scene. To begin a new period or to show elapse of a time period, **'Fade In'** can be used with 'Ten Years later' , or ' After five months' and like on top or bottom as an screen caption. **Fade in** is also used to continue another scene after such periods scenes. Illustrations may be seen in my screenplays in this book.

(xi) Screenplay is required to be comprehensible at a school reading level. Hence, day-to-day, straightforward and simple language should be used in screenplay avoiding convoluted words, phrases, technical jargon or impressive but tedious vocabulary.

(xii) Screenplays are always written in present tense.

<u>Format of a screenplay –</u> There are specimen short stories and screenplays in the next chapters of this book. You may like to see them to learn about the format of the screenplay.

XXXXXXXXXX

1

The Mysterious Combatant
(Short Story)

A group of young tourists, mostly biologists and sculptors, eager to see arctic animals closely, was led by a tour operator to the extreme north of the earth i.e., to the Arctic region. It was summer there with constant daylight for six months, at a relatively low temperature; suitable to be termed as spring that brings a phenomenal resurgence of plant and animal life.

These tourists stayed in their temporary canopy shelters near an Eskimo village, comprising a hundred odd families of Eskimos, in a position to solicit help from Eskimos in case of an attack by arctic wild animals such as Polar bears. They had an Eskimo man as their guide to take them around and to identify and to let them know about Arctic birds, marine and mammal lives. They photographed Polar bears, foxes, ermine, marten, arctic wolf, wolverine, walrus, seal, caribou, reindeer, musk ox, lemming, whale and many other animals. Biologists were very happy to see them in furtherance of their study, whereas sculptors had a rare opportunity to see them to include them in their artistic ventures.

One fine day when everyone was sleeping, a sculptor was unable to sleep. He wanted to explore. He went out of his shelter. It was very bright outside. He walked on solid icy surface and continued walking. After walking about a kilometre, he reached a sludge surface. He was alarmed that he could slip under ice mud if he took one more step. He stopped and checked the sludge area carefully to avoid the ice mud, which was made of snowflakes. He sat there and touched the soft snow. An idea cropped up in the mind of this young sculptor. His idea was to create a icy polar tiger that would scare the polar mammals at night. So he started making tiger sculpture with ice. He was immersed in his work and had no idea about time.

When other tourists in the shelter woke up and found this sculptor missing, they got panicky. They called their guide for help, and four groups set out to search for him in four different directions. The group of six sculptors spotted him. When they saw his work on ice they were amazed and were motivated to do the same in order to leave their artistic imprint in this polar region. After six hours of work, they were satisfied to see their own creation, the magnificent statues of tiger, tigress and five cubs on the icy surface. They returned to their shelter. After a few days they flew back home with a great sense of achievement and happiness.

Winter descended after six months with coldest, darkest, & longest nights. The weather was extremely harsh with windy and stormy conditions which troubled the Eskimos a lot. They mostly lived indoors in igloos and rarely ventured out in search of food such as fish or seal meat. Florence, a tiny tribal habitat, was a Village where lived a couple in their igloo. Kemu and Kelly were married happily.

Snowstorm started and continued for a week and this couple had exhausted their food-stock. Kelly was in advance stage of pregnancy. Kemu grew anxious, as availability of food on time was necessary for his wife. Storm continued and they had to go hungry for two days. Since his wife's condition deteriorated due to hunger and malnutrition, Kemu decided to venture out of his igloo in search of food.

In the dark night, he walked and tried to detect the hollow sound made by his footsteps in order to find a hollow icy cap above an ice-pit. Since wind was blowing hard, it was difficult to detect the sound of footsteps. He continued walking and reached a deserted place very far from his igloo. He did not find a single seal for meat. When the breeze receded, he found an ice-pit and broke the lid with the help of his knife. He tried to immerse himself inside the pit to find fishes. Since it was a dark night, he was not able to see anything. So he did his best by touching and feeling the surface. Finally, he touched a fleshy thing and tried to take it out of the pit. However, he could not as it appeared to be heavy and large. He tried to cut the flesh for meat with his knife. It was a polar snake. The poisonous polar snake bit Kemu at many places on his body. Kemu found it unbearable and came out of the pit immediately. Nevertheless, he could not muster his strength to move away from there to fetch help for survival. He fell unconscious and died.

Kelly grew nervous when Kemu did not return home for six long hours. When snowstorm receded, she came out of her igloo to search her husband. Her neighbour declined help. It was pitch-dark outside. She was feeling weak due to under nourishment. She was hardly able to walk. Still she mustered all her strength to walk. She continued to walk in the chilly dry weather. She stopped and felt dehydrated due to extreme exhaustion. She sat there and waited to relax before starting again. At last, she spotted Kemu lying dead on the icy surface. She was shocked and grief-stricken. She could not hold her emotions and her tears broke the boundary of her eyes. She yelled uncontrollably and the pin drop silence of the area was disturbed. After a few moments due to mental shock, malnutrition, dehydration and exhaustion, she felt a pain in her lower abdomen. She was frightened as she began experiencing her labour pains. Her condition was pathetic.

Up in the sky, Kemu's soul was roaming in the air with five other friendly souls. Cries of Kelly caught the attention of all six souls in the air. They spotted Kelly. Kemu's soul was distressed to see his wife's pathetic condition. He helplessly watched his wife deliver a baby boy and falling unconscious. Actually, Kelly had died after delivering the baby. Thereafter her soul flew up in the sky from the body and found Kemu in the air. Kelly met Kemu. Both were aggrieved to see their helpless baby on the ground. Kemu grew suspicious that his baby was destined to die soon after birth. He raised his head in hopelessness & uttered loudly asking God as to what was the baby's fate. To their surprise, sky echoed and replied his query that the child was destined to live long.

The helpless newborn baby was crying beside the dead bodies of his father and mother, who were of no help. Kemu and Kelly were curious to know whether they can again go back to their bodies on the ground to take care of the newborn child. The other souls were of the opinion that it was not possible to reverse the destiny and that they should not worry, as the child was to live long. It means God would provide help to enable him to sustain his life on the earth.

Baby was crying. Just then, a polar bear at a distance in its icy-cave woke up and heard the baby's sound. The bear was hungry, and became happy to find a prey nearby. Seeing the polar bear approach the baby, Kemu, Kelly, and other souls got frightened as to how this baby could be saved. They waited to see God send some help to bolster the destiny of the child, to give him a long life. When they saw no movement or miracle coming for the rescue of the child, they grew nervous. The polar bear reached near the baby. He was sniffing him before inserting his teeth in baby's flesh. On seeing this, all the souls in sheer rage entered into the icy sculptures of tiger, tigress and five cubs, located nearby. A bright light appeared due to the occurrence of this marvellous phenomenon of nature & God. On seeing and hearing the sudden roars of a group of live polar tigers, the polar bear got scared and had no guts to face them but to run away for safety. Tiger and Tigress i.e., Kemu and Kelly remained near the baby whereas five cubs ran after the polar bear. After a long chase, they grabbed the entire polar bear family consisting of male, female and two kids and killed them. Tiger cubs returned happily.

The Tiger and Tigress soon realized that though they had repelled the polar bears but the life of the baby was still in danger, as there was nothing to feed him or cover him with.

The Tiger raised his head, looked into the dark sky in anger, and said "Now who is going to take care of this baby? The baby will die soon".

"No, he will not die." A sound came from the sky.

"Who is this? Are you God?"

"No, I am not God. I am his accountant."

"Why can't I see you? Please show yourself to me."

Thereafter a bright light descended from the sky and a human shape appeared within the brightness. Everybody was amazed by the event unfolding before him or her.

"I am the accountant of God."

Everybody bowed their heads before this heavenly body.

"This baby will live long."

"How is it possible?"

"I will explain. Tentacles of greedy desire of self-reliance, money, & wealth in human have spread all over the earth. That is why the standard formulation and balance of nature on earth have gone topsy-turvy resulting in serious faults in my balance sheet. Though human virtues have always been supreme all over the universe but devil's special effects have overshadowed these virtues on the earth, resulting natural and unnatural disasters such as mass killings & suicides, epidemics, non-curable diseases, earthquakes, tsunamis, floods, storms, hurricanes, tornados, etc."

Everyone was quiet before the divine body.

"You all were not destined to die. That is why you were not allowed to enter into the heaven or the hell. The boy is to live long but there is no one to take care of him in this polar area. I am in a mess and am forced to do patch up. I have, therefore, allowed you to enter into tiger's icy sculptures and become polar tigers."

"Thanks. Though we scared and repelled polar bears, who would feed and protect this baby? Where is his family?"

"You are the family. Your tigress would breastfeed him. The baby would be able to brave the polar weather due to mother's milk. You, being the polar tigers, made of ice, will not need any food and would live for another twenty years on this earth. When you will die, the baby would be a grown-up and self sufficient to sustain his life on the earth," The accountant said. Soon thereafter bright light disappeared and the celestial body vanished.

Thus they lived in this polar area happily. Tiger, Tigress and five cubs loved this baby and took care of him. As the baby grew, he began playing with his brother cubs, tiger and tigress. He used to have fun while drinking milk of mother tigress, riding on her back, kissing her and his father tiger and brother cubs. While sleeping beneath the sky and looking at the twinkling stars of the night his mother and father used to tell him stories of old kings, queens and princes. Boy was able to communicate with tiger, tigress and cubs. Everybody called him 'Pola' affectionately.

"Mom, where do the Sun uncle and the Moon uncle go for six long months?" Pola asked his mother about the disappearance of the Sun and the Moon. He questions about the six months of long bright daylight and six months of long dark cold night.

"They go to another world," Tigress answered.

"Why can't they remain here with us all the time? I miss them."

"Yes, my baby, you are very lovely. Therefore, they come to meet you. They have many more beautiful boys like you in another world."

"Mom, do they have many more boys like me?"

"Yes."

"I would like to play with them."

"You can't go there."

"Why?"

"It is very far from here. No one can go there."

"How many people are there in another world?"

"Many."

'How many world uncle Sun & Moon have?"

"All the stars in the sky are their world."

"Are there many people there?"

"Yes, there are."

"Are they also looking at us?"

"Yes."

"Is our Sun and Moon uncle very kind?"

"Yes. I will tell you a story of Moon uncle's kindness. There was a man and a woman living in their igloo happily. Once the man went out to fetch food for his lovely wife and was bitten by a polar snake. He died and his wife became restless. She came out from her igloo. She also died leaving her son helpless in the world. They were very unhappy. Moon uncle allowed the man and woman to have another life to look after their baby. He always helps helpless people."

This clarified Pola's curiosity about sun and moon. The boy was very talkative and used to keep his mother and father busy with his talking about many things. Time was happily passing and Pola was growing very strong due to tigress milk.

When Pola attained eighteen years of age, the tiger, tigress and cubs were worried as the time deadline of twenty years was very close, when they were to die natural death. How would Pola manage his life after their death? He would be unguarded. He did not learn human language and habits to mingle with them. These questions worried them.

"We were lost in our love for our child. Now what to do? We are to die." The Tiger was talking to his tigress at night when everybody was sleeping.

The Tigress did not reply. She was sobbing and her eyes were full of tears.

"He has not learnt human habits and language. If we leave him with the humans now at this age, he would be treated as a mentally retarded child. As no human ever held him nor has he interacted with people, it will be hard for him to adjust in the human society. Only love and affection will help him to bring him closure to the society. But, no-one would adopt him now and teach him from scratch," the Tiger said.

"Please do something otherwise how will my child live without us?" the Tigress said while sobbing.

"What should I do? Now we can't even talk like human, and introduce ourselves to our neighbours to request them to look after our child," the Tiger said

Both the Tiger and the Tigress started weeping. The sound disturbed a cub's sleep, lying near them, who woke up and was astonished to see them weeping.

"What has happened? Why are you crying?" the cub asked.

"We are to die soon. Where will our Pola live?"

"Why do you worry for nothing? Don't you remember God's accountant had said that our Pola would live long?"

"Yes."

"It is the accountant's headache to ensure long life for him. Why should we worry?"

The Tiger and Tigress were stunned to hear the indifferent tone of the cub. They had no answer and were silent for a while.

"Didn't you hear that his balance sheet is in mess? We died prematurely due to his erroneous accounts of birth and death," the cub said " Don't worry. He patches up his errors. He allowed us to live with Pola. If he will not find an alternative, he may allow us to live longer with Pola."

"You are right," the Tiger said to find solace from the cub's word.

"You are unnecessarily worried. Just sleep peacefully. Everything would be fine," the Cub said.

"My darling, he is right. Just do not worry. Everything would be fine. Let us sleep now," the Tiger said and stretched himself on the ground to sleep. The Tigress touched and sniffed to kiss Pola in his sleep with love and affection. Thereafter she slept.

XXXXXXXXX

There was a Chinese healer in a neighbouring Kingdom, who used to treat patients with herbs, preserved flesh and bones of different animals including tigers to cure various ailments. He used to have nightmares quite often involving polar tigers and polar bears. Once he consulted a Chinese spiritual specialist about his recurrent nightmares and paid a heavy fee of two thousand gold coins. The specialist did some spiritual chores and meditation. The Chinese healer told him that he was a polar bear in his previous life and was killed by a group of polar tigers. Since he had life still to live, his soul was allowed to occupy the body of a Chinese healer, who died eighteen years ago. The specialist told him that he saw his family of polar bears and the family of killer polar tigers. The Chinese healer asked the spiritual specialist to reiterate whatever he said was truth, as polar tigers made of ice were not found on the earth. He confirmed that unseen facts did occur in spiritual phenomenon. The spiritual specialist offered his services to kill these polar tigers at an exorbitant fee of ten thousand gold coins and some other offerings for rituals.

After the spiritual specialist left, the Chinese healer became restless to take revenge of his death as polar bear. He wanted to kill those polar tigers and use their flesh, blood, and bones as medicines. However, he could not find a way to venture Arctic or Antarctic region in search of these tigers due to lack of facilities and amenities.

Soon after, he found an opportunity to fulfil his wish of revenge. Prince Katoos, son of King Kaboos, fell sick. Despite best efforts of the Royal Physician, he could not be cured. Then the Royal Physician advised King Kaboos to call for help from the physician working for the masses, outside the Royal Palace. A Royal declaration was made that whoever would cure the disease of Prince Katoos will receive an award of one hundred thousand gold coins. Many physicians gathered in the Royal Court to examine the physical condition of the Prince and to suggest medication. The Royal Physician had advised them to write their course of medication on a piece of paper and hand it over to him so that he could check whether any new medication had been suggested which was not administered yet. Only the Chinese healer suggested a new medication. He stated that he would need flesh, blood and bones of polar tiger, a rare tiger in the polar region, to provide an instant cure for the rare disease. The Chinese healer, however, gave some medicines from his stock. Since his medication was new, the Royal Physician advised King Kaboos to kill the polar tigers.

So the King Kaboos ordered and dispatched two groups of hunters to Arctic and Antarctic region to hunt for polar tigers. The hunters returned from Antarctic region, as they could not find polar tigers in the pitch-dark despite their best efforts as it was winter there. It was summer in Arctic region at that time and as a result it was bright all through which helped the hunters to spot seven polar tigers. They chased and shot many bullets to kill them. Fortunately, the polar tigers were able to dodge the bullets and run for safety. They were frightened to see gun-laden hunters chasing them on dog sledges. Pola was also running with them. The tiger and tigress were worried about Pola, as in the process of running he might get hurt.

"Mom, why are they trying to kill us?" Pola asked his mother.

"I don't know," his mother said "Just don't stop and keep running till you reach a safer place."

They were running very fast on icy surface and at times skidded. They were helping each other to save from skidding. At last, a bullet pierced the tiger's body and he felt pain. But he did not stop and kept running. Fortunately, they could dodge the hunters and slip under an ice pit to hide from the hunters. Since the temperature under the ice pit was extremely cold, the tiger was relieved of the paid because the wound was filled and healed by cold. Though they felt safer there, they were extremely frightened. The tigress was hiding Pola under her lap.

Since the tigers have disappeared, hunters decided to bring them out from the ice pit by burning coals to raise the climatic temperature. They thought that by raising the climatic temperature, the ice pits would melt and the hidden animals would have no choice but to come out. So they burnt coals and raised the climatic temperature. The ice pit, where the polar tigers were hiding, started melting.

"These hunters are cruel and cunning. They would surely kill us all as our pit is melting and falling apart. They would be able to notice us very soon," a cub said.

"What should we do to save ourselves?" Pola asked.

"If we can dig further deep and hide ourselves in the snow," the tiger said.

"But we can't dig as our claws are not enough to do that," another cub said.

"I can do that," said Pola. So he started digging the snow with his hands and made a deeper ice pit, where all of them could hide.

"My son is very brave and able. He has saved us," the tigress said and kissed Pola. All of them then kissed and hugged him with affection. Pola was happy. They were safe in their ice pit. Since the ice pit was very deep, it did not melt. Hence, the hunters could not find them despite of their concerted efforts. They had to return empty handed. Thus, the Chinese healer could not carry out his heinous plan of killing polar tigers. Prince Katoos, however, recovered from his sickness because of the Chinese healer's medicine. Therefore, he got an award of one hundred thousand gold coins from King Kaboos.

XXXXXXXX

Almighty God in heaven was worried to see the balance sheet of his accountant concerning the earth. He asked his accountant the reasons for the depleting number of species of different animals and birds and also the extinction of some species. He was very angry with the accountant for his inability and inefficiency to contain the deteriorations and damages on the earth.

The accountant replied very politely that the reasons for these damages created by human beings on the earth are beyond control. Men and women are killing birds and animals mindlessly for food, medicine, etc., resulting in depletion of their number. In their endeavour to achieve self-reliance, money and wealth, men and women have altered climatic conditions, not suitable to most birds and animals, which have resulted in their extinction. Secondly, special effects of devil had also fuelled these reasons. In absence of a couple or eggs, it is impossible to recreate the extinct creature on the earth to fill the void.

God set up a meeting with his advisors. Every body opined that the beautiful earth created by God would become a world of non-living things if devil's special effects and greedy desire of men and women for self-reliance, money and wealth are not contained.

In the meeting it was decided to entrust the accountant to find the ways and means of saving the environment and natural balance of the earth to avoid further depletion and extinction of species.

The accountant was confused about the proper solution of this problem. He thought of taking help from environmentalists. He travelled extensively on the earth on his flying chariot and was disheartened to find that the so-called environmentalists or nature lovers were influenced by commercial motives. They had mask above their personal interests, and were not dedicated to saving the forest. One group had connections with a section of industrialists or producers, whose interest was to save the forest of a particular area in order to get regular supplies of medicinal herbs, whereas the other group had interest in growing woods meant for furniture etc. The accountant did not find a single human being whose help he could seek to contain the deterioration on the earth. He continued his search and continued his journey around the globe on his vehicle.

XXXXXXXXXXXX

Meanwhile the Chinese healer in the neighbouring kingdom was restless, as he could not take his revenge against polar tigers. He paid ten thousand gold coins and sought the help of the spiritual specialist and a black magician to achieve his goal of killing them. Since the Chinese healer could see the polar tigers in a dream and recognize them, the spiritual specialist and black magician made him sit near a pyre and chanted the mantras as recited by him to cast the magic spells on the polar tigers, i.e., wherever they were. This magic spell was to shower rain on the polar tigers, which will result in melting of their exteriors made of ice, bringing their death.

It was summer in arctic region with bright daylight. Pola was sitting amongst his father, mother, and brothers. All of a sudden, rain started to fall. Though Pola liked the rain, the polar tigers were alarmed as their icy exterior had slow melting effect because of rainwater. They ran and hid themselves under an ice-pit from the raindrops.

The Chinese healer under the magic spell could see them hiding beneath an ice-pit. He told this fact to the black magician, who then recited another mantra that the Chinese healer followed to cast another magic spell on these polar tigers.

There was a sudden noise and sound of footsteps. Hearing the commotions, the polar tigers & Pola came out of the ice pit. The rain had stopped and they were frightened to see a sudden presence of hyenas in their area.The polar tigers could not think of braving them as the hyenas were in large number and they could easily become their prey. They started running away from the hyenas. This made the hyenas chase them. Pola and polar tigers were running with their full might and were far ahead of the hyenas.

The Chinese healer saw them far ahead of the hyenas, he told about this to black magician. He put another spell of black magic on Pola and polar tigers. The magical effect was alarming. They found themselves away from polar environment and within tropical surroundings with human habitat. In the tropical surrounding, the climatic temperature was unbearable for them. Polar tigers were losing the ability to run as their icy exterior was melting. To see his mother, father and brothers becoming frail under heat, Pola was worried and panicky as to how he could save them. When they were passing through a human habitat, some tribal men and women also ran towards them holding their weapons in the hand to catch them (the rare tigers). While passing through the human habitat, Pola got a glimpse of a horse carriage kept on the ground without the horse. So he ran towards the horse carriage and brought it to enable the weak polar tigers to sit in the carriage. As they were unable to run fast and would have collapsed any moment, Pola's idea of using the horse carriage had brought a relief and new lease of life among them. He held front rail of the horse carriage and ran as fast as he could from the herd of hyenas and the tribal people. Pola was running frantically to save his family. Pola now realizes the worth of tigress's milk while running fast and saving the polar tiger family.

All of a sudden, whistle of a train was heard. Soon thereafter, a train was running on its track parallel to the road on which Pola and his carriage was racing. The physical condition of polar tigers in carriage were deteriorating. When they saw men, women, and animals and birds in the train, they started shouting and requesting to open the door of the train to get into it. After a few moments, the door of a rail coach opened and the polar tigers jumped into the bogie in motion. Thereafter, Pola left the horse carriage and ran fast. He caught hold of the door handle of the moving rail coach and entered into the bogie. They felt a great relief from an unending run. They sat on the seats and waved hands to greet other passengers in the bogie. The speeding train left the herd of hyenas and tribal people far behind.

When the Chinese healer saw them slipping away from the herd of hyenas and riding a train, he became extremely restless. He told this fact to the black magician, who spelled a new mantra. At the recital of the same by the Chinese healer, a group of flying dragons raced towards the train and started spilling fire and heat from their mouth on the bogie of the train carrying polar tigers. The feeling of being trapped by the dragons flying alongside the train bogie and their staring them in anger and spilling fire made Pola and polar tigers nervous and frightened. After a few seconds, they could realize that fire and heat had no effect on the train bogie and that the chilly condition inside the bogie had helped them recoup the strength lost by melting of icy exterior.

Suddenly it was a pitch-dark in the bogie as the train had entered into a tunnel and a whirring sound could be heard. Again, it was a time of concern for Pola and polar tigers as it was difficult to locate anyone in the darkness.

"Why is it dark now? Where are we?" the tiger asked.

Soon thereafter, a man with halo appeared before them.

"Who are you?" Pola asked.

"Are you the accountant of God?" father tiger asked.

"Yes, I am," the accountant said.

"Where are we?" the tiger asked.

"You are in a train. This is my 'Polar Express-2," the accountant said.

"Where are we going? And who are these passengers?" the tiger asked.

"I have the responsibility to take these pious souls on a tour for fun. They were in heaven and when I set out for extensive journey of the earth, they accompanied me."

"Are you the owner of this train?" Pola asked.

"Yes."

"Why did you name it as Polar Express-2?"

"There are so many vehicles in the heaven. God has a vehicle number 1 to ride and I have number 2 to ride. All the planets have poles, be it hottest or coldest. Since our vehicle can brave any polar condition, hot or cold, it is named as Polar Express. My vehicle being number 2 is called Polar Express-2."

Polar Express-2 had come out of the tunnel but it was pitch-dark as the night had spread in and out of the bogie. Despite darkness, the white snow mountains and blowing of diamond dust could be seen shining outside of the running train.

"Where are we now?"

"We are in the Antarctic polar region."

"How can we reach our place?"

"Are you feeling uncomfortable here?"

"No. Not at all."

The accountant looked at the face of Pola and thought for a while.

"I need your son's help," the accountant asked father tiger.

"What?" he asked.

"I understand that you are worried about your son being not able to learn human language and habits."

"Yes."

"I will empower your son with great knowledge so that he could settle in human habitat and live happily."

"Thanks."

"But he has to do my work."

"What work?"

"There are so many birds and animals which are about to extinct due to devil's effect. This effect has to be contained and reduced to avoid extinction. I need your son's help in information campaign to spread awareness amongst people for the well being of this earth."

"He may not be able to understand this," the tiger replied.

The accountant touched the head of Pola and induced energy in his head, thus empowering him with the total knowledge of Universe and human being.

"I have empowered your son with knowledge and education. He would now be able to live independently in human society. You need not worry about him."

Pola bowed his head before the accountant and touched his feet. He also hugged his mother, father and brothers.

"I would like to take all of you to other planets, which have purity in its natural balance and not been polluted yet. This journey would enable you to compare and find the deficiency cropping up on the earth."

Everybody was happy to hear the offer made by the divine body.

"Would you like to come with me?"

"Yes."

"Thanks for your cooperation."

Just then the flying dragons appeared outside the train window and started spilling fire that lit the area in and out of the train compartment. Despite their best efforts, the dragons were not able to harm the Polar Express or its passengers.

"Who are these dragons? Why are they after us?" the tiger asked.

"These dragons are sent by a Chinese healer. A Polar bear was killed by your cubs, but as he had life left to live, so his soul occupied the body of a Chinese healer who died during that time. Now the Chinese healer is taking his revenge. That is why, he has sent flying dragons."

"How can we get rid of this devil soul?"

"Don't worry. Now we would be flying to another planet and these dragons will not be able to follow us."

"Will this train fly now?"

"Yes, it can run on surface and fly in space too."

Thereafter the train raised its position from surface to air. All its wheels got hidden within the body and it looked like a very long rocket, ascending into the air, having cylindrical compartments with windows, attached with each other to make a long column. The dragons were helplessly standing on the ground, looking up in the sky with utter dismay. It was dark all around the outer space.

"Why is it dark everywhere?"

"Do you like to have light?"

"Yes."

The train compartment was immediately lit. God's accountant vanished from the spot and the Polar Express-2 was flying above the clouds. Watching the clouds closely and flying above it was a matter of pleasant surprise for the polar tiger family. They saw many different species of birds racing with them.

"Open the door, open the door," many of the birds were saying.

The passengers of the train were waving their hands and laughing at them.

"We would like to accompany you all to other world," the birds were conveying.

But no one opened the door and the birds continued their race with the flying train. Ultimately they stopped following as the flying train rocketed fast to leave the orbit of planet earth. It soon slipped deep into the space and there was nothing to see outside the window except vacuum and darkness.

Soon they could see bright light approaching them. The captain of the flying ship declared on his speakerphone that they were about to reach the planet 'Cropper'.

"I am your captain of the Polar Express-2. The bright light outside the window is due to the sun of a planetary system of planet 'Cropper'. This planet is a water ball, the centre of which has hollow football like structure and which works like a submarine. The central part of this planet has life, which uses water energy for sustenance and for lighting of its habitat. We are about to plunge into the sea of this planet before entering into its submarine like habitat," captain of the Polar Express-2 said.

The flying ship, Polar Express 2, plunged into the sea and started working like a submarine. Passengers of Polar Express 2 were fascinated to see the marine life and the inner structures of the sea. Soon it reached at the bottom and a door opened, which gulped the Polar Express-2, leaving a dispersing effect of water. The door immediately closed as Polar Express-2 entered into the habitat. It was bright daylight inside the habitat.

"We will be flying in the axis sky of this habitat. You can see from your window that it does not have a sun for light. They charge themselves from water energy and also light their habitat. Water is the source of oxygen in this habitat and the exhaled carbon dioxide is recycled for oxygen gas and carbon deposits for energy. They switch off the lights to make it dark as a night. They live a hard life but are very wise, knowledgeable and sensitive. They know how to keep their sweet home tidy, orderly and perfect," the captain of the Polar Express-2 said. They stayed in the axis sky to see the breathtaking beauty of the landscape, its habitat, its residential and business facilities. After three hours, it suddenly became dark as the light of the habitat was switched off.

"Now they have switched off the light to consider it as night. I will now put the shutters down of our windows so that light does not go out to disturb them," the captain of the Polar Express-2 said. "We will now slowly make exit of this planet." Captain's voice went off on speakerphone.

Flying ship Polar Express-2 landed on the surface and passengers felt a light jolt. Soon thereafter, it was felt as if a door was opened and the Polar Express-2 was pushed forcefully out with an air storm. The door of the habitat was closed quickly and Polar Express-2 was in the sea as submarine. It started the return journey. Everybody in the Polar Express 2 was excited and happy due to this travel experience. They opened the shutter of the window to catch the glimpse of the beautiful marine life once again. Soon the submarine came on the surface of the sea and then took off as an airplane and after some time flew like spaceship. It soon slipped deep into the space and its vacuum. Passengers still looked outside of the window to see something.

After some time, bright light appeared. The captain of the flying ship again declared on his speakerphone, "We are about to reach a new planetary system. It has a planet 'Cornet' with life."

Soon the spaceship Polar Express-2 was hovering in the outer orbit of planet 'Cornet'. It had a burning yellow-red turbulent outer exterior as the inflammable gaseous cover around the planet was under flame. Polar Express-2 entered into the gaseous boundary and crossed it to find an unbearable hot climate underneath with dense vapour rising in the sky from boiling liquid on the surface of the planet. The surface of the planet was not flat but uneven due to high-rise mountains spread all over the planet and the base of the mountains were dipped in boiling liquid but connected to each other. Its outer atmosphere was not at all suitable for any living being.

The passengers of the Polar Express-2 were fascinated and a bit fearful to see no life but disturbances on the planet.

"I am your captain speaking. The planet that you can see from your window does not have life in its open area. The high-rise mountains that you can see are not solid but hollow from inside and work like very large room connected to each other. These mountains have life within, under tremendously harsh living condition. We would enter into the mountain body to see the inside of it," the captain said.

Soon after, the Polar Express-2 reached near a mountain and a mountain door, made of a large boulder, opened. It had suspended itself in the air like a helicopter and entered into the mountain body slowly and landed on the flat indoor surface. The Polar Express-2 again moved like a train within the mountain body to go all around this compact world. Passengers were engrossed to see the living things of this planet.

"Life within this world gets energy from its outer hot air and liquid. This energy also enable them to light their habitat. They have similar life pattern that we saw on planet 'Cropper'. By now you must have realised that the habitats of these planets have a very harsh and difficult life to lead. This shows that you have been very lucky to be on the earth with extreme facilities and comfortable life with ample sunshine, fresh air and water, fresh food and green vegetations." Captain's sound echoed from the speakerphone.

"He is right," father tiger murmured.

"But people on the earth has not respected the wellbeing of the earth. They are mindlessly destroying forests, killing animals and altering the environment. Unless somebody takes the cudgel to either make them understand their folly or force them to refrain from their heinous act of deforestation, poaching, multiplying pollutions, and fuelling climate changes, the earth will lose its beauty and serenity," said the captain. "Now we would return to the earth." His voice went off. Everybody was silently watching the world within the mountain body from their windows.

Polar Express-2 took off like an aeroplane and made exit from the mountain body through a huge door at the upper end of the mountain. It came out of the mountain and flew in its sky for a few moments. Thereafter, it rocketed to go deep into the space away from the planetary system. After some time, Polar Express-2 entered into the orbit of the earth and flew above the clouds. The flying birds above the clouds were happy to see the Polar Express-2 sailing. They again raced and came closer to the flying plane.

"Welcome back, welcome back from another world," the birds were chirping. The passengers were very happy to see the birds welcoming them.

After a few seconds, it landed on the arctic region of the earth and continued running as train. Pola and polar tiger family were pleased to find that they have returned to their home. The accountant of God appeared before them, surrounded by bright light.

"Pola, now the time has come for you to go to the earth and fulfil the task given by me," he said.

"How would I fulfil this task amongst cunning and cruel people?" Pola asked.

"Don't worry. I would empower you to reform yourself to a lion as well as to become an invisible man. The lion's body would enable you to frighten every one. Secondly, you will have the capability to turn invisible to give a slip to anyone in case of fatal situations. I will give you an ammunition box, which you will be able to operate. It will consist of many forms of gun, such as pistol, machine gun, laser gun, rocket launcher, stealth bomber, anti tank helicopter equipped with missiles and other firepower, etc. This box would always remain full of cartridges, explosives, bombs and missiles. You can also wish or get any type of ammunition from this box. The ammunition box will never be empty."

"Thanks," Pola said in gratitude, while the accountant of God touched his head to induce new capabilities and powers in his body.

Just then father and mother tigers saw from their window a polar bear ascending into the sky, and it was sight of pleasant surprise. The polar bear was waving his hands to polar tigers.

"Look at the flying polar bear," the father tiger said excitedly.

"He is the same polar bear who was after you to take revenge," the accountant replied.

"How come he is flying?"

"He is dead now and going to heaven. He has completed his life."

Everybody was startled to see the event from the running train.

"You and your family have also completed your life except for Pola. He will be taken to a human habitat whereas you all will go to heaven."

"How can we leave without our child?" mother tiger said.

"When you reach heaven, you would forget about worldly emotions and Pola."

"No, but I can't live without my family," Pola said in agitation and anger. " You can't take away my family."

"This is life. Old people have to leave to make way for new ones."

"I cannot live without my family," Pola started sobbing.

"I am sure when you have a family of yours, i.e, having wife, children and grand children in a human habitat you won't have moments to remember your parents. Nevertheless, I grant you the ability to talk to your parents and brothers, whenever you would desire. This gift would, however, not be available to your wife and progeny," the accountant replied.

"But I can't live without my child," mother tiger wept.

"Just bear with me for a while. We will drop Pola on earth and soon enter into the heaven. I am sure you would be comfortable even without Pola. You and your husband would, however, be able to see and talk to Pola from heaven," the accountant tried to console her.

Just then, the train stopped and a human habitat could be seen in the vicinity. Pola got down from the train with heavy heart and the train started moving ahead leaving him behind. The polar tiger family wept bitterly, and looked outside the window to have a glimpse of Pola. Soon Polar Express-2 took off and flew into the air. Pola was looking into the sky to see the ascending heavenly body and was waving his hands. His family was also waving at him.

Pola went and surveyed the city and the forest as well to understand the ways and means to save the earth. He started working as a forest guard. Whenever people with bad motives and Government personnel sent labourers to cut trees, he frightened them by attacking them as a lion. Due to this threat no labourers were ready to go to work in the forest. This made it necessary for bad people and Government personnel to call for hunters to kill all the lions in the jungle. Many hunter groups went into the jungle but never returned as Pola killed those hunters with the help of his divine gun.

A group of hunters went into the jungle and accidentally found the dead bodies of their fellow hunters, which frightened them and they returned with all the corpses. Wounds on the dead bodies could only prove that the attacker was a man. So a decision was taken by the Government to order its military to wipe out this lion man, who was hindering implementation of its order of cutting the trees in the forest. But the military could not do anything, as Pola was able to effectively block them and inflict high casualties on them with the help of his divine gun. At last, the military had to retreat and the forest became safe for all living things.

This was the occasion of celebration for all the animals in the jungle. Nevertheless an incident happened after some time, which worried all the animals in the jungle.

All the animals of the jungle used to drink the water from the river passing through it. One day a tiger became sick and later died after drinking the river water. The old and experienced animals determined that people with bad intentions were contaminating the water of the river with poisonous substances. A beautiful flowering plant was also found dying due to poisonous air. Many animals developed respiratory problems due to poisonous fumes coming from nearby cities. Thus, it became very difficult for the animals to survive in the forest. Pola was hurt by the fact that the animals were facing problems in the forest. So he decided to help them.

He went to the city. There he saw male and female, old and young, baby and infant. He had not yet seen a woman. He was thrilled to find and make a friend. He did not divulge his motive and early life, but could make a very natural and easy friendship with her. She was a nature lover, and used to make portraits of different landscapes and animals. She was a computer analyst by profession. Her name was Pauline and their friendship grew as time elapsed.

To accomplish a pollution free earth, he travelled extensively to locate the factory-sites which were releasing poisonous fumes in the air and harmful liquids in the water canals leading to the rivers. After finding these factories, he went there and scared all the workers by changing himself into a giant lion. There was hue and cry in all the factories. A situation came when no factory-worker was ready to go to the factory for work. Hence all factory work came to a standstill and emission of poisonous fumes and liquids stopped. The bad people were not able to trap and kill this lion as he used to sneak out invisibly. They were unable to understand how a lion could sneak into the factory, scare the workers and then disappear despite of security arrangements. So they installed highly sophisticated automatic surveillance systems in every factory with pre-checks on entry and exit for each and every worker to exclude the possibility of an intruder. After entry into the factory, each and every worker was given a gun or pistol and was authorized to shoot at the sight of any animal or lion. Military men were also requisitioned to guard the internal premises of factories and industrial plants.

Despite the fact that military men were assigned to guard the factories, Pola could turn invisible and enter the factory. Even the workers inside the factory were given guns to shoot the beast. But Pola managed to kill the military men to shake the security arrangements and stop the operations of polluting industries.

Once he was exploring the possibility of entering into an industrial plant along with her beloved friend Pauline, but a surveillance camera traced him. So he had to run from there, as many helicopters and military armoured vehicle were after him either to arrest or kill him. Though Pola had no threat to his life from anyone because of his divine capabilities but he had a hard time protecting his beloved friend Pauline. He could somehow manage to give them a slip.

Pola then decided to go to the jungle and form a group of animals so that they along with him could attack the people responsible for disturbing the environment. He took him divine gun and led a very big contingent of animal to the city.

The city folks panicked when they came to know about the attack, whereas the bad people prepared themselves by prompting public to attack Pola and the animal group. Arms and ammunition were distributed to the general public. Bad people were hopeful that a fight between people and animals would be fruitful to their cause.

Pauline was restless to know that every body in the city was preparing to attack the animals, which would result in widespread bloodshed. She went to a TV-station and delivered a speech outlining the nefarious motives of the bad people and also Pola's concern for all living things on the earth. This made the citizens considerate and sympathetic to the cause of a safe and healthy world. They threw their guns and weapons in the street to refrain from this battle between city dwellers and animal contingent. This friendly attitude of general people towards animals made things very difficult for the bad people.

Ultimately the bad people influenced their Government and in turn the Government ordered a military operation against the advancing animal contingent. But the military could not withstand the firepower of Pola and their soldiers being slaughtered by animals. The military had to retreat. This made the bad people accountable to the Government of their actions regarding harming the environment, so they fled leaving city clean and open for Pola and his animal contingent.

The President met with Pola and the animal representatives. He regretted having placed the responsibilities of the Ministry of Environment and Forest to greedy and dishonest men. The President ordered the arrest of these man along with those responsible for soil, air and water pollution. He vouched for finding and implementing ecologically excellent ways and means of living with peaceful co-existence of human being, animals and plants, in his effort to save the earth.

People in the city espoused the revolutionary cause of Pola and welcomed him along with his animal contingent. Methods and techniques were found to make all the factories environmentally friendly. Scientists were encouraged to invent 'Oxygen Emission Engines and Vehicles' to replace the existing 'Carbon Emission Engines and Vehicles', which effectively eliminated the air pollution and the global warming. Thenceforth, the earth became very safe and sound for all living things.

Pola married Pauline and had a lovely child. Despite the fact that he was happy in his newfound family, he used to remember his parents and often spoke to them. The earth became a sweet, safe home of billions of animals, plants and other species. Pola was always remembered for his marvellous contribution towards the earth. He became an immortal and legendary figure for all living things.

<u>XXXX The End XXXX</u>

The Mysterious Combatant

[Screenplay]

Fade In:

1. Ext: Green lawn in the compound of the Institute of Fine Arts: Morning

Institute of Fine Arts
Copenhagen University, Denmark
[On Screen caption]

Asphalt walkway within the compound of the institute leads to the exit and entrance gate. A group of students, mostly in twenties, is walking on the asphalt walkway, when they meet an elderly man approaching from opposite direction.

Elderly man
"Hello boys! Good morning. What's up? All in one group... And in good mood!"

The students reciprocate, "Good morning, Sir."

One boy [among the students]
"This is a beautiful summer...and vacation time from today!"

Elderly man
"Planning to go home...?"

Another boy [among the students]
"No, we are planning to go on a tour to see some new places. And you Sir?"

Elderly man
"I am visiting my daughter in Stockholm."

Third boy [among the students]

"We are going to meet a tour operator to explore an economical tour to some good places."

Elderly man
"Okay. Wish you all the best in your endeavour."

Then the elderly walks away. The students walk out from the boundary gate of the institute. Just a little away from the metal gate of the institute, is a metallic pole with a board indicating it to be a bus station. These students wait for a bus for some time on the pavement and after a while a bus is seen approaching to the designated bus station. The bus stops at the designated station box and its automatic door opens. All the students enter into it. After that the bus moves ahead on the road.

Cut to:
<u>2. Int : Bus : Day</u>

The bus is full of passengers and all the students are standing inside. They are looking outside of the window.

Cut to:
<u>3. Ext : Downtown, Copenhagen : Day</u>

The bus stops at its designated bus station outside Tivoli Garden in front of SAS Royal Hotel. All the students get down from the bus. The bus moves ahead and is out of sight.

Cut to:
<u>4. Ext: Pavement in front of SAS Royal Hotel, Copenhagen : Day</u>

The students walk on the pavement. They are looking for the office of a tour operator in a small market place adjacent to the hotel. The place is in front of the metro station of the main railway station of Copenhagen. A pedestal signboard bearing 'Budget Travel' is seen outside of an office. The students walk towards the signboard and reach the office of the tour operator. They enter into the office by opening the glass door.

Cut to:
<u>5. Int : Office of the Tour Operator on the ground floor: Day</u>

The office has many clients on its counters. The counter staffs are attending the clients. Since there is no one to attend them immediately, the students get uneasy. Just then, the door of the cabin of the manager is opened and a person approaches them.

<u>Manager</u>
"Gentlemen, I welcome you. Right now, our staffs are very busy but I can help you. I am the manager of Budget Travel. How can I help you?"

<u>One student</u>
"My name is Eddy. We are students, studying sculpture in the Institute of Fine Arts. This summer we decided to go on a sightseeing tour. Can you suggest something good but economical tourist destinations?"

<u>Manager</u>

"That is the area of our speciality, please come into my cabin."

The manager leads them to his cabin door and opens it.

Cut to:

<u>6 : Int : Manager's cabin : Day</u>

The manager gestures and requests them to have their seats placed before his desk. He sits behind the desk. His cabin is tastefully decorated and miniatures of airplane, helicopter and ship are seen on the sideboard adjacent to the desk.

<u>Manager</u>

"We have many packages for the summer like in for Asia, Europe, America and Australia. We have Bangkok, Kuala Lumpur, Sydney, London, Lisbon, Miami and many more on our list. You all need to name your choice and we will make it."

He looks at them to get a response. For a few seconds, all the students are thoughtfully calm.

<u>Eddy</u>

"We have seen these cities and even if there is a new city, all skyscrapers are similar. We need to see something serene and calm."

<u>Manager [Thinks for a while]</u>

"Are you interested to see marine life?"

<u>Eddy</u>

"That may not be a bad idea."

<u>Manager</u>

'Since you all are students of sculpture, this trip may enrich your experience."

<u>Eddy</u>

"How is that?"

<u>Manager</u>

"There are students of Marine Biology who want to go to Arctic region to study arctic animals and birds. They are ten in number and to make a trip economically viable to Arctic I need ten more people. I can see that you all are also ten people. If you agree for this trip then I can draw a tour programme. I assure you that this tour programme would certainly be very enjoyable and memorable."

Eddy [Looks into the eyes of his friends, and they in turn agree to this trip.]

"I think we can accept your proposal. "

Manager

"The total cost of the tour would work out to one thousand Danish Kroner for each tourist. We will take you all in our helicopter and drop you at the designated arctic region with all the accessories, equipments and food. We will pick you up in the helicopter after a week. There would be a local Eskimo man assigned as a tour guide and cook. He will help you in your tour camp and will have a wireless set to communicate with us in case of any emergency."

Eddy

"Where would we stay?"

Manager

"As you know that the area is remote with no hotel facility, we would arrange for a very comfortable stay in our tour camp made of canopies."

Eddy

"Apart from us, there would be ten other students of Marine Biology Institute."

Manager

"Yes."

Eddy

"When can we go? Can we go tomorrow? Our Institute has closed from today."

Manager

"Yes, it is possible for you all to leave tomorrow. But let me speak to the students of Marine Biology Institute."

He dials a number on his landline phone and speaks for a while.

Manager

"Mr. David, I am calling from Budget Travel. I am the manager. You wanted us to make a tour programme for Arctic. I am happy to inform you that I have been able to chalk out this plan but you need to leave for the destination tomorrow. Would it be all right with you?"

He listens with a great satisfaction and happiness appears on his face.

<u>Manager</u>
"Thank you, Mr David, for accepting my tour proposal. Would it be possible for you to deposit the cost of the tour by this evening in my office? It is a thousand kroner for each tourist. We would fly tomorrow from Kastrup helipad at 10 a.m. Kindly be at the helipad at the right time."

He listens to Mr. David's reply.

<u>Manager</u>
"Thank you."

Manager puts down the telephone.

<u>Manager</u>
"They have agreed and now the tour programme is finalized. You all can fly tomorrow to Arctic."

<u>Eddy</u>
"Thanks."

<u>Manager</u>
"Just as I told Mr David, you are also required to pay for the tour by the evening today."

<u>Eddy</u>
"That is not a problem. We will do that."

<u>Manager</u>
"Thanks. Now I will ask my staff to make arrangements for tomorrow's departure."

<u>Eddy [Gets up from his chair]</u>
"We will also take your leave to pack our bags."

All his friends get up from their chairs and shake hand with the Manager before leaving his cabin.

Cut to:
<u>7: Ext : Kastrup Helipad in Copenhagen : Day</u>

There are two helicopters parked in the helipad and the pilots are ready in their cabins to fly. The maintenance staffs are busy with the last minute preparation of the journey. A man wearing a T-shirt bearing 'Budget Travel' on its back, apparently an employee of 'Budget Travel', is leading two groups of students, i.e., ten students in each group, carrying their rolling suitcases towards the parked helicopters.

The helicopters are large enough to accommodate twelve people comfortably and they have a big compartment for baggages.

Each group climbs the metal staircases to get into the helicopter. Once inside, the students take their seats and fasten their seat belts. After that, a maintenance staff closes the glass doors and removes the metal staircases. Thereafter the blades of both the helicopters start speeding and they ascend into the sky. The maintenance staffs keep looking up in the sky until the helicopters disappear.

Cut to:

<u>8: Ext: Igloos, the Eskimo habitat in Icy Arctic region: Day</u>

Two helicopters are visible in the sky above the white Arctic region. The area is a large desert ice plains and rocks. About a hundred Igloos are seen from the sky. An Eskimo is seen standing and waving flag to signal the pilots to descend. Then the Eskimo encircled a large area with a red ribbon, so that the helicopters can come down safely. Seeing the signal, the pilots in the helicopters land inside the encircled area. After the helicopters have touched the ground, the Eskimo runs to the choppers and opens the glass doors.

<u>Eskimo man</u>

"Welcome gentlemen. I am Karu, your tour guide, cook and helper. Please come down. I will lead you all to your tour camp made of canopies."

All the students reciprocate by saying "Thank you". They get down with their rolling suitcases from the helicopters and follow Karu, the Eskimo man.

Cut to:

<u>9: Int : Tour camp for students made of a large canopy : Day</u>

The canopy in the camp is very large and supported by wooden poles which are immersed underneath the icy surface to hold tightly. However, the roof is four feet high and it can brave the windy condition of the area. There are padded mattresses laid on flat wooden boards on the icy floor. All the students got busy with making arrangement of their bed and belonging. They have brought their sleeping bags that are actually a wearable thick quilt to sleep within it and to brave the cold of the night.

Cut to:

10: Int : Karu's canopy : Day

Apart from the canopy's size which is very small, all other arrangements are similar to the student's canopy. He is busy making tea on a gas stove for the students. He pours tea in a ceramic kettle. Thereafter, he warms the tinned food, packets of fish and meat. He takes the kettle along with food and biscuit packets, cups and saucers on a tray, and goes to the student's canopy. His canopy has his sleeping bag apart from the accessories, equipments and the stock of food provisions.

Cut to:

11. Int : Tour Camp of students made of a large canopy : Day

Mr Karu opens the canopy door which is like a curtain but tightly buttoned, to enter inside and serve snacks and tea to the students.

Karu

"You must be feeling hungry and wishing to have a cup of tea."

Everybody looks at him and his tray delightfully. They say in unison, "Yes, you are absolutely right."

Karu

"I have brought warm fish fillets, some biscuits and hot tea. Help yourselves. In the meantime, I am going to arrange for dog-sledges to take you for sightseeing."

Eddy

"Six hours of helicopter journey was very tiring. I am exhausted and think every one feels the same."

Everybody replies in unison, "Yes, that is true."

Karu

"Then all of you can sleep for two-three hours. Thereafter we can go."

Eddy

" But I can sleep at night only."

Karu

"There won't be any night for the next six months in this area. There would always be light. Therefore, you have to sleep in the light only. In this Arctic region, summer months are sunny all-day-long for six months and for the other six months it is night all through."

Eddy

"I will try to sleep. After that where will you take us?"

Karu

"I have been told that you all are interested to see the marine life of this area. So I will take you to a vacant and half-immersed ship and there through the glass cabin you will be able to see the underwater Arctic plants, animals and even birds. It is very beautiful and picturesque, and you can take photos. Thereafter, I will take you all around the area where the natives live in their igloos. You can see also many birds and other overground animals."

Eddy

"Is there overground plants? "

Karu

"It is very rare to find any greenery in this harsh condition."

Eddy

"It is alright. First, we will relish the food and tea that you have brought. Then we will sleep for two-three hours and thereafter we will go for sightseeing."

Everybody nods and few say "Yes."

Karu

"I am going to bring dog-sledges after three hours, and hopefully by that time you all will be refreshed by the nap. Bye for now… "

Karu then leaves the canopy by opening the curtain that is tightly buttoned. Whereas inside, everybody flocks near the food tray. Eddy is serving tea and all the others are either eating biscuit or pre-cooked fish or meat fillet.

Cut to:

12: Ext: Two dog-sledges : Day

There are two dog-sledges, each driven by six robust dogs. Each sledge has a seating capacity of twelve people. So all the students are comfortably sitting in the sledge. Mr Karu is also sitting near the driver of the sledge. The dogs began running fast on the icy surface and at times skid. However, this unique sledge ride gives immense joy to these students, who are laughing and cheering loudly.

Cut to:

13: Ext: Area where half-immersed ship is located : Day

Many dog-sledges are spotted carrying tourists to the site where half-immersed ship is located. This place is a tourist destination in this desolate part of the world. A number of dog-sledges are already waiting for their tourist clients to come back from the cabins of the half-immersed ship. The half of the ship is immersed underneath the icy surface whereas the other half that is above the icy surface has outer metallic wall which prevents the water from flooding into the ship. There are two metallic staircases for climbing onto the ship and then to go to the glass cabin to see the underwater arctic lives.

The students along with Karu reach the site and get down from the sledges. A man approaches Karu.

Eskimo man

"Hello, Karu, will they be interested to go inside?"

Karu

"Yes. What is the discount today?"

Eddy

"Do we need to pay? But why is a ticket needed?"

Karu

"You need not bother, a small fee is charged for proper maintenance and cleaning of this site for tourists. I will pay for this as your trip is fully paid. I am just trying to negotiate with my friend." [He laughs.]

Eskimo man

"No negotiation. Only fixed price..."

Karu

"I will pay you later."

Eskimo man

"It is alright."

Karu [To all the students]

"I will take you to the glass cabin of the ship but before that you will have to follow me and climb that staircase."

Eddy

"That's fine. Let us move."

Everyone climbs the staircase of the ship.

Cut to:

<u>14: Int : Glass Cabin of the immersed ship : Day</u>

There are many tourists inside this glass cabin including the students. They are busy gazing at underwater arctic lives including plants, animals and birds. The birds are trying to catch fishes after diving from the ground above. They took photographs fishes, walrus, seal and many other underwater animals and birds. All the students are busy studying these animals.

Cut to:

<u>15: Ext: Arctic desert with big mountainous chunk of ice rock: Day</u>

Many tourists are looking at a big mountainous rock of ice from a distance. A family of polar bear with six small kids is playing around that. They are in playful mood. The sun is shining in the sky and the temperature is minus thirty-degree celsius. However, the wind is not blowing. This makes the climate very enjoyable, as extremely biting cold is not felt. There are many birds flying around this site and at times sit at the tip of the mountainous rock of ice. The students are taking photographs of birds, playful bears and the surrounding. They are very happy and in good mood. Eddy and David are walking together, whereas the other students are at a distance. Karu is happy to see his tourist clients enjoy the day.

<u>Eddy</u>

"David, this trip is the most memorable one for me."

<u>David</u>

"This is a unique experience for us, which is very refreshing. It has brought us away from the monotonous tourist trips to cities like Europe, America or Asia."

<u>Eddy</u>

"I can use this experience to make my next portraits."

<u>David</u>

"I wish to go to some other natural surrounding next year also."

<u>Eddy [To Mr Karu, his tour guide]</u>

"Mr Karu, where will you take us next?"

<u>Karu</u>

"I will take you to the site of fresh water wells."

Eddy

"How can a well be operational in this area?"

Karu

"Our people have made these wells to draw water."

Eddy

"Snow may cover the opening of the well !"

Karu

"We keep the opening closed with a wooden plank and open it only for drawing water. There are many such wells at one place."

Eddy

"Amazing..."

Karu

"There are many amazing things that you will see here."

Eddy and David keep quiet and move ahead to look at the surrounding.

Cut to:

16: Int : Tour Camp of student tourists : Day

All the students are sleeping in their sleeping bags and a few of them are snoring, whereas Eddy is awake. It is very difficult for Eddy to sleep with light all around. He is watching others sleep deeply. After sometime, he feels tired due to his sleeplessness. He feels uncomfortable and comes out of his sleeping bag and sits for a while with his blanket on him. He watches his friends fast asleep and then gets up. He puts on his warm clothe and opens the tightly buttoned curtain door of the canopy and exits.

Cut to:

17: Ext : Outside of the tour camp of the student tourists: Day

It is still bright at the dawn, though sun appears to be just under the white carpet of the earth. West side of the sky is bright reddish. Eddy is calm and looking at his camp and the camp of Karu. He starts walking in a direction and continues walking while watching the serenity of the surrounding and the red sky. After walking about two kilometres nonchalantly, he finds a sludgy surface. He thinks, "I might have slipped under the ice mud on putting an extra step" [V.O]. He stops and looks at the sludgy area carefully, there the ice mud is made of snowflakes. He sits there and touches the soft snow. An idea crops up in the mind of this young sculptor.

Eddy [Murmurs]
"Icy tiger would scare polar mammals, like bears. That would be fun. Huh."

He starts sculpting an icy tiger. He gets so immersed in his work that he has no idea about time.

Cut to:
18: Int : Tour Camp of student tourists : Day

After eight hours [On screen caption]

Karu enters the student's camp with tea and snacks. All the students are sleeping in their sleeping bags, except Eddy whose sleeping bag is empty. Just then, the alarm of the table clock rings and everybody wakes up.

Karu [a bit loudly]
"Good morning my friends, bed tea is ready."

After yawning and stretching their limbs, they look at the empty sleeping bag of Eddy. David is bit surprised to see that Eddy has woken up early.

David
"Mr Karu, let me empty my bladder first."

He gets up, wears his warm leather jacket, and exits from the camp after opening the tightly buttoned curtain door. Karu is busy serving tea to the students. After a few minutes, David comes back.

David
"Mr Karu, did you see Eddy? Where has he gone? He is not in the toilet."

Karu
"No, I did not see him. When I came, he wasn't here."

David
"He is not in the toilet. He woke up early. Where can he go?"

Karu
"You first take your tea. In the meantime, I will search him around."

Karu goes out of the camp and the students enjoy their tea.

Cut to:
19:Ext : Outside of the tour camp of the student tourists: Day

All the students are in their warm clothes and looking worried.

Karu

"We are twenty people. Let us make four groups of five persons each. We will go in four directions to look for him and return to this camp. Is it clear?"

David

"Yes"

Karu

"Then let us move."

All the students disperse in four groups consisting of five persons in four directions and walk straight. Karu also goes with one group of student.

Cut to:

20: Ext : Far away from the tour camp of the student tourists: Day

Five students led by David are approaching the site where Eddy is busy making the structure of ice tiger. The students are looking for Eddy and recognize him from a distance. They call him loudly.

All the students [In unison]

"Eddy, where are you? What are you doing?"

Eddy's attention is distracted by the clear loud voices of the students. He sees them approaching him. He waves his hand to call them. After a few seconds, the group of five students are with him. They are surprised to see Eddy's creation of the ice tiger.

David [In angry tone]

"Why did you make us worry? Why did you come this far without telling us? We were searching for you in four groups in four directions."

Eddy

"Sorry guys, I had a sleepless night. Therefore, I came out of the camp and strolled. I found this place with snowflakes and could not stop myself from making this ice tiger?"

David

"What would this tiger do in this desolate place?"

Eddy

"This would scare polar bears and other animals at night."

David

"Yes, that is true."

One student [of this group]

"Eddy has made a tiger. Let us make a tiger family from snowflakes."

Everyone in the group welcomes the idea.

David

"But Karu and other guys would be looking for us."

Eddy

"They would return to the camp only. We will also return to camp after the tiger family is ready here. So don't worry and help me create the tiger family."

All the students join together to create the sculpture of the tiger family.

Cut to:

21: Ext: Arctic region with icy sculpture of tigers: Day

After six hours [On screen caption]

All the students remain busy for six hours. Eddy creates a tiger, whereas his friends create a tigress and four cubs. They are very happy and satisfied to see their creations of tiger sculptures in the arctic desert. Thereafter they leave the place and go back to their tour camp.

Cut to:

22: Ext: Two Helicopters parked at a distance away from the tour camp: Day

All the students, in two groups, are approaching towards their respective helicopter with their rolling suitcases to set out on return journey to Copenhagen. Karu is helping them to load their luggage in the helicopters. The students are thanking Karu for his services. Then they climb onto their helicopter one by one. After a while, departure preparations are complete, helicopters start and its blade speeds up. Thereafter, the helicopters ascend into the sky. Karu is watching up in the sky until the helicopters are out of his sight.

Fade Out:

Fade In:

23: Ext: Igloo settlements in a remote Arctic region: Stormy Day

After six months [On screen caption]

There is a bitter winter in the arctic region with snowstorm and pitch-dark night condition even during daytime. Stormy wind is blowing continuously. There are Igloo settlements in this desolate region and snow dust is gathering around the igloos. The condition is unbearably chilly.

A Eskimo man is seen in the dark night, who opens the door and walks some steps to defecate. He quickly finishes nature's call and returns to his igloo.

Cut to:
<u>24: Int: A Igloo in the remote Arctic region: Stormy Day</u>

Kemu and Kelly, both husband and wife, are at their igloo. They are on the bed under thick fur blanket to brave the unbearable chilly condition of the winter but are not sleeping. They are waiting for the weather to be calm and better.

<u>Kelly</u>
"It is the third day. Kemu, I am very hungry. Can you find some food?"

<u>Kemu</u>
"Kelly, I wish I can go for fishing but this weather is terrible. I told Reku's wife to give some food as you are pregnant."

<u>Kelly</u>
"What did she say?"

<u>Kemu</u>
"She said that she is also pregnant like you and that her condition is also the same. She has had all the food at home and there is nothing left."

<u>Kelly</u>
"Kemu, she is a big liar. She has food but she does not want to share."

<u>Kemu</u>
"It is our bad luck. Just tolerate for some more time. When the weather is a bit calm, I will go out and arrange some food for you."

After that, they both keep quiet and wait for the snowstorm to recede as the sound of heavily blowing wind is heard even within the walls of the igloo.

Cut to:
<u>25: Ext : Igloo settlements in a remote Arctic region: Stormy Day</u>

It is pitch dark and the condition in the arctic has worsened. The violent storm kept blowing and is about to destroy the igloo settlements. It has become hard and very difficult for any human or animal to venture out of their Igloo.

Cut to:

26: Int: Igloo home in the remote Arctic region: Stormy Night

Sixth Stormy Night [on Screen Caption]

Kemu and Kelly are in their igloo on a bed under thick fur blanket to brave the unbearable winter.

Kelly

"Kemu, my baby will die and so will I. I am feeling an excruciating pain in my abdomen."

Kemu

"Darling, please hold on a bit. I will go and get food for you. It seems that the wind is subsiding now and becoming weaker."

Kemu is trying to gauze the condition of snowstorm by hearing the sound of wind coming from outside. After a while he finds that the sound has lessen and the snowstorm has receded.

Kemu

"Darling, I am going out to catch fish or seal meat for you. Be careful."

Kelly

"Come, quickly."

Kemu comes out of the bed and wears his leather jacket, cap and knee length fur shoes. He takes out a sharp curved knife hanging from the roof. He carefully opens the door and exits. Igloo door is closed.

Cut to:

27: Ext: Far away from Igloo settlements: Stormy Night

Out of his igloo, Kemu walks a long way to a desolate place trying to detect the hollowness beneath the icy surface by tapping with his boots. It is a pitch-dark night. The wind is still blowing and whirls of snow dust are filled in the air. The velocity of wind is, however, not so fierce. After a long walk in the night, he finds a surface that is hollow beneath. He stops there and breaks the surface of the ice-pit with the help of his sharp knife. He immerses himself in the ice-pit to find fish. In the pitch-dark, he touches something and feels like a flesh, a very big flesh. He guessed it to be a big seal fish. He tries to cut the flesh with the help of his knife. However, it is a snake, which moves his head upward and bites him many times on his face. He quickly moves out from the ice-pit. Nevertheless, snake bites are so deadly that he falls unconscious almost instantly and dies suddenly without a chance of recovering. His dead body is lying on the icy surface.

Fade out:

Fade In

28: Int: Igloo home in the remote Arctic region: Stormy night

After six hours [On screen caption]

Kelly is restless and worried Kemu has not returned even after six long hours.

Kelly [Murmurs]

"O God, why is Kemu not coming? Why so much delay? Please help."

Kelly waits for some more time , then decides to go out of the Igloo to find her husband. She gets off from the bed and wears her leather jacket, cap and knee-length fur shoes. She opens the igloo door and exits.

Cut to:

29: Ext : igloo settlements in a remote Arctic region: Stormy Night

Kelly is out of her Igloo and is knocking on the door of her neighbour, who opens the door and comes out.

Kelly

"Koru, Kemu has gone out to get some food. He has not come back. Can you help me to find him?"

Koru

"I can't go now. My child is sick and I have to be near her bed. It is dark and stormy outside."

Kelly

"What do I do?"

Koru

"What should I say? You either wait or go out and find him. But how can you go in this condition at this night?"

"Papa, where are you? Please come quickly." [O.S]. A child's voice is heard from inside. It was the voice of Koru's daughter. Koru quickly returns to his igloo and closes the door from inside.

Kelly is alone in the dark, stormy and deserted night. She is confused as to what she should do. She thinks for a while and decides to set out to find her husband. She starts walking away from her Igloo. It is very difficult to walk as the wind is still blowing and whirls of snow dust are filled in the air. She musters all her strength and shouts "Kemu". There is no response from Kemu. She keeps walking and in every few minutes would call his name. But her sound disappears in the desolate place. She is very tired and in order to quench her thirst she chews snow dust. She is continuously walking.

Cut to:

30: Ext: A desolate place far away from Igloo settlements: Stormy Night

Kelly walks for a long time and is fully exhausted. She at last finds the body of her husband lying on the icy surface. She is shocked to see him dead. She wails uncontrollably. She feels pain in her lower abdomen, which becomes unbearable. She is frightened. She has no one to help her. She lies down and musters all her strength to push her child out. With all her efforts, she is able to deliver her baby. It is a baby boy. However, she does not have the vitality left and succumbs to her extreme exhaustion, weakness and bleeding. Her helpless baby boy is crying as it is very cold and there is no one to take care of him.

Cut to:

31: Ext: An overview of a desolate Arctic place where a newborn baby is crying: Stormy Night

After death, Kelly's soul moves away from her dead body and goes into the sky, where she finds the soul of her husband Kemu. They are happy to see each other. There are four other friendly souls with Kemu. They greet her cordially. Now Kemu and Kelly are anxious to see their baby crying helplessly on the ground near their dead bodies. Kemu and Kelly are very eager to help their newborn baby. However, by realizing that they are souls now and are barred to enter into their dead bodies, they feel hopeless.

Kemu [raises his head in hopelessness and speaks loudly]

"O God, what is the fate of this newborn baby? Is he going to die?"

To their surprise, the sky echoes and a loud voice is heard.

"The child is to live long." [O.S]

The helpless newborn baby is crying frantically on the ground whereas the dead bodies of his father and mother are of no help.

<u>Kemu</u>
"Oh, my son is crying with on one around. How can I help him? Can I enter into my body?"

<u>A friendly soul</u>
"Once death is granted to you, you can't go back to your body. It has degenerated by now. You cannot change the course of destiny. If God is saying that the child would live long, then you should not worry for him. God will provide help to enable him to sustain his life on earth. Something would certainly happen to save him."

But these words are not able to provide any solace to Kemu and Kelly. They are restless.

Cut to:
<u>32: Int: Icy cave of a Polar Bear family in the Arctic region: Stormy Night.</u>

There is an icy cave wherein resides a polar bear family. The polar bear family consists of the male bear, female bear and their two cubs. They are all asleep, but the baby's cry wakes them up. The sound of a living thing makes them hungry. They all get up and go out to find their prey.

Cut to:
<u>33: Ext: An overview of a desolate Arctic place where a newborn baby is crying: Stormy Night</u>

The polar bear family comes out of their underground cave. Kemu and Kelly become nervous to see the polar bear family. Kemu, Kelly and four other friendly souls are frightened to see the polar bear family approaching to the site where the newborn child is crying helplessly. They are trying to contemplate as to how to save this baby. They wait to see God send some help to save the child. When they see no movement or miracle coming for the safety of the child, they grow anxious.

<u>Kelly</u>
"God said that my child is to live long, but these polar bears will kill my Pola. Where is this God? Why is he not sending any help?

Kemu

"As always... God is not going to do anything. We will have to do something to save our Pola."

Kemu, Kelly and four other friendly souls become restless. They move fast to look for some one, who can render help in saving baby. They cannot find anyone in this desolate place except the amazing icy sculptures of Tiger, Tigress and four cubs. They are surprised to see the icy sculptures of the tiger family.

The polar bear family reaches the place where the newborn baby is lying. They sniff him with satisfaction before inserting teeth in the baby's flesh. When they see this imminent attack on the helpless baby, all the souls in sheer rage enter into the icy sculptures of Tiger, Tigress and four cubs. A bright light appears with the occurrence of this marvellous phenomenon of nature and God. Kemu and Kelly occupy the icy sculptures of Tiger and Tigress and the four friendly souls occupy the sculptures of icy cubs. Therefore, these icy sculptures turn into a lively polar tiger family. Since the souls enter into these sculptures and are in rage, they growl aloud and run towards the polar bear family to save the child.

The sudden appearance and growl of the polar tigers scares the polar bears. They are too frightened to face the polar tigers and in the process run away from there. The tiger family runs after the polar bears. After a long chase, they catch hold of the entire polar bear family consisting of male, female and two kids. The bear family are not able to face the fierce attack of the polar tigers and succumb to their death.

Kelly, the tigress

"We have killed the polar bears, but who is going to feed my child and put him under warm clothes? Without this Pola will die."

Kemu, the tiger

"We are now tigers. We can't do that. We can't go to our igloo as tigers."

Kelly, the tigress

"How can we save our Pola?"

Kemu, the tiger [raises his head and stare into the dark sky in hopelessness] "Now, who is going to take care of my baby? He will soon die."

Again to their surprise, the sky echoes and a loud voice is heard.

"No, he will not die." [O.S]

<u>Kemu, the tiger</u>
"Who is this? Are you God?"

Again, the sky echoes and a loud voice is heard.

"No, I am not God. I am his accountant." [O.S]

<u>Kemu, the tiger</u>
"Why can't I see you? Please show yourself to me."

Thereafter a bright light descends from the sky and a human figure appears within the brightness. Everybody is amazed by the event unfolding before them.

<u>God's accountant</u>
"I am God's accountant."

The polar tiger family bows their head before this heavenly body.

<u>God's accountant</u>
"This baby would live long."

<u>Kemu, the tiger</u>
"How can that be possible? He can be fed and saved only by a human as he is a human baby."

<u>God's accountant</u>
"I will explain it to you. The tentacles of human's greedy desire of self-reliance, money, and wealth have spread all over the earth. That is why the standard formulation and balance of nature on the earth have gone topsy-turvy resulting in serious faults in my balance sheet. Though human virtues have always been supreme all over the universe the devil's special effect has overshadowed these virtues on the earth, resultant effects of which have natural and un-natural disasters such as mass killings and suicides, epidemics, non-curable diseases, earthquakes, tsunami, flood, storms, hurricane, tornado, etc."

The polar tiger family is looking at him in amazement.

<u>God's accountant</u>
"You were not destined to die, that is why you were refused an entry into the heaven or hell. It is a mess here. The boy is to live long but there is no one to take care of him in this arctic area. So I am forced to make things better. I have, therefore, allowed you to enter into the tiger's ice sculptures to become polar tigers."

Kemu, the tiger

"Thanks. Though we killed the polar bear family but who would feed and protect this baby? Where is his human family?"

God's accountant

"You all are his family. The tigress would breast-feed which would make him stronger to brave the harsh weather. You all are made of ice and won't need any food and water to survive. You all would live for another twenty years on this earth. When you die, the baby would be self-sufficient to sustain his life on earth."

Soon thereafter the bright light disappears and celestial body vanishes. The polar tiger family is astonished by the event and is in utter disbelief.

Fade out:

Fade In

34: Ext : Desolate Arctic place with Polar tiger family : Day

After one year [On screen caption]

The polar tiger family is happy in the lonely arctic region. It is summer in the arctic with bright daylight all through. Pola, the infant child is one-year-old now. He is sucking his mother tigress's milk in playful mood. He is laughing as his mother tigress is gesturing to amuse him. After being fed by his mother Pola tries to stand on his feet for the first time but cannot balance himself and fall on his bottom. She is extremely happy to see her son stand on his feet and therefore calls everyone.

Kelly, the tigress

"Kemu, Kola, Keke, Pochu, Naka, come quickly and see my Pola trying to stand on his feet."

Kemu, the tiger and the four tiger cubs are relaxing nearby. After hearing Kelly's sudden call, they get up and come to her. They see that Pola is trying to stand on his feet. After standing for a moment, he tries to balance himself but sits back quickly on ground.

Kemu, the tiger

"Let us help Pola stand."

Kemu and Kelly go near the baby and stand in such a way that Pola is in-between their heads. He holds her mother's head and gets up, whereas his father's head is supporting his back to stop him from falling. With Pola's mother and father supporting him, he does not fall back but gets his balance. While balancing, Pola tries to move his leg ahead in order to walk but he falls. He again tries to stand with the help of his parents. This time he is able to step ahead and walk with the support of his mother and father. Everybody is extremely happy to see him walk.

Kola, Keke, Pochu and Naka, the tiger cubs [In unison] "He is our baby brother. We will play with him and help him walk. He has made our life joyful."

Kelly, the tigress

"He is the treasure of our life."

Kemu, the tiger

"He is the only reason that we have got this second life."

Kemu, the tiger, Kelly the tigress and the four tiger cubs start licking Pola's cheek and body in affection. They shower their love, and play with the baby for quite a long time.

Fade Out:

Fade In

35: Ext: Desolate Arctic place with Polar tiger family: Day

After five years [On screen caption]

Kemu and Kelly are happy to watch Pola, playg with the four tiger cubs in the arctic region. It is summer in the arctic with bright daylight. Pola is now a five-year-old boy. He does not wear any clothes. He is in a playful mood. His brothers are chasing him but he is very fast. Whenever his brother cubs are about to catch him, he dodges them. When he successfully dodges them, he laughs and screams with joy.

Pola

"Brothers, you all can't catch me. Mom, dad, I am the fastest runner."

Pochu, the tiger cub

"We are happy that you are fast, but we will catch you. Just stop."

Pola

"Brothers, if I stop, you will certainly catch me. You all have to run to catch me."

Kemu and Kelly are happy to hear Pola's voice and laughter.

Kemu, the tiger [In low voice to Kelly, the tigress]

"We are lucky to see our son even after our death."

Kelly, the tigress

"With God's grace, he is growing very strong to handle any situation."

Kemu, the tiger

"Your milk has given him enough strength to face the extreme cold."

The tiger cubs come from four sides and do not allow Pola to escape. They catch Pola. But Pola has a reason to protest.

Pola

"Dad, it is not fair. They should run straight run from one direction. Why should they surround me from all four sides?"

Kemu, the tiger

"Yes, I agree. There should be a straight run. I am making a straight line from start to finish for the race."

Kemu gets up and walks from one point to another to mark a straight line for the race. He comes back to the starting point and sits where Kelly is sitting.

Pochu, the tiger cub

"Okay. It is fine. We will now run straight on this line to win."

The four tiger cubs and Pola come to the starting point. They begin their race and are running towards finishing point, where Kemu and Kelly are sitting. Kemu and Kelly are happy to see their son running faster than the tiger cubs.

Fade Out:

Fade In

36: Ext: Desolate Arctic place with Polar tiger family: Night

After six months [On screen caption]

Pola is drinking his mother's milk. Thereafter, he rides on her back and kisses her. Then he jumps and kisses his father and brother cubs. They are all glad to see Pola grow by each day. The winter is approaching. The stars are twinkling in the sky. It is not very dark but dawn-like condition. Pola was lying on the ground and gazing at the twinkling stars. He is eager to know about the stars.

Pola

"Dad, what are those in the sky?"

Kemu, the tiger

"Those are the stardoms."

<u>Pola</u>
"Who... lives... there... ?

<u>Kemu, the tiger</u>
"God grants stardom to kind-hearted souls."

<u>Pola</u>
"Dad, everybody is kind hearted. Does it mean...everyone will get stardom?"

<u>Kemu, the tiger</u>
"A kind heart with kind deed gets stardom."

<u>Pola</u>
"I don't understand."

<u>Kemu, the tiger</u>
"I will make you understand by telling you a story."

<u>Pola</u>
"That is great."

<u>Kemu, the tiger</u>
"A family and friends of a long-legged crane used to migrate every year from the extreme cold in the north to the warmer climate in the south."

Cut to:
<u>37:Ext: Overview of long-legged crane in flight in the sky : Day</u>

This is an overview of long-legged cranes in flight in the clear and ocean blue sky.

Cut to:
<u>38: Ext: Desolate Arctic place with Polar tiger family: Night</u>

Kemu is telling a story to his son in the desolate arctic region. Pola is sitting with his other family members and listening to his father patiently.

<u>Kemu, the tiger</u>
"The crane used to live in a warm habitat, while by feeding on fish of the wetland. Once a tragedy struck as an angler shot these helpless birds and killed all except one aged bird which escaped the shot. The angler tried to kill that bird also but the bird flew away. The angler and his family relished the meat of the dead birds."

Cut to:

<u>39. Ext: A wetland near seashore :Day</u>

A gun-laden angler reaches wetland where a group of long-legged crane birds are busy feeding on fish. The angler fires indiscriminately on these birds. The cranes are unaware about the angler, and are busy feeding on fish with their heads down under water. The bullets hit all the birds except one bird at a distance which flies away. The angler tries to shoot that bird also but missed the target. He is, however, happy to have a big catch of dead birds. He goes where the birds have fallen and collects them in his bamboo basket.

<u>Angler (Murmurs)</u>

"What a big catch? Oh, I am feeling hungry...already."

Cut to:

<u>40: Ext: Desolate Arctic place with Polar tiger family: Night</u>

Kemu continues his story. Pola is listening to his father intently.

<u>Kemu, the tiger</u>

"The fortunate bird was traumatised by the death of his near and dear ones. He had lost his desire to live any more. He took shelter on a tall tree not far from the house of the angler and wished him and his family something bad."

Cut to:

<u>41: Ext: An overview of a tall tree in the area of a wetland :Day</u>

There is a tall tree, where the long-legged crane is sitting on a branch of the tree. No one can see the bird from beneath, as the leaves of the tree cover the bird. There is a village near the tree.

Cut to:

<u>42: Ext: Desolate Arctic place with Polar tiger family: Night</u>

Pola is attentively listening to Kemu.

<u>Kemu, the tiger</u>

"After some time the angler and his family sets out on a sea journey in their fishing boat to catch fish. As it was a sunny day, they ventured for into the deep sea. The bird also followed them into the sea. All of a sudden, the weather became stormy and turbulent. It started raining heavily."

Cut to:

<u>43 : Ext: An overview of in and around the sea :Day</u>

The angler's boat is in the deep sea. He and his family members are alarmed to see the turbulent condition in the sea. There is a high tide in the sea and his fishing boat was moving like a paper boat. The oarsman of the boat loses his balance and the grip of the oars. The wooden oars fall into the sea and is swept away by sea current. Since it is cloudy, it is impossible to navigate the boat towards the seashore as no one can guess the direction without the sun in the sky. The oarsman and the angler are trying to sail the boat by pushing water with their hands from both sides. The crane is also floating above the deep sea and watching the pathetic condition of the angler and his family. The bird is very happy to see them in this condition. The sea currents are getting wild and out of control. The angler is panicking as he sees the imminent death of every one. Everybody of angler's family particularly children in the boat are crying for help. The bird in the sky feels emotional when he sees angler's children crying.

<u>Crane (murmurs)</u>

"Why should his children die? They are innocent and should not suffer due to their father's sin."

The bird sympathises with angler's children. He floats at a lower altitude and helps angler to navigate his boat towards the seashore. The angler feels grateful to this bird and repents for killing its family and friends. On reaching the seashore, the crane falls on the ground and dies due to weakness and extreme exhaustion. The angler picks him up and keep him on his lap. Then he and family wail over the crane's death. They can never forget how crane has helped them reach the seashore safely.

Cut to:

<u>44: Ext: Desolate Arctic place with Polar tiger family: Night</u>

Kemu is nearing the end of the story. Pola is excited.

<u>Kemu, the tiger</u>

"God gave this bird a stardom as he was kind despite of all the odds that he faced but helped the needy. The bird is now living with his family in that stardom."

Kelly, the tigress

"It means that you should be kind hearted towards others."

Pola

"That bird is also there in those stardoms."

Kelly, the tigress

"Yes, my boy."

Pola is very curious and anxious. He keeps quiet for some time, while gazing at the stars of the sky. He again thinks something and blinks his eyes.

Pola

"Mom, where do the sun uncle and moon uncle go for six long months?'

Kelly, the tigress

"They go to another world far away from here."

Pola

"Why can't they be with us all the time? I miss them a lot."

Kelly, the tigress

"You are very lovely, so they come to meet you but they have many more beautiful boys like you in another world."

Pola

"Mom, do they have many more boys like me?"

Kelly, the tigress

"Yes."

Pola

"I would like to play with them."

Kelly, the tigress

"You can't go there."

Pola

"Why?"

Kelly, the tigress

"It is very far from here. No one can go there."

Pola

"How many people are there in another world?"

Kelly, the tigress

"Many."

Pola

'How many world sun and moon have?"

Kelly, the tigress

"All the stars in the sky are their world."

Pola

"Does he go to all the stardoms?"

Kelly, the tigress

"Yes."

Pola

"Those at stardom...are they also looking at us?"

Kelly, the tigress

"Yes."

Pola

"Are the sun and moon kind?"

Kelly, the tigress

"Yes. I will tell you a story of moon uncle's kindness. There was a man and his wife living in their igloo happily. Once the man went to fetch food for his lovely wife in a stormy night and was bitten by a polar snake. He died and his wife became restless. She came out of her igloo. She also died leaving her son helpless in the world. They were helpless as they could not help their son. Seeing this moon uncle resurrected the man and woman so that they can look after their baby. He always helps those who need help."

Pola's curiosity about sun and moon is clarified. He keeps quiet and falls asleep after some time. Kelly and Kemu are by his side and watch him with affection. The four cubs are also lying nearby. Thereafter everyone sleeps.

Fade out:

Fade in

45: Ext: Desolate Arctic place with Polar tiger family: Night

After Eighteen Years [On screen caption]

Pola is now an eighteen-year-old boy. He is sleeping on the ground and so is the tiger family except Kemu and Kelly. They are very disturbed. Kelly is sobbing as she is worried about the time deadline of twenty years given by the accountant of God, which is fast approaching, when they are to die natural death.

Kemu, the tiger

"The accountant have given us only twenty years life. Eighteen years have already passed."

Kelly, the tigress [she is sobbing]

"We have lost track of the time. Now what to do? We are to die soon."

Kemu, the tiger

"I don't know what to do?"

Kelly does not say anything. She just weeps uncontrollably.

Kemu, the tiger

"Pola has not yet learnt the human habit and language. If we leave him in the human habitat now at this age, he would be treated as a mad or mentally-retarded boy. He hasn't been in the company of human beings and has no idea of their daily practices, so he would be considered an outsider."

Kelly, the tigress [She is weeping bitterly]

"Please do something, otherwise how will my child live without us."

Kemu, the tiger

"What should I do? We have lost the ability to talk like human and we can not introduce ourselves to our neighbours to request them to look after our child."

Kelly was heartbroken. Even Kemu couldn't control himself. He too started weeping. Pochu, a tiger cub sleeping nearby wakes up and is astonished to see them weeping.

Pochu, the tiger cub

"What has happened? Why are you both weeping?"

Kemu, the tiger

"We have only two more years of life. We are to die soon. With whom would our Pola live after we are gone?"

Pochu, the tiger cub

"Why do you worry for nothing? Don't you remember God's accountant. He had said that our Pola would live long."

Kemu, the tiger

"Yes."

Pochu, the tiger cub

"It is the accountant's headache to ensure Pola a long life. Why do we worry?"

Kelly is not convinced and so too Kemu.

Pochu, the tiger cub

"Didn't you hear that his balance sheet is in mess? We died prematurely because of his confusion."

Kemu and Kelly are still not very convinced but they are quiet now.

Pochu, the tiger cub

"Don't worry. He patches up his errors. If he does not find an alternative, he may allow us to live longer with Pola."

Kemu, the tiger [finds solace from the tiger cub]

"You are right."

Pochu, the tiger cub

"You are unnecessarily worried. Just calm down and everything would be fine."

Kemu, the tiger

"My darling, Pochu is right. Just don't worry. Everything would be fine. Let us sleep now."

Kemu stretches himself on the ground. He looks up into the sky for some time and then sleeps. Kelly caresses Pola in his sleep with love and affection. Thereafter she also sleeps.

Fade out:

Fade In

46: Ext : Overview of an ancient city's exit gate : Day

An exit door of a walled city is visible, top façade of which indicates the name of a Chinese Kingdom bearing a flag of 'Khirakhao Kingdom'. The exit gate is the thoroughfare for the public. Handheld carts, horse carriages, bullock carts and camel sledges with material loads are seen moving in and out of the gate.

Cut to

47: Ext : Overview of the downtown of an olden city of 'Khirakhao Kingdom' in China: Day

This is an overview of a downtown of the Khirakhao Kingdom in China. The roads and streets look very busy because of movements of people. The market place is bustling with activities due to moving carts having loads of materials, and people buying fruits, vegetables and other food grains from roadside vendors.

Cut to

48: Ext: A clinic of a Chinese healer of herbal and natural medicine in the City's downtown: Day

A bilingual signboard of a clinic of Dr Choo Lai Ho, a Chinese healer of herbal and natural medicine, in city's downtown is seen located adjacent to a busy road. The entrance door of the clinic also mentions in Chinese and English the calibre of Dr Choo Lai Ho, who cures various ailment.

Cut to

49: Int : A clinic of a Chinese healer of herbal & natural medicine in City's downtown: Day

This is a herbal clinic of Dr Choo Lai Ho, the Chinese healer. There are many glass almirahs alongside the four walls of the clinic. The almirahs display glass containers having various herbal and natural medicines duly preserved. Dr Choo Lai Ho, an old Chinese man, is sitting on a broad wooden plank placed a bit higher from the floor, whereas his patients are sitting on the carpeted floor. There are ten patients. He is examining a patient by reading the pulse of his wrist. A young man is assisting him by giving medicines to patients from the glass containers kept in Almirahs.

Cut to:

50. Int: Bedroom of Dr Choo Lai Ho : Night

Dr Choo Lai Ho is sleeping on his bed at night. The moonlight is coming to his bedroom through the window. This improves the visibility of the room. Dr Choo Lai Ho is in sound sleep and seems to be dreaming as his eyeballs appear to be moving under the closed eyelids. He looks uncomfortable in his sleep.

Fade Out:

Fade In

51: An overview of a desolate Arctic place where a newborn baby is crying: Stormy Night

After coming out of the arctic cave from their long sleep, the polar bear family is feeling hungry. They hear a voice of crying. They trail the sound of their prey. The polar bear family reaches the site where the newborn baby is lying. They sniff the baby happily before inserting teeth in the baby's flesh.

All of a sudden, their attention is caught by the loud growl of tigers. The polar tigers approach the polar bear family. Seeing the polar tigers, they become scared and run to their safety. The tiger family chases the polar bears. After a long chase, the tigers get hold of the entire polar bear family consisting of mother, father and two kids. The bear family is not able to face the fierce attack of polar tigers. The polar tigers tear the flesh of polar bears, and kill them. The polar bears are seen lying on the icy ground.

Fade out:

Fade in

<u>52:Int: Bedroom of Dr Choo Lai Ho : Night</u>

Dr Choo Lai Ho is very fond of sleeping and usually gets good sleep. But this night his sleep appears to be disturbed as his eyeballs under the closed eyelids appear to be moving and suddenly he wakes up. He is breathless and after few seconds realizes that he was dreaming.

Cut to:

<u>53: Ext : A clinic of a Chinese healer of herbal & natural medicine in City's downtown: Day</u>

Dr Choo Lai Ho's clinic is located in the city's downtown adjacent to a busy road. His ability to treat various diseases is inscribed bilingually on a signboard placed on a wall. A horse carriage approaches and stops in front of the clinic and an old man gets down with his small bag. He pays money to the driver of the horse carriage. Thereafter, he walks towards the clinic's entrance and enters into the clinic.

Cut to:

<u>54: Int: A clinic of a Chinese healer of herbal & natural medicine in City's downtown: Day</u>

Dr Choo Lai Ho is as usual sitting on a broad wooden plank, whereas his patients are sitting on the carpeted floor. There are six patients. He is looking inside the mouth of a patient. His assistant is making medicines for patients.

The door is opened and the old man enters into the room. The Chinese healer sees the new entrant and gets up from his seat to greet him.

Chinese Healer
"My friend, Kha Ka Shi! I am so grateful that you have come to me."

Kha Ka Shi
"My Dear friend, Choo Lai Ho. I got your letter and have come to you immediately."

Choo Lai Ho [to his assistant]
"Hin Tau Hoo, take my friend inside."

The young man, who is helping the Chinese healer, comes forward and holds the small bag of Mr Kha Ka Shi. He leads him to the inside door which opens to the house of the Chinese healer. Hin Tau Hoo opens the door and they both exit from the clinic.

Cut to:
55: Int: Drawing room of the residence of the Chinese healer: Day

Choo Lai Ho and Kha Ka Shi are sitting on a broad carpet on the floor of the drawing room. They are sipping hot tea. The drawing room is decorated in a peculiar Chinese style.

Choo Lai Ho
"How is everybody in your family?'

Kha Ka Shi
"Everybody is fine. What about you...? You wrote that you see often weird nightmare".

Choo Lai Ho
"For the past few years I am having nightmares. I see a group of tiger chasing and killing a polar bear family. This makes me very frightened and my sleep gets disturbed. Every night I wake up due to this awful experience."

Kha Ka Shi
" Do you see this every day?"

Choo Lai Ho
"No, not daily. Earlier I used to see only occasionally but now it has become regular. That is why I have called you because being a psychologist you will be able to treat me."

Kha Ka Shi
"I will have to perform a ritual tomorrow morning to know the reason of this nightmare. Thereafter I can see what best can be done to treat you for this."

Choo Lai Ho

"Do I also need to get up in the morning?"

Kha Ka Shi

"Yes, you need to take a bath and sit before the deity to worship."

They both look pensive and serious.

Cut to:

56: Ext : Backyard of the residence of the Chinese healer: Early Morning

It is very early in the morning. The has not risen yet. Kha Ka Shi is sitting on a wooden plank and is busy doing some rituals before the deity, whereas Choo Lai Ho is sitting in front of him on the ground on a seat made of tiger leather. Kha Ka Shi burns incense sticks and its smoke and fragrance spreads in the area. Thereafter he touches Choo Lai Ho's head and chants a few spells of verses from a Chinese religious book. Then he concentrates and meditates while keeping both his hands on the head of Choo Lai Ho. After some time Kha Ka Shi completes his meditation.

Kha Ka Shi

"I am not able to read your mind."

Choo Lai Ho

"Why?"

Kha Ka Shi

"Your mind has no scar and deformity."

Choo Lai Ho

"Then why do I see such frightening dreams?"

Kha Ka Shi

"There seems to be some disturbances in your soul."

Choo Lai Ho

"What kind of disturbances?"

Kha Ka Shi

"It is not possible for me to tell as I am not an expert in soul searching. I can read only minds."

Choo Lai Ho

"What should I do for my problems?"

<u>Kha Ka Shi</u>
"You should call Mr Tanaki Kuzawa, the soul specialist. Do you know him?"

<u>Choo Lai Ho</u>
"I know him but he is not a friend of mine. He charges huge amount for consultation."

<u>Kha Ka Shi</u>
"He does not charge any consultation fee for the first time. But he is a true professional and the only person who can help you."

<u>Choo Lai Ho</u>
"Since I find my problem very grave, I will have to consult him."

<u>Kha Ka Shi</u>
"Do as early as possible."

<u>Choo Lai Ho</u>
"Yes."

They both get up from their seats to wrap up the scattered ingredients. By now, there is a bright twilight at the east horizon of the sky.

Cut to:
<u>57: Int : In the Drawing room of the Chinese healer : Day</u>

There are many bowls full of different delicious food. Choo Lai Ho and Kha Ka Shi are sitting on a carpet on the floor and are having lunch. They are talking to each other while eating.

<u>Kha Ka Shi</u>
"Who has prepared these delicious food? Marvellous! "

<u>Choo Lai Ho</u>
"My daughter-in-law is very good at cooking."

<u>Kha Ka Shi</u>
"Everybody can't be such a good cook."

<u>Choo Lai Ho</u>
"She is a very good girl."

<u>Kha Ka Shi</u>
"You are very lucky to have her as your daughter-in-law."

<u>Choo Lai Ho</u>
"No doubt..."

<u>Kha Ka Shi</u>
"Though I am going back to my place, I shall remember these food for many days to come. I shall wait for your invitation again."

<u>Choo Lai Ho</u>
"You are my friend. You don't need an invitation to come to me. You can always drop in."

<u>Kha Ka Shi</u>
"Thank you for this generous invitation."

<u>Choo Lai Ho</u>
"Mention not..."

Thereafter they concentrate on their food and finish eating.

Cut to:
<u>58: Int : A clinic of a Chinese healer of herbal and natural medicine in City's downtown: Day</u>

Dr Choo Lai Ho is examining and patting the stomach of a patient to make a proper diagnosis. His assistant is assisting this frail patient to get up and sit. There are many patients sitting on the ground.

The door is opened and two people enter into the room. One of them is a old man and other is a young man. The Chinese healer sees them and gets up from his seat.

<u>Choo Lai Ho</u>
"Reverend Tanaki Kuzawa at my home! I am thankful to you and God that you have come at my home."

Dr Choo Lai Ho goes ahead to greet him in Chinese style.

<u>Tanaki Kuzawa</u>
"I received your letter and soon thereafter I set out from my home."

<u>Choo Lai Ho</u>
"You are very kind and I am very thankful to you."

<u>Tanaki Kuzawa</u>
"What is your problem?"

<u>Choo Lai Ho</u>
"I will tell you, but first relax yourself and have some food. You have come a long way and must be tired."

Dr Choo Lai Ho carries his luggage and leads him to the inside of his home behind the clinic. He along with Tanaki Kuzawa and the young man exit from the room.

Cut to

59: Int : Drawing room of the residence of the Chinese healer: Day

Choo Lai Ho and Tanaki Kuzawa are sitting on a broad carpet on the floor of the drawing room, whereas the young man is sitting on a wooden plank a little away. Choo Lai Ho and Tanaki Kuzawa are sipping hot tea.

Tanaki Kuzawa
"What is the problem that you have called me for a solution?"

Choo Lai Ho
"For the past few years I am having a nightmare. I see a group of tiger chase and kill a polar bear family. My sleep gets disturbed and I wake up due to this frightening dream."

Tanaki Kuzawa
"Is it happening every day?"

Choo Lai Ho
"Earlier I used to have the nightmare occasionally but now I see it almost every day. That is why I have called you, being a spiritual specialist you can help me get rid of this frightening dream."

Tanaki Kuzawa
"Please lie down here on the ground and keep your eyes shut. I will examine your brain."

Choo Lai Ho lies down on the carpeted floor. Tanaki Kuzawa touches his head and recites few verses in Chinese. Thereafter he closes his eyes and tries to hear something in the quiet drawing room. He opens his eyes and appears to be satisfied with his diagnosis.

Tanaki Kuzawa
"Get up now."

Choo Lai Ho gets up and sits in front of him.

Tanaki Kuzawa
"It seems that it is a problem of soul."

Choo Lai Ho
"Please tell me something more."

Tanaki Kuzawa
"To know every thing in detail, I will have to do certain rituals. Are you ready for that?"

Choo Lai Ho

"Yes."

Tanaki Kuzawa

"You need to submit yourself fully to God. You will have to offer the Almighty two drums of wine and whisky, fifty kilograms of goat meat and two thousand gold coins. Thereafter I will perform my rituals and let you know every detail."

Choo Lai Ho

"The items I have to offer are very expensive. It is beyond my reach."

Tanaki Kuzawa

"I don't want to waste my time here. I will leave now and you can live with your nightmare."

Choo Lai Ho

"What is the purpose of the ritual ? How can I overcome the nightmare? What would be the expenditure for that?"

Tanaki Kuzawa

"I can't say anything right away until I perform my ritual. I don't know whether you will overcome your nightmare."

Choo Lai Ho

"I really want to get rid of this problem. Can you reduce the items to make it affordable for me?"

Tanaki Kuzawa

"No, that is not possible."

Choo Lai Ho is in a dilemma. He is confusingly looking at the face of Mr Tanaki Kuzawa.

Choo Lai Ho

"As I need to know the reason of my nightmare, I have no option but arrange money somehow."

Tanaki Kuzawa

"I can't wait for long. I will have to return by tomorrow afternoon. I will perform the ritual in the early morning. If you are interested, you need to be fast because you don't have much time."

Choo Lai Ho

"OK. I will do my best and bring the money before that. You may kindly relax here."

He gets up from the ground and leaves the room in hurry.

Cut to:

60: Ext : Backyard of the residence of the Chinese healer : Early Morning

The sun has not risen at the east horizon of the sky. Mr Tanaki Kuzawa is in a white robe and is chanting the verses before the deity in a loud voice. He is sitting on the grass, whereas Choo Lai Ho is lying on the ground on a tiger leather sheet. His eyes are shut. Fifty kilograms of meat, two drums of whisky and wine and two thousand gold coins are placed before the deity. The young man with Tanaki Kuzawa is just watching the ritual. Tanaki Kuzawa burns incense sticks, and its smoke spreads in the area. Then he touches Choo Lai Ho's head and chants a few spells of verses in Chinese. Thereafter he closes his eyes and concentrates by keeping his hands on the head of Choo Lai Ho. After some time Tanaki Kuzawa comes out of his state of meditation and opens his eyes.

Tanaki Kuzawa

"Now you can get up."

Choo Lai Ho gets up and sits on the tiger leather sheet.

Tanaki Kuzawa [To the young man]

"Takeda, my son, collect all these offerings and keep it alongside our luggage. We will soon leave for home.

Choo Lai Ho is watching Mr Tanaki Kuzawa keep all the gold coins in a leather bag.

Choo Lai Ho

"Sir, is it possible now to know the details of my problem?"

Tanaki Kuzawa

"Yes, I have come to know the mystery of your soul."

Choo Lai Ho

"What is that?"

Tanaki Kuzawa

"You were a polar bear before occupying the dead body of Dr Choo Lai Ho."

Choo Lai Ho

"I am Choo Lai Ho."

Tanaki Kuzawa

"Dr Choo Lai Ho died eighteen years ago and you got into his mind and body before decomposition."

Choo Lai Ho

"That is unbelievable."

Tanaki Kuzawa

"It was an extraordinary spiritual phenomenon. I will disclose you everything in details."

Dr Choo Lai Ho and Takeda are surprised and looking at Tanaki's face to know the details.

Fade Out

Fade In

61: An overview of a desolate Arctic place where a newborn baby is crying: Stormy Night

After coming out of the arctic cave from their long sleep, the polar bear family is feeling hungry. They hear a voice of a crying human baby. They follow the sound of their prey. The polar bear family reach the site of newborn baby and sniff him with happiness before inserting teeth in the baby's flesh.

All of a sudden their attention is caught by loud growling sound. Then a group of polar tigers are seen approaching the polar bear family. The frightens the polar bear family and they run away from there. The tiger family chases the polar bears and after chasing them for a long time, the tigers grab the entire polar bear family. The tigers fiercely attack the polar bears and in the end the tigers kill the polar bears.

Cut to

62: Ext : Entrance gate leading to heaven and hell on a beautiful landscape: Day

Souls of the bear family along with an attendant of god's accountant reach the entrance gate heading towards heaven and hell. The gateman sees four polar bears approaching him.

Gateman

"My dear, coolie, you were to bring only three souls. This kid was not to be brought."

Coolie

"The God's accountant told me to bring this polar bear family."

Gateman

"Where is the accountant's work order?"

Coolie

"Today was a hectic day and I had to do a lot of deliveries. So when I came, he asked me to rush and bring this polar bear family."

Gateman [looks on to the list in his hand]

"But I don't see the name of this kid in the delivery list. You have made a mistake."

Coolie

"I have worked without work order before also and I do not make this kind of mistakes. I heard the accountant and ran to get the polar bears. I was in a hurry and didn't collect the work order. But I am sure, he told me to bring the polar Bear family. "

Gateman [Dials a number in his walkie-talkie]

"Sir, you gave me the delivery list of three members of the polar bear family."

"Yes, that is true". [A Loud voice is heard from the walkie-talkie]

Gateman [speaks into his walkie-talkie]

"But, Sir, the coolie has brought all the four souls of the polar bear family. I don't see the name of this kid in your list."

"The coolie has made a mistake. He did not collect the work order and ran just after hearing my words. It appears that he did not even listen to my words carefully". [The loud voice is heard from the walkie-talkie]

Gateman [speaks into his walkie-talkie]

"Now what to do sir...?"

"I can see that the body of the kid is irreparably damaged because of the coolie's negligence. Ask the coolie to take the kid and put him in to the body of Dr Choo Lai Ho, a Chinese healer in Khira Khao Kingdom, who is to die after fifteen minutes. The coolie should rush and bring Choo Lai Ho's soul. " [The loud voice is heard from the walkie-talkie]

Gateman [Speaks into his walkie-talkie]

"Sir, where should I put these three members of polar bear? Heaven or Hell...?"

"Let them go to hell. They have been mercilessly killing innocent lives". [The loud voice is heard from the walkie-talkie]

Gateman [puts off his walkie-talkie]

"Mr Coolie, did you hear about your foolishness?"

Coolie

"I am really very sorry, Sir. It is the pressure of work that leads us to mistakes."

Gateman

"Now that you have heard the course of duty, take this kid and rush to the dying Chinese healer."

Before the coolie could take the kid, the other three bear souls feel emotional of separation from the kid. Then they hold the kid together and touch his head to show love and affection. Thereafter, the coolie takes the kid with him. He holds him in his arm and flies away. The three members of the polar bear family look at the gateman for further instructions. Just then, another coolie is seen passing by.

Gateman [to the other coolie]

"Hello, my dear coolie. Take these three polar bears from here and put them in hell."

The coolie takes the polar bears on the road that leads to the hell.

Cut to:

63:Int: Bedroom of Dr Choo Lai Ho : Day

Dr Choo Lai Ho is seen unconsciously lying on his bed. His relatives are standing around his bed with their grim faces. A Chinese doctor is administering some medicine in his mouth with the help of a tiny funnel. He examines the pulse of his right wrist.

Chinese doctor [to relatives]

"His condition is very serious. His vitality is falling very fast. If he does not recover quickly on the medication which I am giving, then he will die very soon."

A relative

"Is there anyway that his health can be improved?"

Chinese doctor

"There is nothing more to do. I have done my best. Now just pray to god."

The same relative

"We want to thank you for giving your best to help Choo Lai Ho."

Everybody is looking helplessly at the calm face of Dr Choo Lai Ho.

Cut to:

<u>64 : Ext : Backyard of the residence of the Chinese healer : Day</u>

Dr Choo Lai Ho's dead body is seen lying on a hand-held cart made of bamboos. His relatives are weeping and a priest is making preparations of the funeral.

Just then, the coolie arrives at the site with the kid's soul. They both have a aura surrounding them. They are invisible to the people there.

<u>Coolie</u>

"Dr Choo Lai Ho, do come out of the body as you have to go with me."

Dr Choo Lai Ho's soul comes out of the body and stands alongside the coolie.

<u>Coolie [to the kid of polar bear]</u>

"Kid, now you should occupy the body of Dr Choo Lai Ho."

The kid's soul does what the coolie says. He occupies the dead body of Dr Choo Lai Ho. Thereafter the coolie flies away with the soul of Choo Lai Ho. When his relatives are about to lift the hand-held cart to proceed with his dead body, Choo Lai Ho becomes conscious and opens his eyes. He gets up and sits on the cart. The relatives are alarmed to see him sitting, but after some time everything is normal and they are to see him alive."

<u>Priest</u>

"God is very kind that Choo Lai Ho has risen from his deathbed."

Dr Choo Lai Ho is surprised to see himself on a deathbed and people preparing for his funeral procession. He quickly stands up. All his relatives come near him and hug him with joy and affection.

Fade out

Fade In

<u>65: Ext : Backyard of the residence of the Chinese healer : Early Morning</u>

It is early morning and Dr Choo Lai Ho is patiently listening to Tanaki Kuzawa. He concludes his anecdote.

<u>Choo Lai Ho</u>

"It's very difficult for me to believe the story, but tell me why do I see the nightmare?"

<u>Tanaki Kuzawa</u>

"When they come to know that they are doomed to hell, your mother, father and brother can not believe it. But when they hear that you have to return to the earth in another life, they hold you with affection and love. While hugging you, they desired that you, being the member of polar bear family, should take revenge against the killer polar tigers. It is their desire that reminds you in your dream. This nightmare will continue until you take the revenge and fulfil the desire of your ancestors. This is a rare but fantastic spiritual phenomenon, which you may or may not believe. "

<u>Choo Lai Ho</u>

"Where are these tigers now?"

<u>Tanaki Kuzawa</u>

"They are in the Polar region."

<u>Choo Lai Ho</u>

"Can you help me to locate and kill these tigers ?"

<u>Tanaki Kuzawa</u>

" Yes, I can help you."

<u>Choo Lai Ho</u>

"Kindly do that for me."

<u>Tanaki Kuzawa</u>

"You need to submit to God ten thousand gold coins, hundred kgs of goat meat and ten drums of wine and whisky. Thereafter, I will start my rituals."

<u>Choo Lai Ho</u>

"This is beyond my capacity. I am already in debt because of the present ritual."

<u>Tanaki Kuzawa</u>

"I will take your leave now. I am always there to help you, provided you have got the offerings ready for my rituals."

<u>Choo Lai Ho</u>

"It may not be affordable for me at all unless you reduce the scale of offerings."

<u>Tanaki Kuzawa</u>

"Takedo, my son, let us go."

Takedo has already collected all the offerings, then he and Tanaki leave Choo Lai Ho's residence.

Fade Out:

Fade In

66: Ext : King's Palace in Khira Khao Kingdom : Day

There is a white-marbled palace on a beautiful green landscape within a fortified compound of a thousand acres. The palace has three floors. The security personnel with their guns and weapons keep patrolling within the compound to safeguard the palace against intruders. The main entrance door of the palace has two flags on its top. One of the flags have the inscription of 'Khira Khao Kingdom' and the other 'Long live King Kaboos'.

Cut to:

67: Int : Palatial bedroom of Prince Katoos : Day

Prince Katoos is unconscious on his large bed made of mahogany that is carved with gold and other precious stones on it. King Kaboos and his queen are sitting on stools near the head-side of the bed of Prince Katoos. Their faces look grim. There are Royal Physician and three Ministers including the Chief Minister in the room. Everyone is serious and thoughtful.

King Kaboos

"My dear Royal Physician, why is my son not coming to his senses?"

Royal Physician

"Your Excellency, our beloved prince is apparently suffering from some unknown disease. I have tried my best to diagnose his ailment but have failed. I have studied most medicinal book that are available to ensure that I may not falter in diagnosing his ailment. Till this time I can say that I did not find the specific symptoms in any of these books."

King Kaboos

"My dear Royal Physician, you are my only hope and I expect from you an advice as to how my son can be saved?"

Royal Physician

"I would advise you to announce a big reward to anyone who will come forward and suggest medicines that will cure the ailment of Prince Katoos. Before that medicine is administered, I would check whether it was given to the Prince earlier."

King Kaboos

"My Dear Chief Minister, please make a public announcement as suggested by the Royal Physician."

Chief Minister
"Yes, Your Excellency, I will."

The Chief Minister bows his head in honour of King Kaboos and leaves the room, whereas others are still praying for the ailing Prince Katoos.

Cut to:
68 : Ext : Road in market place in front of the clinic of Chinese healer of herbal and natural medicine in City's downtown: Day

A person with a big sound system is riding on a Royal horse carriage on the road. An announcement is heard from the sound system.

[Announcement made by Sound System]
"Prince Katoos, son of our beloved King Kaboos, is seriously sick and suffering from an unknown disease. Each and every physician of the Khira Khao Kingdom is invited at the Royal Palace today in the evening to examine the illness of Prince Katoos and suggest medication for his recovery. King Kaboos will give a reward of one hundred thousand gold coins to the physician whose extraordinary prescription of medicine would cure Prince Katoos."

Cut to:
69: Int : Clinic of the Chinese healer of herbal and natural medicine in City's downtown: Day

Dr Choo Lai Ho is scratching his head and thinking about the remedy of the sickness after examining a patient. His assistant is waiting for the instructions from him to prepare the medicine. There are many patients sitting on the ground.

Just then, the sound of an announcement is heard by Choo Lai Ho inside the clinic.

[Announcement made by Sound System]

"Prince Katoos, son of our beloved King Kaboos, is seriously sick and suffering from an unknown disease. Each and every physician of the Khira Khao Kingdom is invited at the Royal Palace today in the evening to examine the illness of Prince Katoos and suggest medication for his recovery. King Kaboos will give a reward of one hundred thousand gold coins to the physician whose extraordinary prescription of medicine would cure Prince Katoos."

Dr Choo Lai Ho attentively listens to the announcement and is very pleased.

Choo Lai Ho [Murmurs]
"O God, you are great. You have given me a royal chance to earn gold coins."

Cut to:
70: Int : A large hall of the Palace near the bedroom of Prince Katoos : Evening

This is a highly decorated hall of the King's palace, where large number of physicians from different places have gathered. They are waiting for the instruction before they could examine Prince Katoos. The Royal Physician comes and stand on a podium to make an announcement. Dr Choo Lai Ho is also seen amongst the physicians.

Royal Physician
"Our beloved Prince Katoos is seriously sick from an unknown disease. I as a personal physician of the Royal family have used all the knowledge and resources that is available with me. Unfortunately, the condition of our beloved Prince has not improved. On my advice, the King has called all of you to examine the ailing prince and suggest medication. You can prescribe your medication on a piece of paper and give it to me so that I can see whether I have tried the medical course that you have proposed."

Dr Choo Ho Lai
"Can we suggest something outside of the traditional medicines?"

Royal Physician
"Yes, you can. Now all of you need to form a queue before the bedroom of the Prince. He is lying unconscious on his bed. You need to examine him and come out of the room and write your prescription."

Thereafter all the physicians start making a queue before the bedroom adjacent to the hall.

Cut to:
71: Int : Palatial bedroom of Prince Katoos : Night

The physical condition of Prince Katoos is frail and he is unconscious. King Kaboos and his queen are standing near the head-side of the bed of Prince Katoos. The Royal Physician and three Ministers including the Chief Minister are also in the room.

Royal Physician

"Sir, I have received prescriptions of all the physicians and I didn't find a prescription with a new medical treatment except in the case of Dr Choo Lai Ho."

King Kaboos

"What is his prescription?"

Royal Physician

"An unbelievable prescription...! He has given one medicine to Prince Katoos made of cat's bone and snake's flesh. He has also suggested that he would need bones of Polar tigers to make another medicine for fast the recovery of Prince Katoos."

King Kaboos

"Do Polar tigers exist?"

Royal Physician

"I am not sure but he says that there are six Polar tigers in the Polar region and these tigers should be killed so that their bones can be used for medicine."

King Kaboos

"If we have to try this medication of Dr Choo Lai Ho then let us send our hunters immediately to find these tigers in Polar region."

Royal Physician

"Yes Sir, we do not have any other option."

King Kaboos

"My Dear Chief Minister, let all the hunters of our kingdom set out in the Polar region to find and kill those six polar tigers for my son's life."

Chief Minister

"Yes, Your highness, I will do just as you have said."

The Chief Minister then leaves the bedroom.

Fade Out

Fade In

72 : Ext : Overview of Antarctic region : Day

Antarctic in winter [On Screen Caption]

It is a pitch-dark night in the Antarctic as it is winter there. However, the white layers of snow are dimly visible. Two batches of hunters consisting of ten people each sent by King Kaboos are riding two dog-sledges. Among them two hunters are holding torches to show in and around in the region.

A hunter

"We have not been able to spot a single polar tiger even after two weeks of being here. I doubt whether Polar tigers exist."

Another hunter

"There may be such Polar tigers in Arctic region."

A hunter

"What to do now? "

Another hunter

"We have nothing to do but to return home and report the matter to the Chief Minister."

A hunter

"Let us not waste our time here and return back."

Another hunter

"Okay, let us return."

Both the teams return back in their dog-sledges.

Cut to:

73: Ext : Overview of Arctic region in summer : Day

Arctic region in summer [On Screen Caption]

Two other groups of hunters are riding on dog-sledges in the day light of the Arctic region in search of polar tigers. They are not sure whether they will find polar tigers or not. But luckily it is summer in the Arctic region at this time and due to bright light, the hunters ultimately spot six polar tigers relaxing near a big ice rock. The hunters speed up their dog-sledges to reach the polar tigers. The speeding sound of dog-sledges catches the attention of polar tigers and they are astonished to see aliens in this desolate area. The polar tigers get up and go away from there. Seeing the polar tigers moving away, the hunters shoot bullets with their firearms to kill them. Fortunately, the polar tigers are alert and are able to dodge the bullets. They are frightened to see the gun-laden hunters after them on dog-sledges. Pola is also running with the polar tigers. Kemu, the tiger and Kelly, the tigress, along with tiger cubs are keeping Pola in between to save him from getting hit by bullets. They are anxious about Pola as he might be injured by the bullets. They all are running very fast to save themselves.

<u>Pola [while running]</u>
"Mom, why are they trying to kill us?"

<u>Kelly, the tigress [while running]</u>
"I don't know. Just don't stop running until we reach a safe place."

They are running very fast on a icy surface and at times skid. They are helping each other against skidding. At last, a bullet pierces Kemu's body and he feels pain. But he does not stop and keeps running. The others are able to dodge the hunters and escape from their sight. Immediately they all slip under an ice pit to hide from the hunters.

Cut to:
<u>74 : Int : Inside the ice-pit : Day</u>

Since the temperature is extremely cold under the ice pit, Kemu feels better as his wound caused by a hunter's bullet is being filled and healed by the cold. Though the polar tiger family feels relieved from strenuous running on icy surface, they are extremely frightened. Kemu and Kelly are worried about Pola's life. Pola is hiding himself on his mother's lap. Everybody is frightened.

Cut to:
<u>75: Ext : Arctic plane in summer : Day</u>

Since the tigers are not in sight, the hunters are puzzled. They stop their dog-sledges to locate the tigers.

<u>A hunter</u>
"Where have these tigers vanished?"

<u>Another hunter</u>
"They must have slipped into some ice pit."

<u>A hunter</u>
"Let us burn coal to increase the temperature of this area so that the ice pit melts and they are forced to come out in open."

<u>Another hunter</u>
"Yes, let us do that."

Thereafter the hunters of the Khira Khao Kingdom burn coal to raise the climatic temperature. Slowly the temperature rises.

Cut to:

<u>76 : Int : Inside the ice-pit : Day</u>

The ice pit where the polar tiger family have taken shelter starts melting. The polar tiger family is extremely worried about their life.

<u>A tiger cub</u>

"These hunters are cruel and cunning. They would surely kill us as our ice pit is melting and falling apart. They would be able to notice us very soon."

<u>Pola</u>

"What should we do to save ourselves?"

<u>Kemu, the tiger</u>

"We can save ourselves if we dig further deep and hide ourselves in the snow."

<u>Another tiger cub</u>

"But we can't dig. Our claws are not enough to do that."

<u>Pola</u>

"I can do that."

Pola starts digging the snow with his hands and makes a deeper ice pit, where all of them slip into hide.

<u>Kelly, the tigress</u>

"My son is very brave and able. He has saved us."

Kelly then kisses Pola. Everyone else also show their love and affection towards him. This makes Pola happy. They are safe in their deeper ice pit made by Pola. Since this ice pit is very deep, the melting of its upper layer does not matter.

Cut to:

<u>77: Ext : Arctic plane in summer : Day</u>

The hunters are worried to see their efforts going in vein, as despite the melting of the upper layer of the ice pit, polar tiger family is able to hide themselves.

<u>A hunter</u>

"We have exhausted our coal stock."

<u>Another hunter</u>

"These Polar tigers must have gone somewhere else. They are not here. We have to find them for our beloved Prince Katoos."

Another hunter

"Let us go and search for them somewhere else."

They are dejected and are seen leaving the particular area.

Fade Out:

Fade In

78. Int : Beautiful scene of heaven: Day

Almighty God in heaven is comfortably sitting on a seat, padded with lotus flowers and petals. He is worried when he sees the balance sheet of his accountant concerning earth's environment. His accountant is standing before him with head down. After checking the balance sheet of the accountant, almighty God becomes disappointed and angry.

Almighty God

"My dear accountant, could you let me know the reasons about the depleting number of species of different animals and birds, and also the reasons for extinction of some species. To me it seems that you are an inefficient person and incapable of controlling the damages."

Accountant

"O my almighty God! I pray for your mercy. It is the human beings on earth, who have created these damages, which are beyond control now. The people are killing birds and animals mindlessly for food and pleasure, this is resulting in depletion of their number. In their endeavour to be self-reliant and financially strong, men and women destroyed the eco-system, which have resulted in the extinction of birds and animals. Secondly, special effects of devil have also fuelled the reasons. In absence of a couple or eggs it is impossible to recreate the extinct creature on the earth to fill the void."

God is very upset with the events going on in earth.

Cut to:

79 : Int ; Beautiful meeting room of heaven :Day

While comfortably sitting on a snake-laid seat, God worried about the balance sheet of his accountant concerning earth. God is busy in a meeting with the advisors, who are standing nearby.

Almighty God

"I would like to know your opinion about the depletion and extinction of the number of species in earth and also your suggestions how this trend can be stopped?"

<u>One advisor</u>

"O my almighty God, the beautiful earth created by you would destroy soon if devil's special effects and selfish desires of men and women are not contained."

<u>Another advisor</u>

"As the accountant has the responsibility to reconcile the accounts of various species on earth, we should entrust him to seek the ways and means of saving the environment and natural balance of the earth to avoid further depletion or extinction of species.

God agrees with the suggestions offered by his advisors.

Cut to:

<u>80: Int: Beautiful scene of heaven: Day</u>

Almighty God calls for his accountant. Within a minutes he is standing before God with head down.

<u>Almighty God</u>

"My dear accountant, you need to safeguard the environment and make efforts to redeem the losses. It is your duty."

<u>Accountant</u>

"O my almighty God, I shall be able to perform my duty with your gracious blessings and power."

<u>Almighty God</u>

"I need to see the earth regaining its old beauty and charm."

<u>Accountant</u>

"O almighty God, your desire is supreme."

<u>Almighty God</u>

"Now you can go."

<u>Accountant</u>

"O almighty God, as you wish."

The accountant goes away.

Cut to:

<u>81: Int : Drawing room of the house of God's accountant : Night</u>

The drawing room of the accountant of God is tastefully decorated. The accountant is sitting on a couch. He is in a pensive mood. His wife is worried about him.

<u>Accountant's wife</u>
"Dear, I can see that something is bothering you."

<u>Accountant</u>
"Darling, as you already know that my balance sheet is in mess, so God has ordered me to stop the damage and recover the losses."

<u>Accountant's wife</u>
"So have you thought of an idea to correct your balance sheet?"

<u>Accountant</u>
"I am not able to conceptualize as to what to do and how to do."

<u>Accountant's wife</u>
"You being a divine personality, it is beyond your capacity to do this work. You need the help of a worldly being, may be an animal or a human, to take over this cause."

<u>Accountant</u>
"You have made a vital point. But how to have the goal achieved?"

<u>Accountant's wife</u>
"There may be many animals or human beings who are equally disturbed about the worrisome condition of the earth. You need to identify and entrust them the cause of recovering the earth. You need to go around the earth to find such a noble soul. You can empower him to take up your cause."

<u>Accountant</u>
"How to be sure if he is a noble soul."

<u>Accountant's wife</u>
"You will be able to know about him by the way he behaves and conducts. I believe there are environmentalists, who are passionate about saving the earth."

<u>Accountant</u>
"Then I should find these environmentalists."

<u>Accountant's wife</u>
"Yes."

<u>Accountant</u>
"I will set out on my journey tomorrow."

The accountant is satisfied.

Cut to:

<u>82 : Ext : Overview of Earth from high up in sky : Day</u>

The God's accountant is riding in his flying chariot and descending from the cloud to the ground.

Cut to:

<u>83 : Ext : Downtown of a metropolitan city : Day</u>

The God's accountant is floating in the air and moving along the crowded street as per his wish. He comes across a neon signboard that reads 'Save Green Earth'. This catches his attention. He moves towards the office of the 'Save Green Earth'.

Cut to:

<u>84: Int : Office of the Save Green Earth: Day</u>

This office is well decorated. Very few people are seen in the office. Among them is the Chief Coordinator of 'Save Green Earth' and two of his associates. God's accountant stops for a while to listen to their conversation. These people cannot see the accountant, as he is invisible.

<u>Chief Coordinator</u>

"To promote the slogan of 'Save Green Earth', we have got the attention of few government agencies. They have agreed to help and support our NGO by paying a regular yearly aid to save the herbs meant for medicinal use. They are asking our report on how a new legislation can be made to ban the deforestation."

<u>His associate</u>

"Our efforts to promote 'Save Green Earth' are paying us a good fortune as many furniture-producing companies have paid us hefty sums to formulate our report to the Government in such a manner that the deforestation is not banned but the ban may be limited to herbs only."

<u>Chief Coordinator</u>

"Let us open a new outlet of our NGO titled 'Save wild cat and other precious species'.

<u>His associate</u>

"What should be our motto?"

<u>Chief Coordinator</u>

"Our motto will be to earn more money! We will, however, as

environmentalists advocate the safety of wild cats and other precious species and I am sure our hue and cry would make many Government functionaries and their accomplices restless. They would pay us a considerable amount to keep our mouth shut, which will, of course, open periodically to fleece money from them."

<u>His associate</u>

"My dear friend, you are superb. You have made us rich. You have an excellent mind to earn money without doing anything except some hue and cry and come out with catchy slogans."

<u>Chief Coordinator</u>

"In fact, I am going to join hands with all the other Coordinators of different NGOs dealing with 'save the earth' or 'save green earth' or 'save animals' to make an impenetrable shield to avoid any exposure of our hollowness and treachery."

God's accountant is disheartened to find them dishonest as they are using cunning methodology to earn money. He is very worried as to how he can find an honest person for his cause. He is very disgusted with the whole issue and leaves the place immediately.

Cut to:

<u>85: Ext: Downtown of another metropolitan city: Day</u>

God's accountant is on an extensive tour of the earth in his flying chariot and is floating in the air. Later he moves along the crowded street as per his wish. He is thoughtful.

Cut to

<u>86: Ext: Overview of Earth from the sky: Day</u>

God's accountant is riding in his flying chariot. He ascends into the air and above the cloud and after some time descends on the ground.

Fade out:

Fade In

<u>87: Int : Palatial bedroom of Prince Katoos : Day</u>

Prince Katoos is physically better now. King Kaboos and his queen are very happy to see Prince Katoos recovering from his ailment. There are Royal Physician, Dr Choo Lai Ho and three Ministers including the Chief Minister in the room. Everybody is sitting comfortably on wooden settee. The the queen gets up and gives a glass of juice to Prince Katoos. He takes the glass and drinks it. Everybody is happy to see him in good condition.

King Kaboos

"Though it took some time for recovery, I am very happy that my son is hale and hearty. I am really grateful to Dr Choo Lai Ho."

Dr Choo Lai Ho

"It was my duty to treat my beloved Prince. Had I received the flesh and bones of polar tigers, the recovery would have been much faster. Unfortunately I did not get that."

King Kaboos

"Never mind, now you will hold the position of 'Physician Extraordinary in the Royal Court'.You will also receive a reward of one hundred thousand gold coins."

Royal Physician

"He deserves this position."

Dr Choo Lai Ho

"I am extremely grateful to my beloved King to give me the opportunity to serve a cause of my nation. Prince Katoos is our future King and he will certainly grow leaps and bounds in his Kingship also."

King Kaboos

"My dear Chief Minister, make arrangements for the grand ceremony where I will personally honour Dr Choo Lai Ho for his outstanding services."

Chief Minister

"As you wish, my lord...."

The Chief Minister leaves the bedroom in a hurry.

Cut to:

88: Ext: A large compound in front of the King's palace: Day

There is a large gathering of men and women in the compound in front of the King's palace. The musicians are entertaining the crowd. There is a large podium, where the King, Queen, Ministers, Royal Physician, Dr Choo Lai Ho and other religious persons are present. After some time, the King honours Dr Choo Lai Ho and hands him over a box containing hundred thousand gold coins. Dr Choo Lai Ho is delighted to receive the reward, and everyone in the gathering applauded.

Cut to:

89: Int: Bedroom of Dr Choo Lai Ho : Night

Dr Choo Lai Ho is sleeping on his bed at night. Though dark, a beam of moonlight is coming in from the window, which makes the bedroom visible. Suddenly Dr Choo Lai Ho's sleep is disturbed. He wakes up and sits on his bed. His breathing is heavy and he is perspiring. He is fearful until he realizes that he was dreaming.

Dr Choo Lai Ho [Murmurs]

"What a terrible dream? I have to do something about these polar tigers."

He appears to be thoughtful.

Cut to:

90:Int : Drawing room of the residence of the Chinese healer : Day

Dr Choo Lai Ho and Tanaki Kuzawa are sitting on a broad carpet on the floor of the drawing room, whereas Takeda, his young son is sitting on a wooden plank a little away. Dr Choo Lai Ho and Tanaki Kuzawa are sipping hot tea.

Tanaki Kuzawa

"What is the problem now that you have called me again?"

Choo Lai Ho

"You are well aware of the problem regarding my nightmare. As you suggested, I am now ready with the offerings. I would like you to kill those polar tigers so that I can get rid of this nightmare."

Tanaki Kuzawa

"You have got ten thousand gold coins!"

Choo Lai Ho

"Yes, I have got them."

Tanaki Kuzawa

"As usual, tomorrow in the morning I will perform my spiritual and magical spells to kill those polar tigers.

Choo Lai Ho

"I shall remain grateful to you for this help."

Tanaki Kuzawa and Takedo are happy to get the ten thousand gold coins.

Cut to :

<u>91:Ext : Backyard of the residence of the Chinese healer : Early Morning</u>

It is cloudy outside and Mr Tanaki Kuzawa in a red robe is chanting mantras in loud voice before a deity and a pyre. Dr. Choo Lai Ho is sitting on the ground on a tiger leather sheet with his eyes closed. Hundred kilograms of meat, ten drums of whisky and wine, and ten thousand gold coins are placed before the deity. Takedo, son of Tanaki Kuzawa, is watching him performg the rituals. Tanaki Kuzawa burns incense sticks and its smoke spreads all around. Thereafter he closes his eyes and touches Choo Lai Ho's head and chants a few spells of mantra in Chinese. Then he began to concentrate and after some time Tanaki Kuzawa comes out of his meditation and opens his eyes.

<u>Tanaki Kuzawa</u>

"I am going to cast some magic spells that will hypnotize you. You will then be able to see those polar tigers and answer my questions regarding them."

<u>Choo Lai Ho</u>

"Okay."

<u>Tanaki Kuzawa</u>

"Now lie down on the tiger skin."

Choo Lai Ho lies down on the tiger skin.

Tanaki Kuzawa casts magic spell on Dr Choo Lai Ho. And after sometime he slips into a semiconscious state.

<u>Tanaki Kuzawa</u>

"Now, can you see the tigers? If yes, then let me know their whereabouts."

Dr Choo Lai Ho is not responding.

<u>Tanaki Kuzawa</u>

"Choo Lai, tell me, what do you see? Where are these tigers? What are they doing? If you tell me the location and their condition, then I shall cast magic spells accordingly to kill them."

<u>Choo Lai Ho</u>

"I can see them in Arctic region. There are six of them. They are made of ice. I can see a human boy with them.

Fade Out

Fade In

<u>92: Ext : Desolate Arctic place with Polar tiger family : Day</u>

The polar tiger family is happy in the lonely arctic place. It is summer there with bright daylight. Pola, an eighteen-year-old boy, is also among them. Though he is young and strong, he still drinks the tigress's milk. He is laughing as mother tigress is gesturing to amuse him.

Pola was sitting amongst his tiger family. All of a sudden, it starts raining.

<u>Pola</u>

"What is this Mom? Why is it raining?"

<u>Kemu, the tiger</u>

"Rain in arctic region is not possible. This must be some powerful force. We can't face rain as our body is made of ice."

Though Pola likes rain the polar tigers are alarmed as their icy exterior is slowly melting due to the drops of water on their bodies.

<u>Kemu, the tiger</u>

"Let us hide ourselves in the ice pit otherwise we would die."

They are running to find a ice pit. Pola is following them. After running for a few yards, they find a ice pit. They hide under the ice-pit to save their exterior from the rain drops.

Fade Out

Fade In

<u>93:Ext : Backyard of the residence of the Chinese healer : Early Morning</u>

It is still dark in the early hours of the morning. Mr Tanaki Kuzawa is busy performing some rituals before his deity and a pyre while sitting on a wooden plank placed a bit higher from the ground, whereas Dr Choo Lai Ho is lying on the ground on a tiger skin with his eyes shut.

<u>Choo Lai Ho</u>

"I can see that the tigers and a human boy have slid themselves and immersed under a ice pit to save themselves from the rain drops."

<u>Tanaki Kuzawa</u>

"They appear to be smart enough. Let me cast another magic spell that will definitely kill them."

Tanaki Kuzawa is performing incantation.

Fade Out

Fade In

<u>94: Ext : Deserted Arctic place with Polar tiger family : Day</u>

The polar tiger family come out of the ice pit and they look at the sky to find out the source of rain drops but to their surprise the sky is very clear and there is no cloud.

<u>Kemu, the tiger</u>

"As there is no cloud in the sky, then where did the rain come from? Let us, however, sit near this ice pit, in case rain falls again, we will be able to save ourselves."

They sit near the ice-pit. After some time the tiger cubs lie on the ground. Then a few minutes later they hear a sound and get up. They can see a big group of hyenas approaching towards them. They are alarmed by the sudden appearance of hyenas. They are frightened.

<u>Kemu, the tiger</u>

"Someone wants to kill us and that is why he has sent the hyenas. Let us run away from these hyenas."

<u>Pola</u>

"Can we not fight against them?"

<u>Kemu, the tiger</u>

"They are in thousands. We can't face them. Don't waste your time and run my son."

The polar tiger family is running with full might to get out of the reach of the killer hyenas. They are running very fast and are far ahead of the hyenas. The hyenas are not able to match the speed of polar tiger family.

Fade Out

Fade In

<u>95: Ext : Backyard of the residence of the Chinese healer : Early Morning</u>

Now the sun can be seen at the east horizon of the sky. Mr Tanaki Kuzawa is still busy doing some rituals before his deity and a pyre. Dr Choo Lai Ho is still lying on the ground on a tiger skin with his eyes shut.

Choo Lai Ho
"I can see the tiger family running very fast and are ahead of the hyenas. The hyenas are not able to match their speed."

Tanaki Kuzawa
"I will have to diminish their physical strength. Let me cast another magic spell."

He is chanting some magic spells.

Fade out

Fade In
96: Ext : Desolate Arctic place with Polar tiger family : Day

Polar tiger family is running with full might to get out of the reach of the killer hyenas. They are running too fast and are far ahead of the hyenas.

There is a sudden climatic and environmental change in the arctic area. The polar tiger family finds themselves away from polar environment and within the tropical surroundings with human habitat. Polar tiger family is nervous to see the sudden magical change in climatic condition.

Kemu, the tiger [slows down his speed]
" Oh God, what a calamity? Are we destined to die now?"

Kelly, the tigress [shouting in panic]
"Kemu, don't think. Come on... run fast."

Polar tiger family is running far ahead of the hyenas. In tropical surroundings, the climatic temperature is unbearable for the tiger family. Polar tigers are losing the ability to run fast as their icy exterior is melting. To see his mother, father, and brother becoming frail due to hot climatic condition, Pola is worried and panicky about their life. While passing through human habitat, some tribal men and women also see the polar tigers.

A man from the habitat [shouts while watching the running polar tigers]

"Look at these peculiar tigers made up of ice. They are different from anything that we have seen before. Come all of you, let us catch them."

Men and women start chasing the polar tiger family. They are holding their weapons to catch the rare polar tigers. Pola is worried to see the sudden onslaught of hyenas, tribal men and women. Polar tiger family's hope to survive is fading away. Pola can see his mother, father and brothers getting weaker and gradually losing speed in the hot climatic condition. He is thinking as to how he can save them. While running through the human habitat, Pola has a glimpse of a horse carriage without a horse around. He runs towards this horse carriage and brings it near to enable the frail polar tigers to sit in the carriage because they can collapse any moment. Pola's idea of using the horse carriage has brought a relief and lease of new life to the tiger family.

<u>Pola</u>
"Mom, Dad and my dear brothers, please jump in this and sit. I will take you."

Kemu , Kelly, and his four brother cubs take their seat in the horse carriage. Pola holds the neck hold of the horse carriage in front and runs very fast , leaving behind the herd of hyenas and the group of tribal people. Pola is running frantically to save his family. Pola realises the worth of mother's milk now while running faster and saving the polar tiger family. He is running with the horse carriage on a footpath along a garden. All of a sudden, whistle of a train is heard. Soon thereafter, a train is seen running on its track across the garden and parallel to the road on which Pola is racing the horse carriage with polar tiger family. The condition of the polar tigers in the carriage deteriorate due to the heat of tropical climate. So when they see men, women, and animals and birds making journey by the train, they wave their hands indicating them to stop. Pola speeds, takes the horse carriage across the garden and runs along the running train.

<u>Pola [shouts]</u>
"Please open the door."

<u>Kemu, the tiger</u>
"Please open the door."

<u>Kelly, the tigress</u>
"Please, for God's sake, open the door."

<u>Four tiger cubs [in unison]</u>
"O God, please help."

Pola is running along the moving train almost at the same speed of the train. After a few moments the door of a rail coach opens.

When they see the door open, a sense of relief sets in the polar tiger family. The tiger family jumps and enters into a compartment of the train in motion. Thereafter Pola leaves the horse carriage and runs fast. He catches the door handle of the moving rail coach, and enters into the bogie.

Cut to:

97: Int : Rail Train: Day

Polar Tiger family is inside the bogie of the running train. They all feel relieved from an unending run. They take their seats and greet other passengers in the bogie. They see from the windows of the speeding train the herd of hyenas and group of tribal people being left behind.

Fade out

Fade In

98: Ext : Backyard of the residence of the Chinese healer : Early Morning

Clouds have dispersed. Morning sun is shining in the sky. Mr Tanaki Kuzawa is busy doing rituals before his deity and a pyre while sitting on a wooden plank placed a bit higher from the ground, whereas Dr Choo Lai Ho is lying on the ground on a tiger skin with his eyes shut.

Choo Lai Ho

"I can see a train. The polar tigers have taken refuge in it."

Tanaki Kuzawa

"I will cast another magic spell."

So he starts chanting some magic spells.

Fade out

Fade In

99: Int : Rail Train : Day

Tiger family is inside the bogie of the running train. Suddenly groups of flying dragons appear near the running train and they spill fire from their mouth towards the train bogie The polar tigers and Pola become nervous and frightened. The flying dragons kept spilling fire towards them, but after a few second, they realize that the fire have no effect on the train bogie and that the chilly condition inside has helped the tigers to recoup the strength lost due to melting of their icy exterior. The polar tigers have regained their health and happiness.

Suddenly it is pitch-dark inside the bogie as the train enters into a tunnel and a whirring sound can be heard. Again, it is a time of concern for Polar tiger family as it is difficult to locate anyone in the darkness.

Pola
"Why is it dark now? Where are we?"

Soon thereafter, a light in the shape of a man appears before them.

Pola
"Who are you?"

Kemu, the tiger
"Are you the accountant of God?"

Accountant of God
" Yes, I am."

Kemu, the tiger
"Where are we?"

Accountant of God
"You are in a train. This is my 'Polar Express-2'."

Kemu, the tiger
"Where are we going? And who are these passengers?"

Accountant of God
"I have the responsibility to take these pious souls on a tour for merriment. They were in heaven. When I set out for the extensive journey, they accompanied me."

Pola
"Are you owner of this train?"

Accountant of God
"Yes."

Pola
"Why did you name it as 'Polar Express-2' ?"

Accountant of God
"There are so many vehicles in the heaven that it becomes necessary to number them. God has vehicle number 1 and I have vehicle

number 2. All the planets have poles, either hottest or coldest. Since our vehicle can brave any polar condition, hottest or coldest, we call it 'Polar Express'. My vehicle is numbered as 'Polar Express-2'."

The accountant's answer satisfies Pola. 'Polar Express-2' has come out of the tunnel but it is still very dark and quiet in and out of the bogie. Despite darkness, the white snow mountains and blowing of diamond dust of Antarctica can be seen shining outside of the running train from its windows.

<u>Kelly, the tigress</u>
"Where are we now?"

<u>Accountant of God</u>
"We are in the Antarctic polar region."

<u>Kemu, the tiger</u>
"How can we reach our place?"

<u>Accountant of God</u>
"Are you feeling uncomfortable here?"

<u>Kemu, the tiger</u>
"No. Not at all..."

God's accountant looks at Pola and thinks for a while.

<u>Accountant of God</u>
"I need your son's help."

<u>Kemu, the tiger</u>
"What?"

<u>Accountant of God</u>
"I know that you are worried about your son being unaware of the human language and human behaviour."

<u>Kelly, the tigress</u>

"Yes."

<u>Accountant of God</u>
"I will empower your son with special power and knowledge so that he can settle in a human habitat and have a family of his own."

<u>Kemu, the tiger</u>
"Thank you."

<u>Accountant of God</u>
"But he has to do my work."

Kelly, the tigress
"What work?"

Accountant of God
"There are many birds and animals in the verge of extinction due to the devil's effect. This effect has to be contained and reduced to avoid extinction. So I need someone like your son to spread awareness amongst people for the well being of this earth."

Kemu, the tiger
"He may not understand this."

Accountant of God
"Don't worry. I will empower him."

The accountant puts his hand on Pola's head and induces energy to empower him with total knowledge of the Universe and human being. Polar tiger family is watching the spiritual procedures done on Pola with delight.

Accountant of God
"I have empowered your son with all the knowledge of the Universe. He would now live independently in the human society. You need not worry about him."

Pola bows his head before the accountant and touches his feet. He also hugs his mother, father and brothers.

Accountant of God
"I would like to take all of you to other planets which have purity in its natural balance and are not polluted yet. This journey would enable you to compare and find the deficiency cropping up on the earth."

Polar tiger family is not able to understand what the accountant means and are spellbound.

Accountant of God
"Would you like to come with me?"

Kemu, the tiger
"Yes."

Accountant of God
"Thank you for your cooperation."

Just then, the flying dragons again appear outside of the train and start spilling fire which envelopes the area outside the train compartment. Despite their best efforts, the dragons are not able to harm the 'Polar Express-2' or its passengers.

Kemu, the tiger

"Who are these dragons? Why are they after us?"

Accountant of God

"They have been sent by a Chinese healer. When the Chinese healer died, a polar bear's soul occupied his body. This polar bear had life left to live but was killed by your cubs. So, now he is taking revenge by trying to kill all of you."

Kemu, the tiger

"How can we get rid of this devil soul?"

Accountant of God

"Don't worry. Now we would be flying to another planet. These dragons can not follow us."

Pola

"Will this train fly now?"

Accountant of God

"Yes, it can run on any surface and fly in space too."

Thereafter the train raises its position from surface to air. All its wheels get hidden within the body and it looks like a very long rocket ascending into the air. It has cylindrical compartments with windows attached with each other to make a long column. The dragons are no longer able to follow the 'Polar Express-2' and are staring up in the sky with utter dismay. Suddenly it is dark all over the outer space.

Pola

"Why is it dark everywhere?"

Accountant of God

"Do you like to have light?"

Pola

"Yes."

The train compartment is immediately lit. Thereafter God's accountant disappears from the spot.

Cut to:

100: Ext : Polar Express-2 in the sky : Day

'Polar Express-2' is flying above the clouds. It is a pleasant surprise for the polar tiger family to watch the clouds closely and to fly above it. They are happy to see out from their windows. There are many birds flying alongside the 'Polar Express-2'.

Birds [saying in chorus]
"Open the door, open the door."

Passengers sitting inside the 'Polar Express-2' are waving their hands at the birds.

Birds [saying in chorus]
"We would also like to go to other world."

However, no one opens the door of the 'Polar Express-2' but the birds continue their race with flying 'Polar Express-2'. The birds cannot match the speed of Polar Express-2 and are left behind. Soon the 'Polar Express-2' moves rapidly and leaves the orbit of planet earth. It soon slips deep into the space.

Cut to
101: Int: Polar Express-2 in space: Day

As Polar Express-2 enters deep into the space, there is nothing to see outside of the window except vacuum and darkness.

After some time, bright light appears and the speakerphone within the compartment rings and the voice of the Captain is heard.

Captain
"I am your captain of the 'Polar Express-2'. The bright light outside the window is due to the sun of a planetary system having planet 'Cropper'. This planet is a water ball, and its centre has hollow football like structure and which works like a submarine. The centre part of this planet has life, which uses water energy for sustenance and lighting of its habitat. We are about to plunge into the sea of this planet before entering into its submarine like habitat."

Everybody in the compartment of the Polar Express-2 is excited and fascinated.

Kemu, the tiger
"This is a rare chance to see a new world."

Kelly, the tigress
"We are fortunate."

Tiger cubs and Pola are looking outside the window. There is nothing but bright light everywhele. The flying ship 'Polar Express-2' plunges into the sea and starts working like a submarine. Passengers of 'Polar Express-2' are fascinated to see the various marine lives and the inner structures of the sea. Soon it reaches at the bottom and a door opens which gulps the 'Polar Express-2', leaving a dispersing effect of water. The door immediately shuts down as 'Polar Express-2' enters into the enclosure of the habitat.

Cut to
<u>102: Ext : Axis sky of the Planet Cropper :Day</u>

Axis sky of the planet Cropper appears like an inner enclosure of a very large circus where outer areas are used as sitting arrangements and middle space is used to perform. Planet Cropper does not have a sun and its middle space have a very large but self-hanging arrangement of floodlight that lights the habitat, whereas its outer area has buildings and gardens for human and other living beings.

Cut to
103: Int : Polar Express-2 in Axis sky of the Planet Cropper:Day

Everybody including Polar tiger family is looking outside of the window to see the habitat of the Planet Cropper. Everyone is excited to get the view of outside.The speakerphone within the compartment rings and the voice of the Captain is heard.

<u>Captain</u>
"We are flying in the axis-sky of this habitat. You all can see from your windows that it does not have sun to provide light. They charge themselves from water energy to light their habitat. Water is the source of oxygen in this habitat and the exhaled carbon dioxide is recycled for oxygen gas and carbon deposits for energy. They switch off the lights , and are ready to sleep at night. They live a hard life but they are very wise, knowledgeable, and sensitive. They know how to keep their home tidy, orderly and perfect."

The captain keeps the 'Polar Express-2' flying in the axis sky to show the passengers the breathtaking beauty of the landscape, its habitats, its residential and business facilities. After three hours, it is become totally dark as the lights of the habitats are switched off.

<u>Captain</u>
"Now they have switched off the light to represent it as night. I will now put our shutters down so that the light does not go out of the windows and disturb them."

Thereafter windows of the compartments of 'Polar Express-2' close automatically. There is light inside but no one can see outside.

Pola
"Mom, Dad, what a beautiful place!"

Kemu, the tiger
"Though it looks very beautiful but there is extreme hardship to maintain life here."

Kelly, the tigress
"That is true. Our planet earth is very comfortable and freindly."

The speakerphone inside the compartment rings again and the voice of the Captain is heard. Everybody in the train compartment is alertly and attentively listening to the voice of the captain.

Captain
"We will now slowly make exit of this planet."

Captain's voice goes off on speakerphone.

Flying ship, 'Polar Express-2' lands on the surface and passengers feel the light jolt. Soon thereafter, it is felt as if a door is opened and the Polar Express-2 is pushed forcefully out with pressure to make a dispersal effect for water.

Cut to:
104: Int: Polar Express-2 in deep sea:

Door of the habitat on the planet Cropper has closed. The 'Polar Express-2', which is now in the sea as submarine, starts return journey. Everybody in the Polar Express is again excited and happy due to this travel experience. They open the shutter of the windows to catch the glimpse of the beautiful marine life once again.

Cut to:
105: Ext: Sea and sky of the Planet Cropper : Day

Soon submarine like 'Polar Express-2' comes on the surface of the sea and continues sailing for some time before taking off as an airplane into the sky. After that, it flies like spaceship and then slips deep into the space.

Cut to:
106: Int : Polar Express-2 in space :Day

'Polar Express-2' is deep into the space and there is nothing to see outside of the window except vacuum and darkness.

After some time, there is bright light and the speakerphone inside the compartment rings and the voice of the Captain is heard.

<u>Captain</u>

"We are about to reach a new planetary system. It has planet 'Cornet'."

The outer orbit of planet 'Cornet' is seen from the window of the compartment. It has burning yellow-red and turbulent outer exterior, as the inflammable gaseous cover around the planet is under flame.

Cut to:

<u>107: Ext: Polar Express-2 in space of the Planet Cornet : Day</u>

'Polar Express-2' enters into the gaseous boundary and crosses it to find an unbearable hot climate underneath dense vapour rising in the sky from the boiling liquid on the surface of the planet. The surface of the planet is not flat but uneven due to high-rise mountains spread all over on the planet, bottoms of which are dipped in the boiling liquid but connected with each other. Its outer atmosphere is not at all suitable for any living being.

Cut to:

<u>108: Int : Polar Express-2 in planet Cornet :Day</u>

Passengers of the 'Polar Express-2' are fascinated and a bit fearful to see no life but disturbances on the planet Cornet. Bright light is coming in from the windows. The speakerphone Inside the compartment rings and the voice of the Captain is heard.

<u>Captain</u>

"I am your captain speaking. A planet that you can see from your window does not have life in its open area. The high-rise mountains that you can see are not solid but hollow from inside and work like very large room connected to each other. These mountains have life within it but under tremendous harsh living condition. We would enter into the mountain body to see inside of it."

After 'Polar Express-2' reaches near a mountain, it enters the mountain door made of a large boulder.

Cut to:

<u>109: Ext: Polar Express-2 in the Planet Cornet : Day</u>

'Polar Express-2' suspends itself in the air like a helicopter. It enters into the mountain body slowly through its wide door.

Cut to:

110 : Int : Large mountain body of planet Cornet with life: Day

'Polar Express-2' lands on a flat indoor surface. It again moves like a train within the mountain body to go all around this compact world. Passengers are engrossed to see the living things of this planet.

Cut to:

111: Int : Polar Express-2 inside the planet Cornet :Day

Passengers of the 'Polar Express-2' are fascinated. Bright light is coming in from the windows. Speakerphone within the compartment rings and the voice of the Captain is heard again.

Captain

"Life within this world gets energy from its outer hot air and liquid. This energy also enables them to light their habitat. They have similar life pattern that we saw on planet 'Cropper'. By now you must have realised that you have been very lucky to be on the earth with extreme comfort and easy life with ample sunshine, fresh air and water, fresh food and green vegetations."

Captain's voice echoes from the speakerphone.

Kemu, the tiger

"He is right."

Captain

"But human on earth has not respected the wellbeing of the earth. They are mindlessly destroying forests, killing animals and altering the environment. Unless somebody takes the cudgel to either make them understand their folly or force them to refrain from their heinous act of deforestation, poaching, multiplying pollutions and fuelling climatic changes, the earth will lose its beauty and serenity."

Kemu, the tiger

"I agree with him."

Captain

"Now we would return to earth."

Captain's voice goes off from speakerphone. Everybody is silently watching the world inside the mountain body from their windows.

Cut to:

112: Ext: Polar Express-2 in the planet Cornet : Day

'Polar Express-2' takes off like an aeroplane and exits from the mountain body through a huge door at the upper end of the mountain. It comes out of the mountain, flies in its sky for a few moments, then rockets to go deep into the space away from the planetary system.

Cut to:

113: Ext : Polar Express-2 in space : Day

After some time, 'Polar Express-2' enters into the orbit of the earth and flies above the clouds. The flying birds above the clouds are happy to see the 'Polar Express-2' sailing above the clouds. They are flying speedily towards 'Polar Express-2'.

Birds [chants in chorus]

"Welcome back, welcome back, how is the other world?"

To see them chanting and welcoming, passengers are very happy and waving their hand from inside of windows. The birds are welcoming the passengers , and this make them very happy.

Cut to:

114: Ext: Polar Express-2 on the earth surface: Day

Rocket like body with cylindrical compartments and windows of Polar Express-2 is changing its shape from spacecraft to a train. All its wheels hidden within the body comes out while descending from the air and a long column of 'Polar Express-2' is landing on the arctic region of the earth and is running as a train.

Cut to:

115: Int : Polar Express-2 compartment: Day

Polar tiger family is happy to find that 'Polar Express-2' has landed on the surface of the earth and that they have returned to their home.

Pola

"Mom, Dad, we have come back to our beloved earth."

Kelly, the tigress

"Yes."

The accountant of God appears again.

<u>Accountant of God</u>
"Pola, it is now time for you to go back to the earth and do the task assigned by me."

<u>Pola</u>
"How would I fulfil this task amongst cunning and cruel people?"

<u>Accountant of God</u>
"Don't worry. I would empower you to reform yourself to a lion as well as to become invisible. Lion's body would enable you to frighten everyone. Secondly, you will have the capability to turn invisible to give a slip to anyone in case of fatal situations. I will give you an ammunition box which only you will be able to operate. The box will contain many forms of weapons such as gun, pistol, machine gun, laser gun, rocket launcher, stealth bomber, anti-tank helicopters, fighter jets equipped with missiles and other firepower, etc. The ammunition box would always remain full of cartridges, explosives, bombs and missiles. You can wish for any type of weapons and ammunition and it will be there in this box. The ammunition box will never be empty and would appear before you when you would desire to have it for usage."

<u>Pola</u>
"Thank you."

The accountant touches Pola's head to induce new capabilities in his body. Pola's bare body gets a new outfit. Suddenly he finds himself dressed in a shirt, a short and a pair of shoes. The tiger family is pleasantly surprised to see Pola in charming outfit. Pola himself feels very happy.

<u>Kelly, the tigress</u>
"How beautiful my son is! He looks very handsome."

<u>Kemu, the tiger and four tiger cubs [in unison]</u>
"Yes, very handsome looking boy!"

Due to the blessings of the accountant, Pola is enlightened with deep knowledge of the world. He is grateful to the accountant and also the tiger family. He touches the feet of the accountant and his mother, father and elder brothers. Everyone hugs and kisses him with affection and love.

Just then an unusual sight outside the window catch the attention of everyone including the tiger family. They see a polar bear gradually ascending to the sky. It is a sight of pleasant surprise. The polar bear is waving at the polar tigers.

Kemu, the tiger

"Look at the flying polar bear!"

Accountant of God

"He is the same polar bear who was in the body of a Chinese healer and was after you, to take revenge of his death as a polar bear."

Kemu, the tiger

"How come he can fly?"

Accountant of God

"He is dead now and going to heaven. He has completed his life."

Polar tiger family is surprised to know this fact.

Accountant of God

"You have also completed your life. I will drop Pola in the human habitat and will take you and your tiger family to heaven."

Kelly, the tigress

"How can we leave without our child?"

Accountant of God

"When you would reach heaven, you would forget about worldly emotions and about Pola."

Pola

"But I can't live without my family. You can't take away my father, mother, brother, my family."

Pola is agitated and disheartened to find sudden turn of the event.

Accountant of God

"This is life. Old-ones have to leave and let new-ones live."

Pola

"I can't live without my family."

Pola starts weeping and sobbing.

Accountant of God

"I am telling you that when you have your family in the human habitat having wife, children and grand children, you won't have moments to remember your parents. Nevertheless, I grant you the capability to talk to your parents and brothers in heaven, whenever you would desire. This capacity would, however, not be available to your wife and progeny."

<u>Kelly, the tigress</u>
"But I can't live without my child."

Kelly, the tigress is also weeping.

<u>Accountant of God</u>
"You would be able to watch Pola and his activities from the heaven."

<u>Kelly, the tigress</u>
"But I want to live with my child."

<u>Accountant of God</u>
"Just bear with me for a while. We will drop Pola on the earth and will soon enter into the heaven. I am sure; you would be comfortable even without Pola."

The accountant is trying to console her and the tiger family.

Cut to:
<u>116: Ext: Tropical Region of the earth : Day</u>

'Polar Express-2' is moving along a tropical region on the earth, where ample green vegetation including dense tree plantation is visible. The train stops where a human habitat is in the close vicinity.

Cut to:
<u>117: Int : Polar Express-2 compartment: Day</u>

Pola is not happy to leave his mother, father and the brothers. He has been sobbing. He has to face the reality and painful situation. The accountant is looking at Pola and suggesting him to get down from the train. But Pola is unmoved.

<u>Accountant of God</u>
"My Dear Pola, you need to get down here and undertake the mission that I have assigned to you."

Pola does not say anything. He hugs his mother, father and four tige cubs with tears in his eyes. His mother, father and brother cubs are weeping bitterly. The tiger family is aggrieved to be separated from Pola. Pola bows and touches the feet of God's accountant and moves towards the wide open door of the train and exits with a heavy heart. Soon after, the train starts moving ahead and leaves Pola behind.

Cut to:

<u>118: Ext: Tropical Region of the earth near human habitat: Day</u>

Pola gets down from the train with heavy heart and the train starts moving ahead on its track leaving him behind. Polar tiger family are bitterly weeping while looking outside and waving hands to have a last glimpse of Pola. Soon 'Polar Express-2' takes off, raising its upper end into the air and fly away into the sky. Pola is looking into the sky and is waving his hands. 'Polar Express-2' goes out of sight.

Cut to:

<u>119 : Ext: A tropical forest : Day</u>

Pola is walking and making his way ahead in a dense tropical forest. He is pleasantly overwhelmed to see greenery, flowery plants, and tall trees of the forest.

<u>Pola</u>

"Mom, Dad, what a beautiful place? Everywhere green… beautiful flowers…"

<u>Voice of Kelly, the tigress [O.S]</u>

"Yes, my dear. You are in a forest."

<u>Voice of Kemu, the tiger [O.S]</u>

"Be careful my son."

<u>Pola</u>

"Mom, Dad, how do you know that I am in a forest? Can you see me?"

<u>Voice of Kelly, the tigress [O.S]</u>

"Yes, my son. We can see you from the heaven."

<u>Pola</u>

"But I can't see you. Why?"

<u>Voice of Kelly, the tigress [O.S]</u>

"You are on the earth. The God's accountant has allowed you to speak to us whenever you wish."

<u>Pola</u>

"Mom, I am feeling hungry. I need to drink your milk."

<u>Voice of Kelly, the tigress [O.S]</u>

"My dear son, now you need to eat fruits and drink cow's milk."

Pola
"Mom, where can I get them?"

Voice of Kemu, the tiger [O.S]
"Carefully watch around you. I am sure you will find some fruits hanging from the trees. Pluck and eat them. Pola, my dear son, you need to manage with these fruits. You will find cows also for milk."

Pola
"Dad, how would it taste?"

Voice of Kemu, the tiger [O.S]
"Cow's milk will taste like your mother's milk. Fruits are mostly sweet, but there are bitter fruits also. Sp you need to bite first and taste it. But don't swallow. If you find it tasty, then eat otherwise spit it out."

Voice of Kelly, the tigress [O.S]
"My son, be careful and seek our advise whenever you need."

Pola
" Okay, Mom. Okay, Dad."

Pola continues his journey through the dense forest and find many guava trees at a place. He plucks them and eats. He is happy to eat the guava fruit. Then he continues walking for a long distance within the forest. After some time, he listens to the growls of tigers and finds a herd of tigers approaching towards him. He finds the tigers with bone and flesh altogether different from his mother and father tiger. He is not astonished as he is now enlightened due to the blessings of the accountant of God.

Pola
"Hello, my dear tigers. Why are you growling? I am one of you."

The tigers are astonished to find that a human is speaking their language and is able to communicate. They do not hold their wild and attacking posture and become friendly with him. One old tiger comes forward.

Old tiger
"Who are you? How come you speak our language?"

Pola
"My mom and Dad were also tigers like you. I drank my mother's milk since my birth."

<u>Old tiger</u>
"Where are your mother and father now?"

<u>Pola</u>
"They are in the heaven now."

<u>Old tiger</u>
"How can we trust you? Humans have always been a threat to us. They kill us including other animals and destroy our habitat, our forest."

<u>Pola</u>
"That is the reason the God's accountant met me and assigned a duty to go to forests and do something to save the deteriorating condition of wildlife and forests on the earth."

<u>Old tiger</u>
"Did you meet God?"

<u>Pola</u>
"No, I met his accountant. He keeps the accounts of lives on this earth."

<u>Old tiger</u>
"God or a member of his clan meets only kind souls. You must be a kind soul."

<u>Pola</u>
"My name is Pola, I am here to help you. You need to narrate the actual problems that have threatened the existence of lives on this earth."

<u>Old tiger</u>
"Now, you are our man. We will tell you everything that we suffer from."

<u>Pola</u>
"Thank you for confiding in me."

<u>Old tiger [to other tigers behind him]</u>
"No need to worry. He is a God-sent man to save our lives and our forest. Let us take him to our home and welcome him. He must be very tired."

The old tiger leads Pola along with other tigers to a cave, the home of tigers.

Cut to:
<u>120: Ext : Cave of tigers in a forest: Morning</u>

This is the morning hour and Pola is sleeping amongst many tigers, lions and other animals on the ground. A crow on the tree is crowing to wake them up. All the animals and Pola wake up.

<u>Old tiger [to his tigress]</u>
"O my dear tigress. Our Pola must be hungry after a long sleep at night. Could you kindly give him milk to drink?"

<u>Tigress</u>
"He is just like my child. Of course, he can drink my milk."

<u>Pola</u>
"I need to know as to what is the reason of threat that looms large?"

<u>Old tiger</u>
"Knowledge and shrewd mind of human have made us helpless despite of our strong physical make up. These humans are killing us for our skin. They are destroying our habitat by cutting trees and burning bushes. They have made our environment dangerously polluted. It has resulted in premature deaths of animals and birds living in the wild."

<u>Pola</u>
"Why are these human so inhumane, so heartless and dangerous?"

<u>Old tiger</u>
"We don't know. You need to find out for us. We are ready to live in harmony but they are not ready."

<u>Pola</u>
"Where do they live?"

<u>Old tiger</u>
"They live just a little distance away from the periphery of this jungle. They live in concrete buildings."

<u>Pola</u>
"I will go to see their activities and their behaviour."

<u>Old tiger</u>
"Be very careful."

<u>Pola</u>
"Are they very dangerous?"

Old tiger

"They may not be dangerous for you. But they have made our lives miserable."

Everybody nods in agreement. They look thoughtful.

Cut to:

121: Ext: Downtown of a modern City : Day

Pola is walking on a crowded pathway of a downtown city and is feeling uneasy to breath in a heavily polluted environment due to emission of gases on combustion of fossil fuel in motor vehicles and factories. He sits on a roadside settee to rest. He watches his surrounding with astonishment. He sees a person sitting on a nearby pavement and coughing profusely due to the effect of pollution. He feels pity about this man. He goes near him and tries to pat on his back to comfort him. The man lies down on the pavement and feels relief.

Pola walks further and finds a very big building, outer gate of which has a neon signboard of 'Ministry of Environment and Forest.' There are four guards on the gate. They are allowing only those persons to enter into the building who are carrying identification card. Nevertheless, he goes there.

Pola

"I would like to go into this building."

The security guards at the gate look at him suspiciously, as he does not carry any identification card.

One security guard

"Do you have an appointment?"

Pola

"No"

Other security guard

"Then you can't go inside."

Pola moves away from there and watches them from a distance. After a while, he can see that the security guards are busy checking the identification cards of four visitors. So Pola closes his eyes to become invisible. Soon he becomes invisible.

Cut to:

122: Int : Office door of the Minister of Environment of Forest: Day

There is a large size office door, outside of which has a hanging wooden board, which shows 'Minister of Environment and Forest'. Four waiters are entering into this room with trays having tea and snacks. They open the door and close it after entering inside.

Cut to:

123: Int : Office room of the Minister of Environment and Forest: Day

There is a very large room. The ceiling is very high and gives the feeling of a palatial hall. This is the office room of the Minister of Environment and Forest, which has a very large and elaborately decorated Minister's desk. There are nine chairs around this desk, one for the Minister and eight for the visitors. There is a large meeting table within this room, where twenty-five people can sit and have their group discussions, etc.

There are twenty-four people sitting around this large table and the Minister is seated on his chair, made up of mahogany and placed a bit higher than the other twenty four chairs, indicating the leading position of the Minister. The four waiters are serving tea and snacks to everyone on the table. Pola suddenly appears and is standing behind a side pillar of the room, which is covered by a thick curtain hanging from ceiling to the ground. Pola is trying to hear the conversation of the meeting.

Minister

"I am personally very thankful to all of you who have contributed for successful ascent of our political party to power in the recently concluded general election in the country. Though everybody has contributed heartily but today I would like to extend my special thanks to Mr David Burn and Mr Carter Greenwood, who have not only contributed financially but have always managed the electioneering affairs very personally."

Mr David Burn

"I thank you Mr Jackson Green, our beloved Minister of Environment and Forest, for your personal compliments to me."

Mr Carter Greenwood

"I too thank you Mr Jackson Green, our beloved Minister of Environment and Forest, for your personal compliments to me."

Mr Jackson Green

"Though I am in power now, I still need support of every one of you."

Mr David Burn

"Same thing applies to us. We also need your support."

Mr Jackson Green

"Please go on...".

Mr David Burn

"As you know we are engaged in the construction work, cement production and furniture export business, it is because of the hopeless policy of the outgoing Government to protect the trees, forests, lime deposits of the mountains, and also the minimal use of backed clay and bricks, etc which had badly affected our business. Now you have taken over as the Minister in charge of the portfolio that directly holds this policy, we would like a shift in the policy of the outgoing regime."

Mr Jackson Green

"The outgoing political party is to sit in the opposition in the parliament, so it would be very difficult to alter the policy, which is largely environmental friendly."

Mr Carter Greenwood

"But my dear friend, this policy is not at all friendly to us."

Mr David Burn

"Mr Green, my dear Minister, we need to remain friendly so that our businesses run smoothly. Every one of us has decided to transfer one million US dollar to your Swiss account."

Mr Jackson Green

"I welcome your contribution to my account, but you know to alter a policy there should be very strong justification."

Mr David Burn

"We would provide you written justifications on the basis of which you may order change in the policy."

Mr Jackson Green

"To take that kind of courage to change the policy of erstwhile regime, I would like the contribution to my Swiss account be doubled."

Mr David Burn

"As you desire... transfer of money to your account is not a problem."

Mr Jackson Green

"Can you tell me the point of justifications that you propose to enlist?"

Mr David Burn

"Our country is facing serious problem on account of hard currency reserve and this policy has contributed to this scarcity as it had restricted the export growth. Secondly, for the last ten years, there has not been any tree felling in the forests, that has resulted in wild fire due to high density of forest. Hence tree felling and deforestation is necessary now."

Mr Carter Greenwood

"We will transfer the fund in your Swiss account forthwith but you need to take care of our requirement. This should be done very soon. I would personally like to start felling of trees in the forest to start by next week. I shall be highly grateful if you could effect change in Government's policy within this week."

Mr Jackson Green

"I would do my best to help you. We are friends and would continue to be friends."

Mr Carter Greenwood

"Can I start tree felling by the next week? Would you issue order to that effect?"

Mr Jackson Green

"I would do everything within this week to help all of you."

Everybody present in this meeting applauses whey they hear the encouraging words of the Minister.

Cut to:

124: Ext : Cave of tigers in a forest: Morning

Pola is sitting amongst the tigers, lions and other animals near the cave. Everyone is worried to know that the work of deforestation would soon start that threatens their habitat.

Pola

"There is nothing to worry. You all need to hide. I will take care of those who would come to execute the orders of criminals."

Old tiger

"You are our only hope."

Everybody is alarmed to know the plan of criminal men.

Cut to:

125: Int: An office room of Mr Carter Greenwood: Day

Mr Carter Greenwood is sitting in his office room. The office is decorated in an oriental fashion. He is talking to his manager Mr Garry.

Mr Carter Greenwood

"Mr Garry, you need to hire a thousand workers to be engaged in felling of trees in the forest."

Mr Garry

"Do we have the government's sanction? Sir..."

Mr Cater Greenwood

"If I don't have a sanction, I won't ask. I have a written Government-sanction. So go ahead and start felling of trees quickly. We need to accelerate our work fast to catch up the export business."

Mr Garry

"This is good news for us."

Both appear to be happy and cheerful.

Cut to:

126: Ext: Dense Forest : Day

Ten buses carrying large number of labourers in green uniforms go on a concrete road and stops near the periphery of a dense forest. All the labourers get down of the bus. The cleaner of the bus gets down and goes to the backside of the bus to open the luggage holder to allow labourers to collect their battery-operated saw. The empty Bus goes away, whereas the labourers step forward to move into the forest holding their saw in hand. There is a person among the labourers, who is in red uniform with a handheld mike. He is seen leading the contingent of labourers in the forest. The forest is green and very dense.

Person in red uniform [into his mike]

"We need to cut mature trees, basically which are straight and fit in furniture making."

One labourer in green uniform

"Felling the trees would be very difficult. Mr Larry, you can see the thick bushes which might be the shelter of poisonous snakes."

Mr Larry, in red uniform [into his mike]
"You can burn the bushes to clear your hurdles in tree felling."

Labourers move into the forest and reach a segment of the forest, where they find trees with very thick trunks and branches. They stop and start burning the bushes.

A little away from this location, Pola, tigers, lions and other animals are watching from behind a bush the activities of the labourers. The animals are frightened to see bushes put on fire.

Pola
"You may move away from here. I will stay here and tackle them."

Old tiger
"You need to stop them."

Pola
"That is what I will do. Please go away with everybody."

The old tiger is leading the animal contingent and going away from that place. Pola moves ahead towards the place where labourers are busy burning the bushes. He turns himself invisible and reaches near a labourer and reform himself as a Lion. He roars aloud, attacks this labourer and injures him. When the other labourers hear the lion roar and the cries of the injured labourer, they get fearful. All the labourers encircle Pola, the lion, in order to kill. Pola, the lion hides himself behind a bush and turns invisible. Labourers are alarmed to see that the lion has vanished. After a few moments, when labourers see no threat, they help clean the wound of the injured labourer and make bandage. Pola, the lion again turns himself visible, attacks on another five labourers and quickly turns invisible. Now everybody is fearful to continue their work.

One Labourer
"This is a forest full of lions. If all the lions attack on us, we will die without any funeral and grave. Let us go back and report to our boss. They should first kill the lions, and then we would engage ourselves in tree felling."

Another worker
"Yes, you are right. Let us return."

Mr Larry in red uniform [into his mike]
"Right now we can't work until the lions, tigers and other dangerous animals of this forest are killed. We will return now and report the situation to our boss."

Everybody nods in agreement. They hold their saw and return.

Cut to:
<u>127: Int: An office room of Mr Garry : Day</u>

Mr Garry, the manager of Mr Carter Greenwood, is sitting on a chair behind his office desk, whereas Mr Larry in red uniform is sitting on another chair opposite him.

<u>Mr Garry</u>
"Mr Larry, I am amazed that you did not complete the task that was assigned to you."

<u>Mr Larry</u>
"Sir, no labourer was ready to work because the attack of that lion was sudden and fierce."

<u>Mr Garry</u>
"You were in large number. Why did not all of you try to catch this lion alive or dead for its skin and fur? You had saw in your hands. What was the problem in killing or catching this Lion?"

<u>Mr Larry</u>
"Hunters can do the work of catching or killing a lion, not labourers like us. Secondly, killing of endangered animals such as lions and tigers is a crime in this country. We need Government's approval for carrying out killing of these animals."

<u>Mr Garry</u>
"Our Boss, Mr Carter Greenwood, has a firm hold in the Government's decisions and getting an approval would not be a problem. I will report the matter to him."

<u>Mr Larry</u>
"I would wait for the approval."

<u>Mr Garry</u>
"Go and find hunters and kill all those who come in our work of tree felling. Getting the approval is my business. You need to carry out my orders."

<u>Mr Larry</u>
"Okay, Sir."

<u>Mr Garry</u>
"Do it tomorrow itself so that the tree felling may start immediately."

Mr Larry
"Okay, Sir."

Mr Larry gets up and exits from the room.

Cut to:
128: Ext: Dense Forest : Day

It is a bright sunny day when two buses carrying hundred hunters come near the periphery of a dense forest. All the hunters get down from the bus. The driver of the bus also gets down and goes to the backside of the bus to open the luggage holder to allow hunters to collect their guns and ammunition. The empty Bus moves away, whereas the hunters step forward to move into the forest holding their guns in hand. One hunter, wearing a hat, is guiding the contingent of the hunters in the forest. After walking for some time, they reach a location where Pola, the lion had attacked the labourers.

Guide hunter
"This is the location where the lion had attacked the labourers. Now we need to disperse ourselves and few of us should climb on the trees and shoot the lion at sight."

Thereafter three hunters climb on three different trees and sit on the branches with loaded guns. Other hunters move ahead in search of lion.

Pola and other animals are standing and watching these hunters from behind the bush. When the animals see these gun-laden hunters they become frightened. Pola makes a gesture to them to hide themselves under the bushes. He steps forward to face the challenge of these hunters.

He closes his eyes and he becomes invisible. There is a hunter on a branch of a tree and looking for the lion on the ground. Pola appears behind his back on the branch of the tree and closes his eyes to turn himself in a lion form. He attacks on the hunter, who shouts, "O God" and in fear jumps from the tree. The tree is very tall and that is why when the hunter falls he is critical and succumbs to his injury. Pola in the lion form roars aloud and then becomes invisible. All the hunters gather near the dead body of the hunter and are astonished.

One hunter
"How can a lion go climb the branches of a tree and attack him?"

<u>Other hunter</u>
"There are strange things happening in this world. This can be possible."

<u>One hunter</u>
"Should we return with his dead body?"

<u>Other hunter</u>
"We will avenge the death of our friend first and then we will return. Now there is no need to be on the branches of the trees. Let us find the lion on the ground. Let us be more alert."

Thereafter two hunters on the branches of the tree climb down from the trees and moves in a group with fully loaded guns to shoot the lion at sight.

A little away Pola shuts his eyes and remembers his ammunition box. A very sophisticated machine gun comes into his hand. He holds the machine gun tightly and starts firing bullets towards the hunters. The sudden burst of bullets pierce the bodies of hunters, who start falling on the ground. Hunters at the backe hear the sudden burst of bullets and are alarmed. They can see Pola firing his machine gun on their fellow hunters.

<u>One hunter [shouts]</u>
"Just run away. There is no lion. He is a man holding a machine gun to kill us. Let us run away."

Hunters, who are alive, picks up corpses of fellow hunters on their shoulders and tries to escape from there. Pola runs after them and fire bullets mercilessly to kill all the hunters. At the end dead bodies of all the hunters are lying on the ground.

Pola is happy to kill all the hunters.

Cut to:
<u>129: Int: An office room of Mr Garry : Day</u>

Mr Garry, the Manager of Mr Carter Greenwood, is sitting on a chair behind his office desk, whereas Mr Larry is sitting on another chair opposite him.

<u>Mr Garry</u>
"Mr Larry, did you get a confirmation, whether lions have been killed by our hunters."

<u>Mr Larry</u>
"No, Sir. I am shocked and clueless as to why our hunters have not returned despite of forty-eight hours. "

Mr Garry

"What? Forty-eight hours...? There must be something terribly wrong in your plan."

Mr Larry

"I have sent a hundred gun-laden experienced hunters. I can't say as to why they have not returned yet?"

Mr Garry

"Then, you may send another batch of hunters to find these missing hunters in the jungle."

Mr Larry

"That is the only option left with me."

Mr Garry

"Please do fast. My boss needs result."

Mr Larry gets up and exits from the room.

Cut to:

130: Ext: Dense Forest : Day

There has been a drizzle. Though all the trees are wet, the earth surface is still dry. Two buses with hundred hunters stop near the periphery of the dense forest. All the hunters get down from the bus. The cleaner of the bus gets down and goes to the backside of the bus to open the luggage holder to allow the hunters to collect their guns and ammunition. The hunters step forward to move into the forest holding their guns in their hands. Mr Larry is guiding the contingent of hunters in the forest. After walking for some time, they reach the location where Pola, the lion had attacked the labourers. They find the dead bodies of hunters scattered in and around the area. They are alarmed and fearful. Mr Larry checks the wound of a dead hunter and finds that it is a bullet wound.

Mr Larry

"This is a bullet wound. A man with a machine gun has killed them. They have not been killed by an animal or lion."

One hunter

"Let us collect all their guns to check whether they fought with the lion or not and whether bullets have been fired."

Mr Larry

"Yes, in case they did not fire, then it would be a case of assault by someone else with machine gun."

Another hunter [checks three guns]
"They did not fight. There was an assault on them. Let us return quickly. The assailants will come after us."

Mr Larry
"We need to carry the corpses on our shoulders to return home."

Everyone carries a corpse on his shoulder and leaves in a hurry.

Cut to:

131: Int : Office room of the Minister of Environment and Forest: Day

Mr Jackson Green, the Minister of Environment and Forest, is meeting with Mr Carter Greenwood in his office room. Mr Greenwood is discussing about the hindrances coming in his way.

Mr Carter Greenwood
"My dear Minister, my plan of felling trees in the forest has not yet started because the laborers refused to execute the orders as lions attacked and injured many of them. I sent hunters to kill these lions, of course with your permission, who did not return. When I sent some more hunters to find out the reasons, they returned with their corpses with bullet wounds."

Mr Jackson Green
"Lions and bullet wounds?"

Mr Carter Greenwood
"Lions can't fire bullets. I am sure some of your opposition politicians are behind this. Are the opposition protesting your new policy of allowing deforestation?"

Mr Jackson Green
"Maybe the Green activists are taking up arms to dispel deforestation."

Mr Carter Greenwood
"This must not show that your government is handicap in implementing its order."

Mr Jackson Green
"No one can put hurdles in implementation of my orders. I would order military operation in the forest to kill all those who would become a hurdle in your work."

Mr Carter Greenwood
"I appreciate that you have sensed the gravity of this problem."

Mr Jackson Green

"I am ordering the military to move its troops to the forest. Anyone going against the felling of tree will be killed instantly."

Mr Carter Greenwood

"Thank you, Minister. I am extremely grateful for your instant action."

Mr Carter Greenwood shakes hand with the Minister and gets up to leave the room.

Cut to:

132 : Ext : Dense forest : Day

A very large number of machine gun-laden soldiers of five military troops are getting down from fifty armoured military trucks. Five military tanks are also rolling on the road near the periphery of the forest. The gun-laden soldiers and five military tanks are moving into the dense forest. The soldiers are alert and ready to shoot at any slightest sign of danger.

A little away from this location, Pola and the animals are watching the movement of soldiers. The animals are frightened to see gun-laden soldiers.

Pola

"You may again to move away from here."

Old tiger

"How are you going to stop them? They are in a large number."

Pola

"They can't beat me. I will force them to stop their movement and return to barracks. God has given me that power, so don't worry and go away to a safer place."

Old tiger

"God is very kind. He has sent you as our saviour."

The old tiger is leading the animal contingent and going away from that place. Pola moves ahead towards the place where the soldiers are alert and moving towards the centre of the forest. He closes his eyes and remembers his ammunition box and ten military tanks appear which fires bombs towards the forward moving enemy tanks and soldiers. Sudden attack baffles the commander of the troops as a very large number of casualties take place and his military tanks become dysfunctional in this gun battle.

Military Commander [into his wireless set]

"May day, may day. Hello, I am Commander Jerome speaking. We are under attack of tremendous firepower that has resulted in large number of casualties to our side and dysfunction of all five tanks. Send enforcement to wind up this operation quickly. Send military fighter planes or helicopters to identify the assailants from above the sky."

The Military Commander is hiding himself behind a thick trunk of tree along with few other soldiers. It is a calm for some time and there is no gunfire.

Cut to:

133: Ext: Overview of dense forest: Day

Fighter jets and helicopters are flying in the sky above the forest. They start firing on the suspected targets by shelling remote controlled missiles and cluster bombs. Smoke billows into the sky due to spread of fire in a very large area of the forest. The animals are running here and there to save their lives. They are frightened whereas Pola is very angry with the large-scale destruction in the forest. He closes his eyes to remember the ammunition box. A fighter helicopter appears suddenly, which is equipped with missiles, bombs and ammunition. Pola gets into this helicopter and quickly ascends into the sky and chases the enemy fighter jets and helicopters. The enemy fighter jets and helicopters are firing continuously but Pola's helicopter is smart enough to dodge them and instead fires missiles and destroy the enemy helicopters and jets one by one. After some time enemy contingent falls silent and meet its end in the forest.

Cut to:

134: Ext: Dense forest : day

Soon the animals realize that the enemy contingent has found its grave in the forest and there is no danger anymore, so they come out in the open to express their joy as Pola has defeated their enemy.

Old tiger

"Pola is our true saviour. He has defeated our staunch enemy and dispelled them to run away from the forest. He is our true man."

Another tiger

"He has shown his mettle. I am sure that our enemy would not dare to come to the forest again."

He takes Pola on his back and runs in joy. Other animals also do the same with Pola. They dance together to express their gratitude to Pola for being their saviour.

Cut to

135: Int : office room of the Minister of Environment and Forest: Day

Mr Jackson Green, the Minister of Environment and Forest, is meeting with a military commander in his office room.

Mr Jackson Green

"It gives me extreme pain to know that a large number of soldiers have died in the 'Operation forest'. Whoever is fighting against us is challenging the decision of a sovereign nation, which is not acceptable to this country."

A Military commander

"I had sent five troops to the forest, which came under fierce attack. Thereafter I sent ten fighter jets and ten fighter helicopters, which were also brought down. It appears that the challenger is much more equipped and smart."

Mr Jackson Green

"Our government can't face a situation of helplessness. We have to enforce the order of the government and wipe out the challenger. Put all our military might and air power to defeat and kill this challenger. This is the order of the President."

A Military commander

"Okay, Sir. I will issue instructions accordingly."

Mr Jackson Green shakes hand with the military commander, who gets up to exit from the room.

Cut to:

136 : Ext : Overview of the forest : Day

There is a large movement of military force. Soldiers are getting down from a hundred armoured military trucks. Numerous military tanks are also rolling in the forest. Soldiers and military hardware are moving fast into the forest. They are alert and ready to shoot at any slightest sign of danger. Many fighter jets are flying in the sky above the forest.

Fighter jets start firing on the suspected targets by shelling remote controlled missiles and cluster bombs. Smoke billows into the sky and fire spreads throughout the forest. The animals are running here and there to save their lives. They are frightened. The military tanks and soldiers are moving ahead to face the challengers.

Pola is upset with the large-scale destruction in the forest. He closes his eyes to remember the ammunition box. Many auto fighter jets appear instantly, which are equipped with missiles, bombs and ammunition.

<u>Pola [to fighter jets]</u>
"Go and fight with enemy jets and helicopters. You should also pound on the enemy tanks and soldiers."

All auto fighter jets follow the instruction of Pola and quickly fly into the sky and chase the enemy fighter jets and helicopters. The enemy fighter jets and helicopters are firing continuously but Pola's auto fighter jets are smart enough to dodge them and instead attack the enemy at a close range. It fires missiles and destroy them one by one. Pola's auto fighter jets pound on the enemy tanks and soldiers continuously. There are large number of dead bodies of soldiers and demolished enemy tanks, scattered all over the forest. Fierce battle continues for some time between the enemy and Pola's auto fighter jets. After some time the enemy contingent falls silent in the forest.

The animals come out in the open to express their joy as Pola has again defeated the enemy. They take Pola on their back and dance happily.

Cut to:

<u>137: Int : Office room of the Minister of Environment and Forest: Day</u>

Mr Jackson Green, the Minister of Environment and Forest, is meeting with Mr Carter Greenwood in his office room.

<u>Mr Jackson Green</u>
"We have lost thousands of our soldiers, enormous military hardware, tanks, fighter jets and helicopters in this fight with the challenger. We cannot afford to continue this fight. This battle has shaken our government and economy."

<u>Mr Carter Greenwood</u>
"We are a sovereign nation. How can we accept defeat from this challenger?"

<u>Mr Jackson Green</u>
"We accepted the challenge and fought but we lost heavily. We have realized that we cannot continue our fight. This is the considered decision of our parliament, to make forest out of bound, so that green forest remains preserved."

<u>Mr Carter Greenwood</u>
"Then I will lose heavily."

<u>Mr Jackson Green</u>
"You have to diversify your business to eliminate your dependence on wood and forest."

<u>Mr Carter Greenwood</u>
"You need to help me."

<u>Mr Jackson Green</u>
"I will return your contribution from my Swiss account. I cannot act against the decision of our parliament. If you can go to forest alone and face the challenger, you are free to do that."

<u>Mr Carter Greenwood</u>
"You must be joking. How can I dare to go to the forest alone?"

<u>Mr Jackson Green</u>
"Forest remains out of bound for everyone including you. You need to change your business to remain sound."

<u>Mr Carter Greenwood</u>
"I will take your leave now."

Mr Carter Greenwood shakes hand with the Minister and gets up to leave the room.

Fade out

Fade In
<u>138 : Ext : Dense Forest : Day</u>

After some time [on screen caption]

A herd of lion, tiger, bear and other wild animals are sitting under a big tree. They are worried to see the deteriorating physical condition of five cubs. The cubs are restless due to abdominal pain and respiratory trouble. They are not able to breathe properly due to pneumonic condition. The reason of their sickness is not known. The old tiger often looks at the pathway as if he is expecting someone. After some time Pola is seen approaching them.

Old tiger

"Pola, where were you for so many days? We were eagerly waiting for you."

Pola

"I used this opportunity to see various places of the forest including mountains. But why are you waiting for me? Is there a problem here?"

Old tiger

"Yes, for the last few days, we all are having breathing problems. These five cubs are restless due to abdominal pain and are not able to breathe properly. We do feel some abdominal discomfort."

Pola

"Why?"

Old tiger

"We do not know the reason."

Pola

"Let me examine."

Old tiger

"Today when I drank water from the river, its taste was a bit different."

Pola

"Let me check the water of the river."

Old tiger

"Come with me. I will show you."

The old tiger takes Pola, whereas other animals follow them. After walking for a while, they reach the riverbank. The river passing through the forest is the source of drinking water for the animals of the forest. The water surface seems unusually black.

Old tiger

"I think something has been mixed in the water. In the morning it was not like this but the taste was different."

Pola

"It seems that someone has contaminated this water by putting crud petroleum in the river water. This is the reason of abdominal discomfort and pain."

Pola then breathes deeply for two minutes.

Pola

"Something is wrong with the air also. That is the reason for breathing problems."

The old tiger sees a flowering plant and a creeper at the riverbank, they are dying as its leaves and flowers have dried and fallen on the ground. He goes near this flowering plant and touches it. Everyone looks at him.

Old tiger

"These beautiful flowering plants at the riverbank have died suddenly. It may be due to the contaminated water and air."

Pola

"Yes, that is the reason. Can you tell me as to wherefrom this river comes into this forest?"

Old tiger

"The river comes from the city, the human habitat."

Pola

"It is very clear that the oil spill in water and poisonous gas emission is the doing of the city dwellers. Perhaps, it is done willfully to harm the animals in the forest."

Old tiger

"It might be true because you defeated them. They are taking revenge now. But they must understand that it is not good for them also."

Pola

"There are a handful men who are greedy to earn money by any means, whether good or bad for mankind. There is no place on the earth where human cannot go and live, whether chilly cold arctic or antarctic or hottest desert."

Old tiger

"What should we do now to save ourselves?"

Pola

"I will have to go to the city and stop them. Now confrontation with the city dwellers is the only way out for survival of animals in the forest. I am leaving for the city tomorrow."

Old tiger

"You are the only hope for our existence."

Pola

"Don't worry. I will do everything in my power."

Everybody appears to be satisfied with Pola's answer. They hope that everything would be fine.

Cut to:

<u>139: Ext: A Modern city : Day</u>

Pola sets his foot in the city for the first time. He is stupefied to see the skyscrapers and the modern men and women. People are sitting and relaxing on the riverbank. He is surprised to see young men and women kissing each other in broad daylight. He reaches a lush green garden with a very beautiful landscape. There are many men and women in this garden and they are enjoying each other's company in the summer climate. He sees them engrossed in reading something or talking heartily or playing cards. He continues walking and is awestruck with the newfound world. He wants to take someone's help to let him know about this city.

After some time, he finds a young and beautiful woman, who is busy painting a portrait of the beautiful landscape on a canvas. Pola is flabbergasted to see the exact portrait of the landscape on the canvas. He is so impressed that he applauds for her beautiful work. Pola's clap deviates the focus of the young woman. She sees Pola standing near her with appreciating eyes for her artwork.

<u>Pola</u>

"Very beautiful artwork indeed...!"

<u>Young woman</u>

"Thank you. Who are you?"

<u>Pola</u>

"My name is Pola. What about you?"

<u>Young woman</u>

"My name is Pauline. Thank you for appreciating my artwork."

<u>Pola</u>

"Everybody would appreciate your work."

<u>Pauline</u>

"No one has time to look at other's work."

<u>Pola</u>

"Why?"

<u>Pauline</u>

"Do you not live in this city?"

Pola
"No."

Pauline
"People in small towns have still some time for others but city dwellers are self-centred and selfish."

Pola
"Why do you say so?"

Pauline
"They are after money and materials. Everything else is worthless for them."

Pola
"Please educate me."

Pauline
"They care for money and matter and nothing else. They don't even take care for their own health."

Pola
"Is there any health problem?"

Pauline
"I am very fond of nature. But natural beauty is diminishing. Air and water pollution is killing everybody including animals, plants and human but the rampant increase in industrial activities, increase in waste product, continuous spilling of poisonous liquid and gas on the earth is unabated. Despite of the fact that the top industrialists of this city are also suffering from breathing problems, they have no sense to find a solution to eliminate this problem. Instead they prefer finding a medicine for mass production and then earn from the sale of it."

Pola
"You sound very enlightened and interesting. What do you do?"

Pauline
"I am a computer programmer by profession. And you?"

Pola
"I am a fighter."

Pauline
"Do you fight in rings? Boxing...?"

Pola
"No...no... I am from a place in the wild. The water we drink has been poisoned. I think someone in this city is contaminating this river with poisonous substances. I have come to fight with him."

<u>Pauline</u>

"You are a fool. There are so many industrialists and factory owners who are responsible for spilling poisonous liquids in the water canals leading to rivers. You are alone and you will not be able to fight with them. They will kill you."

<u>Pola</u>

"I have extreme courage and I am sure I will be able to effectively curb their activities."

<u>Pauline</u>

"How?"

<u>Pola</u>

"If I get your support and guidance, I will be able to fight them. You appear to be truly aggrieved by the natural disaster and wish to save it."

<u>Pauline</u>

"Yes, I do."

<u>Pola</u>

"Then you are my friend. If we put our shoulders together, we will have the power of eleven and not two."

<u>Pauline</u>

"What kind of help do you need from me?"

<u>Pola</u>

"Kindly take me to the industrial areas, where the heinous act of self destruction is carried out."

<u>Pauline</u>

"That would not be a problem for me."

<u>Pola</u>

"Can you take me to one of these today?"

<u>Pauline</u>

"Yes. Just wait."

Pauline is wrapping her canvas and accessories to keep in a bag so that she can go with Pola.

Cut to:

<u>140: Ext: A factory site: Day</u>

Pauline is accompanying Pola. They reach the backside of a very big factory. The factory is emitting black smoke into the air.

There is a big sewerage pipe, which originates from the factory and ends in a water canal. From that sewerage pipe, black liquid is oozing out.

Pauline

"This is a fertilizer factory, which is polluting the water."

Pola

"Thank you for guiding me till here."

Pauline

"I won't go any further. Whatever you would like to do, you can do on your own."

Pola

"I won't put you in danger. But you need to show me other places as well."

Pauline

"That won't be a problem."

Pola

"I have to meet you tomorrow. Where will I find you?"

Pauline [takes out a paper from her bag]

"This is my address. You can come to my residence."

Pola

"Thank you. Now you can go. I will meet you tomorrow."

Pauline hurries from there, whereas Pola is watching her go. Thereafter he walks and reaches the front side of the factory, which has a gate with mechanized access control mechanism under the supervision of many security personnel. Pola closes his eyes and becomes invisible.

Cut to:

141: Int : Fertilizer factory : Day

Pola invisibly reaches the inside of the factory, where a large number of workers are assigned. There are very huge machines on which these workers are engaged to execute required instructions in order to make the fertilizer, the product of the factory.

Pola changes himself into a large sized lion and roars aloud. He runs towards these workers. Seeing a lion approaching them, all the workers become fearful and run for safety. Pola, the lion, attacks one factory worker and injures him. Soon thereafter security personnel of the factory step in with their firearms. One security guard spots Pola, the lion and fires his gun. Pola, the lion, is alert. He escapes the bullets and hides himself. Thereafter he becomes invisible.

The security personnel search for the wild animal everywhere in the factory but do not find a lion.

Security Chief [into his walkie-talkie]
"Sir, we have checked everywhere but surprisingly we do not find the wild animal anywhere. Sir, kindly check up the video file of the surveillance camera to know whether there was a lion or was it an illusion of some factory worker."

[Voice from walkie-talkie]
"Ask your security guards to check again thoroughly. The lion must be there because a worker is injured due to wild attack. Of course I am going to check the video file."

Security Chief [into his walkie-talkie]
"Okay, Sir."

Cut to
142: Int: Overview of internal premises of the fertilizer factory: Day

There is an overview of the activities of security personnel. The security guards are engaged in searching the wild animal within the factory. After some time, the security guards come to the security chief in the middle of the factory and encircle him.

One security guard
"Sir, we have thoroughly checked and did not find any animal."

Security Chief
"Is that true? It is very surprising that a lion roared, injured a factory worker and vanished."

Another security guard
"Now what to do sir...?"

Security Chief [into his walkie-talkie]
"Sir, did you see a lion in the video file. We did not find the animal."

[Voice from walkie-talkie]
"Yes, there is a very big sized lion in the video file of surveillance camera. Ask your security men to guard the inside premises and shoot at sight of the animal. Ask all the workers to resume the work of the factory."

Security Chief [to his security men]

"You shall be guarding the internal premises and shoot at the sight of the animal. Be vigilant and ask all the workers to be vigilant. They should resume the work of the factory."

All the security guards disperse after receiving the instruction and take up their positions. An announcement is made on an internal microphone of the factory.

[Loud Voice]

"A thorough search has been carried out and all the security personnel have been asked to take positions inside the factory premises to ensure safety against the animal. All the workers are, therefore, requested to resume work in the factory and be vigilant. The security guards are authorized to shoot the animal at sight."

After the announcement, workers come and take their positions near the large machines of the factory. Thereafter the factory functions normally. Pola appears again and takes the shape of lion just behind a security guard, standing at an elevated platform on a steel pillar of the factory. The lion roars very loudly and attacks the security guard from behind. This security guard is caught by surprise and is not able to hold his gun on hearing the loud roars of the lion behind him. He gets scared and his gun falls from his hand. Pola, the lion, pounces on the security guard and injures him. In order to save himself, this security guard jumps down from the steel pillar and injures himself very badly. Other security guards see the lion and fire bullets at him. Pola, the lion, is alert. He hides himself and becomes invisible.

The roars of the lion creates fear among the factory workers and they panic. The security personnel resumes their thorough check in the factory.

Cut to:

143: Ext: Crud Refinery Plant : Day

Pola is standing outside the refinery plant and trucks carrying petrol and diesel are moving in and out of the plant's entrance gate, which has a mechanized access control mechanism under the supervision of many security personnel. Pola closes his eyes and becomes invisible.

Cut to:

144: Int : Refinery Plant : Day

Pola goes inside the refinery plant. A large number of workers are working near big oil reservoirs to execute required instructions to store refined petrol or diesel that comes into reservoir through big pipes.

Pola turns himself into a large sized lion and roars aloud. He runs towards the workers. When the lion approaches, the workers become fearful and run away from their position to safety. The lion attacks many factory workers with his teeth and claws. The lion injures them to the extent of minor external injuries. Soon thereafter security personnel of the factory step in with their firearms. One security guard spots the lion and fires his gun. As the lion is alert he dodges bullets and hides himself. Thereafter he becomes invisible but the bullets fired by the security guard brings devastation as the bullets pierces the reservoir of a fuel tanker and fire breaks out. Fire spreads very quickly to other areas.

One security guard (into his walkie-talkie)

"May day, may day. Please rush fire tenders immediately. There is a large fire in the factory."

Cut to:

145: Ext: Overview of Refinery plant: Day

Smoke billow up into the sky from the refinery plant due to devastating fire. The fire tenders rush into the factory through its entrance gate to put off the fire. Firefighters come out of the fire tenders. They are seen putting off the fire in the refinery plant.

Cut to

146: Int : Pauline's home : Day

Pauline is sitting on a couch in the drawing room at her residence. Her mother is also sitting beside her and is sipping tea. Both are watching TV and her attention is caught by a TV-news.

[Loud Voice from TV]

"Unbelievable incidents have been reported from many factories and industrial plants, which are security fortified. Today a lion appeared at these factories and injured many workers. Fearful factory workers stopped their work and when security personnel confirmed that there is no lion, the factory workers resumed work in the presence of security guards. However, the lion reappeared again and injured security guards. Security personnel are clueless as to how this lion comes into the factory and disappears. Fire broke out at many places due to bullets fired at this lion during search and kill operation carried out by the security personnel. This incidence has shattered the confidence of the workers of all the factories and industrial plants. They have decided not to resume their work until this lion is killed."

<u>Pauline's mother</u>
"How can a lion go inside a factory?"

<u>Pauline</u>
"Perhaps, I know."

<u>Pauline's mother</u>
"What do you know?"

<u>Pauline</u>
"I am sure, Pola has done this."

<u>Pauline's mother</u>
"Who is Pola?"

<u>Pauline</u>
"A friend...."

<u>Pauline's mother</u>
"Boy friend...! I am happy that at last you have got a boy friend."

<u>Pauline</u>
"No, not a boy friend... I just met him today. He is a man from the wild and very innocent. He has come to fight those who contaminate the river water that they drink. I think he has managed to ward these workers off so that poisonous liquid is not spilled in the river."

<u>Pauline's mother</u>
"Is he a lion?"

<u>Pauline</u>
"No, he is a young man. Perhaps he has disguised himself as a lion to frighten the workers, otherwise the security guards could have traced an animal. I am sure; he has disguised as a lion, did his tricks and then reappeared as a man and escaped from there."

<u>Pauline's mother</u>
"He is an interesting young man. I would like to meet him. Can you bring him home?"

Pauline

"I don't know where he lives? He has my address. He may come to me."

Pauline's mother

"Why did not you take his address?"

Pauline

"I did not expect a man from wild to be so smart. But don't worry mom, I guess, he will come to me tomorrow. "

Both look at each other's face.

Cut to:

147: Int : Office room of the Minister of Environment and Forest: Day

Mr Jackson Green, the Minister of Environment and Forest, is in a meeting with many factory owners and industrialist. Mr Green is discussing about the sudden stoppage of industrial activities due to a wild animal.

Mr Jackson Green

"My government is very concerned about the total shut down of industrial activity. It must start immediately."

One Industrialist

"We have tried our best but the workers are not ready to come for work until the lion is killed."

Mr Jackson Green

"What is the problem in killing this animal?"

Another Industrialist

"Our security personnel have tried their best to search and kill this animal, which gives a slip and vanishes."

Mr Jackson Green

"We can take the help of technologists to improve the surveillance system and to track this animal in the factory."

One Industrialist

"But it would be a costly affair for us."

Mr Jackson Green

"We can't afford to keep our economic activity shut due to an animal. This is dangerously costly. My government would not charge any duty on import of any surveillance system or technology from abroad. So don't sit but improve your system and catch or kill the animal."

Another Industrialist
"Okay, Sir. We would try our best."

Everyone gets up and shakes hand with the Minister before going out of the office.

Cut to:
148: Int : Pauline's home : Day

After one month [on screen caption]

Pauline is sitting on a couch in the drawing room at her residence. Her mother is also sitting beside her and is sipping tea. Both are watching TV when her attention is caught by a TV-news.

[Loud Voice from T.V]
"It is expected that the industrial activity of the city would resume by tomorrow that has remained shut during the last one month mainly due to threat of a lion. Association of the workers is now ready to resume the work. Every worker will be given a personal firearm to shoot an animal at sight within the factory. Due to government's intervention, every factory or industrial establishment is equipped with modern surveillance system now, which would effectively track the movement of an animal."

Pauline's mother
"Pola did not come to meet you. Do you think that he will do such tricks again when every worker is gun laden? "

Pauline
"Perhaps, not...never."

Pauline's mother
"You should have taken his address. He is a noble man fighting for nature."

Pauline
"I did not realize that he is such a courageous man. He is worth for a friendship."

The doorbell rings, which makes both of them anxious as to who is at the door? Pauline's mother gets up and goes to open the door. She opens the door. Pola is in front of her and she is not able to recognize this handsome young man.

Pauline's mother
"Whom do you want to meet?"

Pola
"My name is Pola. Is this the home of Pauline, my friend?"

Pauline's mother [happily smiles]
"Yes, Pauline lives here. I am her mother. Please come in. Pauline told me about you."

Pola
"Thank you, mom."

Pauline's mother leads him to the drawing room, where Pauline sees Pola in disbelief. She is very happy to see him.

Pauline
"Pola, you have done a great job. Every factory was closed for the last one month."

Pauline's mother
"Let him sit and relax first."

Pauline gestures and requests Pola to sit on the couch. Pola sits on the couch and looks at the beautiful interior of the house in amazement.

Pauline
"What are you looking at with so much disbelief?"

Pola
"I am a man from the wild and have not seen a house so beautiful like this."

Pauline
"It means you need to see more as this is nothing compared to interiors of the rich people."

Pauline's mother
"Where did you live all these years?"

Pola
"I am from an Eskimo family and lived in igloo. My parents died right after my birth and I lived with animals in the wild."

Pauline's mother
"Wild animals could have killed you."

Pola
"The animals are kind hearted. I can talk to them. I lived with them

freely. I am here because of them as their lives are threatened due to poisonous air and water."

Pauline

"That is amazing. You are great. You have done something that no one could do yet."

Pola

"How do you know as to what I have done?"

Pauline

"The industrialists of this city are reeling under your threat. You have disguised yourself as a lion and every worker got scared to work in the factories. The factories have shut down for the last one month, but they are going to resume their work from tomorrow."

Pola

"How do you know this?"

Pauline

"That is a television, which telecasts news of prime importance."

Pola

"I have to stop them again."

Pauline

"You can't stop them this time as every worker would be equipped with a gun to shoot the lion at sight. So don't ever dare to go again otherwise it may be fatal."

Pola

"Don't worry. I will be able to deal with them."

Pauline's mother

"What would you like to eat?"

Pola

"Milk and fruit would be good for me."

Pauline's mother goes to the kitchen whereas Pauline is happily watching the glowing face of Pola.

Cut to:

149: Ext: One roadside telephone booth in the modern city: Day

Pola is in the roadside telephone booth. He dials a number and waits to respond.

Pola (speaks into the phone)
"Is it the Office of the Minister of Environment and Forest?"

He listens carefully.
Pola (speaks into the phone)

"Can you connect me to the Minister? Tell him that the lion of the factories and plants is calling."

He again listens carefully.

Pola (speaks into the phone)
"Hello, Mr Minister, my name is Pola. I would like to tell you that you are working contrary to your duty of saving the environment and forest. You have allowed rampant spilling of poisonous liquids in the river water. The animals of the forest drink this contaminated water and then die. You have also allowed emission of poisonous gas beyond the dangerous limits that kills animals and plants alike in forests. You are a dangerous mole in the humankind. You have joined hands with criminals, who are dangerous to the mankind and the beautiful nature on this earth."

He again listens carefully.

Pola (speaks into the phone)
"Listen Mr Minister; there is no one who can kill me. You need to keep these polluting industries shut otherwise your workers will have to bear the consequences."

He again listens carefully.

Pola (speaks into the phone)
"Then, you need to see further actions of mine. I will teach you a lesson or two."

He replaces the telephone receiver.

Cut to:
150: Int : Office room of the Minister of Environment and Forest: Day

Mr Jackson Green, the Minister of Environment and Forest, is in meeting with the military commanders, many factory owners and industrialists. Mr Green is discussing about resuming of the industrial activities.

Mr Jackson Green
"I have called this meeting due to a sudden development. I received a telephone call from one Mr Pola, the so-called lion, who disrupts

the industrial activities. He threatened me that if the activities of the polluting industries are resumed, then he would inflict serious damages to the workers."

<u>Military Commander</u>

"Sir, if he is the same guy, whom we faced in the forest, then we must take his threat very seriously. He has sophisticated firepower. He has the capacity to inflict damages."

<u>Mr Jackson Green</u>

"But we can't stop our economic activities. Our nation would perish without economic backbone."

<u>One Industrialist</u>

"We have given gun to every worker to shoot the moment they see him. I think he may not succeed this time."

<u>Military Commander</u>

"But he has the firepower to blast the industries, plants...".

<u>Mr Jackson Green</u>

"That is where military's role is crucial. I am sure; he will not come inside the plants or factories. He would try to blast bombs and create panic. Military has to safeguard the life of people and repel any such attack."

<u>Another industrialist</u>

"We have to seal the border of this city so that undesirable elements can be screened and caught before they approach us. Military can undertake this task."

<u>Military Commander</u>

"We can do any duty that would be assigned to us. But this man is seriously addressing the issue of pollution. If we also join hands, it would be beneficial to everyone."

<u>Mr Jackson Green</u>

"We are open to discussions. But we are not open to threats. We are a sovereign nation and have the capacity to formulate our policy against the will and wish of anybody. I would, therefore, ask our military to prepare itself to face the threat of this lion man."

<u>Military Commander</u>

"Sir, military is always ready to obey orders of the Government."

The industrialists are happy.

Cut to:

<u>151 : Ext: Lawn in front of the house of Pauline : Morning</u>

This is a summer season. Pauline and her mother are sitting on chairs in the lawn in front of their home. Both have just finished their morning breakfast and tea and are busy reading morning newspaper. Pola approaches them. He knocks at the wooden gate of the fence around the lawn. Pauline and her mother are happy to see him.

<u>Pauline's mother</u>

"Hello, Pola, my son."

<u>Pola</u>

"Good morning, mom. Good morning, Pauline."

<u>Pauline</u>

"Where were you these days? The Government has ordered its military to deal with you."

<u>Pola</u>

"What is the news?"

<u>Pauline</u>

"There would be military men in the factory premises to guard against you."

<u>Pola</u>

"Don't worry. I know the course of actions that I need to do. But why is the Government taking side with the criminals, who are polluting environment and destroying forests. They are supposed to save the environment."

<u>Pauline</u>

"It appears that the Minister of Environment and Forest is also a criminal. He is portraying you as a criminal against these industrialists. That is why there is hatred against you in the public. You must do something to correct this impression in the public."

<u>Pola</u>

"I don't know as to what I should do."

<u>Pauline's mother</u>

"Let us leave this subject. Did you have your breakfast? Or should I make for you?"

<u>Pola</u>

"Thank you. I have had my breakfast."

Pauline's mother
"Where did you live?"

Pola
"I lived in the wild. I slept beneath the open sky. This city is much more orderly and clean surfaced to stretch my body and sleep."

Pauline's mother
"Can you tell me something more about you?"

Pola
"As I told you, I am a boy of an Eskimo family. My parents died and I lived in the wild."

Pauline's mother
"But you appear to be intelligent and educated."

Pola
"I did not have a regular education. But I have knowledge due to God's grace."

Pauline's mother
"You appear to be a God-fearing person. An innocent person like you is rarely seen these days."

Pola
"Thank you."

Pauline's mother
"Pauline talks about you all the time. In fact she likes your innocence and straightforwardness."

Pola
"I also like her."

Pauline's mother
"Do you have a girl friend in the wild?"

Pola
"No."

Pauline's mother
"Pauline also does not have a boy friend. Both of you can be friends."

Pola
"We are friends and that is why I like to meet her and talk to her."

Pauline's mother
"I wish that your friendship grows thicker and you become partner for life."

Pauline

"Mom has gone mad. She wants me to marry and go away."

Pauline's mother

"I don't ever wish to be away from my child. I wish to live with you till my death."

Pola

"Mom's wish is very natural. You must fulfil that."

Pauline does not say anything but smiles. Pola looks at her with affection and so does Pauline. Pauline's mother leaves them there and goes inside the house.

Cut to:

152: Int : Refinery Plant : Day

Pola appears inside the refinery plant. There is large number of workers, who are working near big oil reservoirs to execute required instructions to store refined petrol or diesel that comes into reservoir through big pipes.

There are a large number of military men guarding the internal premises of the refinery plant. Pola appears just behind a military man. He turns himself in a large sized lion and roars aloud. The military man is shaken and his gun falls from his hand. Pola, the lion, attacks the military man with his teeth and claws and injures him to the extent of external injuries. Soon thereafter military men, guarding at various points of the factory, come running towards the site, where the lion is mauling the military man. One military man spots the lion and fires his gun. The lion is alert. He escapes the bullets and hides himself. Thereafter he becomes invisible. But the bullets fired by the security guard pierces the body of the military man mauled by the lion.

Pola, the lion, turns himself into Pola. He finds a uniform hanging from a nail on a wall. He quickly wears the uniform and looks like a worker of the factory. He comes out from the hiding and sees that the wounded military man mauled by him is lying on the ground. His fellow colleagues have encircled him. They are comforting him before taking him to hospital.

Pola goes to a higher platform and closes his eyes to get a sophisticated gun in his hand. He fires at the crowd gathered around the wounded military man. He kills every military men present there.

There is an outcry among the workers, who are running away from their workstation.

Cut to:

<u>153: Ext: Downtown of city : Day</u>

There is a market place in the downtown of the city, bustling with crowds. A hawker is selling newspapers and is telling important news for public attention.

<u>Hawker</u>

"The so-called lion, Pola, pounds again within the security fortified plant and kills all the military men guarding the workers. The workers decide again to refrain from going to work due to the failure of military men to provide foolproof security."

People are thronging around this hawker to buy a copy of newspaper.

Cut to:

<u>154: Int : Drawing cum dining room of Pauline's home :Day</u>

Pola and Pauline are sitting on dining chairs before the dining table, whereas Pauline's mother is serving lunch to them.

<u>Pauline</u>

"I am surprised as to how you killed these military men."

<u>Pola</u>

"I need to confess."

<u>Pauline</u>

"What?"

<u>Pola</u>

"I am blessed with God's power to kill anyone, who is found destroying the natural balance of the world. I have the responsibility to save the forest and animals, who are not capable of protecting themselves against the heinous act of human being."

<u>Pauline</u>

"That is incredible!"

<u>Pauline's mother</u>

"How did you get this power?"

<u>Pola</u>

"This is God's desire that I should be his weapon to fight against wicked human being."

<u>Pauline</u>
"Do you mean that you met God?"

<u>Pola</u>
"Yes."

<u>Pauline</u>
"Incredible. You are God-sent man."

<u>Pauline's mother</u>
"God has chosen Pola because he is an innocent and kind person."

<u>Pauline</u>
"Don't you have fear against bullets and guns?"

<u>Pola</u>
"No, I don't fear because I am on a duty assigned by God."

<u>Pauline</u>
"Will you take me with you?"

<u>Pola</u>
"It may be dangerous for you."

<u>Pauline</u>
"Can you not save me?"

<u>Pola</u>
"I will do everything in my capacity to save you."

<u>Pauline's mother</u>
"That is like a brave man. I am impressed. Pola is the perfect match for my daughter. Pola, will you marry my daughter?"

<u>Pola</u>
"I will be very happy to have Pauline as my wife but I will have to ask my parents."

<u>Pauline's mother</u>
"But you said that your mother and father are no more."

<u>Pola</u>
"Yes, that is true but there are some who are just like my parents. I would like to take their blessing."

<u>Pauline's mother</u>
"Pauline is fascinated by you. I had some doubts before but now I am pretty sure that my daughter's choice is perfect."

<u>Pola</u>
"I am extremely delighted that Pauline is fond of me."

Pola is sitting just near Pauline. He holds her hand lovingly and smiles at her and so does Pauline. Pauline's mother watches them happily.

Cut to:

155 : Ext: A Garden of the City : Day

Pola is sitting alone in a garden. As this is a working day in the city, the garden is almost empty.

Pola

"Mom, Dad, where are you? Do you hear me?"

Voice of Kemu, the tiger [O.S]

"Yes, my son. We can hear you. Go on...."

Voice of Kelly, the tigress [O.S]

"Pola, I am very happy that you have found yourself a woman."

Pola

"So you both know what I have come across so far."

Voice of Kelly, the tigress [O.S]

"Yes, my son. We have no other work but to see you."

Pola

"Heaven must be very beautiful."

Voice of Kelly, the tigress [O.S]

"No doubt... but for us, watching your activities is most enjoyable."

Pola

"Mom, should I marry Pauline?"

Voice of Kelly, the tigress [O.S]

"I can see that you like her very much, the way she likes you. And the yearning for each other is the main reason for success of married life."

Voice of Kemu, the tiger [O.S]

"She is very pretty, good natured and wise. I hope she would make a good wife for you."

Voice of Kelly, the tigress [O.S]

"You can go ahead and marry her. "

Voice of Kemu, the tiger [O.S]

"We would then be extremely happy to see our grandchildren."

Voice of Kelly, the tigress [O.S]

"Your would-be mother-in-law is also a very good lady."

Pola

"Mom, dad, I am very happy to receive your blessing."

Voice of Kelly, the tigress [O.S]

"Take good care of yourself and whenever you need our advice, call us immediately."

Pola

"Thanks. I am going to take Pauline with me today to a polluting factory."

Voice of Kemu, the tiger[O.S]

"Be careful, son.

Pola gets up and walks out of the garden.

Cut to:

156: Int: Office room of the Minister of Environment and Forest: Day

Mr Jackson Green, the Minister of Environment and Forest, is having a meeting with military commanders, many factory owners and industrialists.

Mr Jackson Green

"It is very unfortunate that one sympathizer of animals comes into the factories and no one stops him for being an outsider. He comes inside and terrorise the area. He kills military men and escapes easily. What is this?"

Military Commander

"We did not know him as no one had seen him earlier. Now we know him. Our security cameras have filmed him while he was shooting at the military men. He was wearing a worker's uniform and managed to escape luckily."

Mr Jackson Green

"Let us publicize his photo."

Military Commander

"If we want to eliminate him, then we need to keep this secret otherwise he may become alert and resort to some other tactics. We will inform all our detectives and police personnel to look for this man and if found, kill him."

Mr Jackson Green

"Let police, military and administrative departments know about this man and be made authorized to eliminate him at sight."

<u>Military Commander</u>
"I will issue orders accordingly."

<u>Mr Jackson Green</u>
"Is there any possibility to persuade the workers to resume work?"

<u>One industrialist</u>
"If we can show the video footage, where he was shooting at the military men and then if his dead body is produced before them, then the workers would resume the work immediately."

<u>Mr Jackson Green</u>
"How soon should we be able to eliminate this threat perception."

<u>Military Commander</u>
"It depends upon him as to when he comes out in open to make his move and we have a glimpse of him. We will then shoot him at sight."

<u>Mr Jackson Green</u>
"Please execute this task at the earliest, as our nation is losing its economic stability."

Everybody in the room looks grim as they are worried about the prevailing situation.

Cut to:
<u>157: Int : Moving Bus : Morning</u>

This is a city bus, which is crowded in the peak hour. The bus is moving on a broad city road. Passengers are sitting as well as standing. Some are talking to each other. Pola and Pauline are also travelling in this bus. While they are sitting, two passengers, sitting in front of them, are talking, which Pola and Pauline are listening.

<u>1st Passenger</u>
"The lion man has again terrorised the city. This time he has killed military guards. He has gone mad and is creating hurdles in the industrial activities."

<u>2nd Passenger</u>
"What is the motive of this man? Why does he want to cripple our economy and our nation in the name of saving the forest?"

<u>1st Passenger</u>
"Yes, he is the same person, who forced this Government to abandon its plan involving deforestation. He portrays himself to be the saviour of the environment."

<u>2nd Passenger</u>
"He may be an agent of our enemy country, which wants our country to go to the doldrums."

<u>1st Passenger</u>
"How can a person be so smart that he can't be contained? Even our military appears to be helpless."

<u>2nd Passenger</u>
"There must be many people helping him in his assignment."

<u>1st Passenger</u>
"If this situation continues, our country would become pauper."

The bus stops on its stoppage shade. Pola and Pauline gets down from the bus.

Cut to:
<u>158 : Ext: Footpath of broad city-road : Day</u>

Pola and Pauline are walking together on the footpath. The footpath is not very crowded.

<u>Pauline</u>
"Did you hear what those two passengers were talking?"

<u>Pola</u>
"Yes."

<u>Pauline</u>
"People are under wrong impression. They must know your noble cause."

<u>Pola</u>
"It is very difficult for me to change this."

<u>Pauline</u>
"Don't worry. You continue your work. I think people will come to know the benefits of this."

They continue walking on the footpath.

Cut to:
<u>159: Ext: Exit gate of Industrial Plant : Day</u>

Pola and Pauline are in front of an industrial plant. The top fitted exhaust pipe is emitting black poisonous smoke in the air. The smoke is billowing up in the sky. Since this is a time of shift change, incoming workers are in queue at the entrance to get into the industrial plant after security frisking whereas outgoing workers are getting out of the plant from a side exit gate.

Pola

"Let the workers get into the plant, then you can talk to the sentry and request him to allow you to go into the factory to watch the internal operation."

Pauline

"Will they allow me? What about you?"

Pola

"You are a pretty girl. I am sure, they would allow you."

Pauline

"What about you? How would you come inside?"

Pola

"I can't afford to come with you. I know my secret routes. Don't worry about me. I will meet you inside."

Cut to:

160: Int : Security Room of the industrial plant: Day

This is a security room of the industrial plant. There are a large numbers of security monitors, which show the images of video pictures taken by hidden security cameras in and around the industrial plant. There are five security personnel stationed to keep a continuous watch on these monitors. All of a sudden, the security alarm is heard in the security room that attracts the attention of security personnel. The video film of Pola is on the monitor. Since Pola's photo is earmarked as wanted man in the security system, it beeps to find Pola's photo on its monitor. Pola is standing outside the factory, a little away from Pauline. An alert security guard takes his walkie-talkie in his hand to flash the news.

Security Guard

"Sir, the wanted lion man has been seen outside the entrance gate."

[Voice from Walkie-talkie]

"All security personnel may rush to the site and shoot him dead. If he runs away, airborne security may chase him; locate him and shoot him dead. Do, it fast."

Cut to:

161: Ext : Overview of site near entrance gate of the industrial plant: Day

Pauline is standing three yards away from Pola and watching the formalities of worker's entry at the entrance gate. Gun laden military soldiers get out of the factory and are approaching towards Pola, which he notices instantly. The military men starts firing at Pola. Pola ducks himself on ground to save from the bullets.

Pola

"Pauline, run from here."

Pauline has understood the gravity of the situation. Pola and Pauline are running on the road dodging the bullets, when a scattered bullet hits a car driver and he brakes his car that stops just near Pola. The car driver dies instantly. Pola and Pauline take out the dead man and get into the car, then speeds. After a few moments, three military helicopters are flying above the road to chase Pola's speeding car.

Pauline

"They have recognized you. That is why they are chasing you."

Pola

"Yes."

Pauline

"This is very dangerous. They may kill you."

Pola does not answer but he is thinking.

[V.O]

"This is a dangerous situation for you and not for me. I can disappear but you can't. I have to save you."

Three helicopters are flying and chasing Pola's car. They are firing machine guns, bullets of which are piercing the body of car. All of a sudden, Pola changes the direction of his car and gets into the staircase of an underground metro station. The roof of the staircase leading to the underground metro station provides safety from the chasing military helicopters. Pola jumps out of the car and Pauline follows him.

Cut to:

<u>162: Int : Underground metro station</u>

Pola and Pauline come down of the stair and reach the station, where a train is standing. Passengers are getting in and out of the train. After a few moments, the platform looks deserted as there is no one on the platform except Pola and Pauline.

<u>Pola</u>

"Pauline, please get into the train and go away from here. If they recognize you with me, it will be fatal for you"

<u>Pauline</u>

"But it is dangerous for you also."

<u>Pola</u>

"Don't worry about me. I know how to fight for my cause. You take this train and just go away from here."

<u>Pauline</u>

"Come with me..."

<u>Pola</u>

"No. Just leave me and go away."

Just then, the military soldiers are seen coming down the staircase into the station. Pola sees them. He pushes Pauline inside the train, door of which closes quickly after Pauline is inside the rail bogie. The train moves fast, whereas Pola turns himself invisible. The military men are trying to find a glimpse of Pola from within the moving train coaches. The train goes away and military men are huffing-puffing on failure to catch Pola alive or dead.

Cut to:

<u>163: Ext: Road facing entrance of the underground metro station : Day</u>

Military soldiers are emerging out from the underground metro station. There is an armoured vehicle waiting for them on the road. The soldiers approach this vehicle and get into it to move ahead. There are a few military helicopters flying in the sky.

<u>One soldier [into his walkie-talkie]</u>

"The lion man has fled in metro train approaching Burnham station. Kindly check Burnham station to arrest or shoot him."

There is a roadside tree, where Pola reappears. He closes his eyes to remember his ammunition box. A rocket launcher appears in his hand. He launches a series of rocket attacks on the armoured vehicles running on the road as well as the flying helicopters in the sky. He destroys them. There is a big fire which spread in and around a very large area. The debris of destroyed helicopters and armoured vehicles is spread in a large area, whereas corpses of dead soldiers are scattered on the road. Soon ambulances and rescue vehicles are seen approaching to this site. Pola moves away from this site.

Cut to:

<u>164: Int : Dining cum drawing room of Pauline's residence: Day</u>

Pauline and Pauline's mother are tense and sitting on the couch to watch TV news.

<u>[Voice of TV news reader]</u>

"The lion man was spotted today in front of an industrial plant. Soldiers chased him but he gave them a slip. Eyewitnesses say that he was fleeing in a car with his girl friend, whose identity is not known as no one could see her face. The soldiers understood him to be fleeing away in the running metro train at Brantley underground station and stopped chasing. When soldiers returned to their armoured vehicle and were heading to Burnham, the next metro station, the lion man, in hiding, attacked them with a rocker launcher. He killed all the soldiers, destroyed armoured vehicles and three military helicopters. Every citizen including leaders of this country has condemned this dastardly attack of lion man."

Pauline switches the TV off.

<u>Pauline's mother</u>

"Pola is being portrayed as villain. People of this city are not aware about his noble cause. If they come to know, I am sure, they won't think of him as villain."

<u>Pauline</u>

"Yes, that is true. But how to do that...?"

<u>Pauline's mother</u>

"Until people come to know that Pola is fighting not only for animals and forest but for them also, they would not espouse his cause. It is very necessary for Pola to make people aware of his cause to have success in his assignment."

Pauline and Pauline's mother are anxious about the turn of the event.

Cut to:

165 : Ext : A tropical forest : Day

This is a dense forest, where animals in large number encircle Pola. They are ready to listen what Pola has to say.

Pola

"I have tried my best to stop the polluting industries from operating but stubborn criminals are adamant to continue with their heinous crime. Their evil motives have empowered them to disregard the God-given principles of peaceful co-existence. To instill the system of peaceful co-existence, evenly balance of power appears to be extremely necessary. Bad people have understood that the power is heavily in their favour and that is why they recklessly turn blind eyes from the silent sufferings of animals and plants."

Old tiger

"What should we do to install the God-given system of peaceful co-existence?"

Pola

"We have to fight and show that animals are not harmless, helpless or powerless. They can also pose a serious threat to the existence of human being. When human beings realize this threat, they will come to the task of finding ways and means for peaceful co-existence of every living thing on this earth."

Old tiger

"How can we fight? We are really helpless against the lethal weapons of human being."

Pola

"I have power and can effectively fight against them. But my fight won't be considered animal's fight and it cannot symbolize animal's power. We have to generate animal's power, a power of wild and forest."

Old tiger

"What should we do? Tell us."

Pola

"Kindly call every animal, big or small, to join hands together and to advance towards the city to attack city dwellers and pose a serious threat to them. We have to make them realize that they have to mend their ways of living and to follow the system of peaceful co-existence. They should know that even animals have the capacity to fight for their right to exist in their forest on this earth."

Old tiger

"However, large in number we may be, how can we be a threat against their lethal weapons?"

Pola

"I will join you and lead the contingent. I will use my power to match their lethal weapons but your presence in large number would prove this fight to be yours."

Old tiger

"Is everybody present here agrees to fight against city dwellers?"

"Yes, we are ready." An echo is heard as every animal present there agrees.

Old tiger

"I am going to call everybody else to be ready to join hands and to proceed towards city on the Sunday morning, which is three days away."

Everybody appears to be excited to this proposed fight against the city dwellers, who are the culprits of water and air pollution that kill animals and plants in the forest.

Cut to:

166: Int : Office of the Minister of Environment and Forest : Day

Mr Jackson Green, the Minister of Environment and Forest, is in a meeting with military commanders, many factory owners and industrialists.

A factory owner

"Sir, I have come to know that the lion man is organizing a massive attack of animals on city dwellers on the Sunday morning. He has given a call to every animal to join hand and advance towards city to attack city dwellers, who in their opinion, are the main culprits of air and water pollution."

Military Commander

"This is rather a good development as military will not be involved in the fight. Now people of this city have to fight for survival against the lion man and his animal contingent."

Mr Jackson Green
"But we have the responsibility to provide arms and ammunitions to our citizens, who would be fighting against the rogue band of lion man."

Factory owner
"But this fight may prove fatal for both sides. City dwellers may also die in large number."

Military commander
"At least soldiers won't die. And casualty is a must in any fight."

Mr Jackson Green
"My government would like that every city dwellers are equipped with lethal weapons by the evening today so that they can effectively fight on the Sunday morning."

Military commander
"Yes Sir, we will successfully carry out this task today."

Mr Jackson Green
"This fight will reduce the population of the city dwellers. It is quite beneficial to our government as we would toil for lesser number of citizens."

Every body is happy after the discussions.

Cut to:
167: Ext : Downtown of a city : Day

A military armoured vehicle is parked on a broad pathway of the downtown area. One military man, carrying a handheld mike, is about to speak into his mike. Five other military men are holding guns for distribution amongst public.

Military man [into his handheld mike]
"There is an intelligence report that reveals the lion man is bringing all animals of the forest for a massive attack on this city's dwellers on the Sunday morning. He would lead this animal contingent. They consider you, the city dwellers, main culprits for their woes. That is why they are coming in large numbers to attack. But your government has the responsibility to equip you with lethal weapons so that you can fight effectively and kill these advancing animals. You need to wipe out the rogue band of the lion man. Please be in a queue and collect firearms from us."

The public present there makes queue before the armoured vehicle to collect the firearms. People are going away after collecting guns from the military men.

1st Gun laden man
"We need to kill these animals and eat their flesh."

2nd Gun laden man
"Apart from pigs, goats or similar animals, you can't eat lions or tigers."

3rd Gun laden man
"We can use the skin of tigers, lions or other animals for domestic purpose. It is a good opportunity for us as the Government is arming us to kill these animals."

4th Gun laden man
"I will shoot the lion man into his head."

People present there are happy as guns give them the sense of power .

Cut to:
168: Int : Drawing cum dining room of Pauline's residence: Day

Pauline and Pauline's mother are sitting on couch and watching TV news.

[Voice of a TV newsreader]
"Mr Jackson Green, the Minister of Environment and Forest, has urged the citizens of this city to come in open and fight against the rogue band of the lion man. It is learnt that the lion man is contemplating to lead the animal contingent in large number and attack city dwellers on the Sunday morning. He considers city dwellers as the main culprits for all the environmental woes that kill animals. The Government has delivered lethal weapons to city dwellers, urging them to fight effectively against the advancing contingent of animals. Sunday may be a fateful day which would decide the supremacy, either of human being or animals."

Pauline switches off the TV.

Pauline
"Mom, this Minister appears to be a bad person. He instead of supporting the efforts of Pola has taken side of these industrialists

polluting the environment. He has put city dwellers in illusion and made them believe that Pola is putting their economic life at stake. He wants to see this fight between city dwellers and animals that would result in large scale casualty."

Pauline's mother

"That may also be beneficial to this man."

Pauline

"I need to stop the fight otherwise innocent city dwellers as well as animals would die."

Pauline's mother

"What can you do?"

Pauline

"I know someone in the TV station. I would like to air my message on TV to urge city dwellers not to take up arms against animals as their fight is our fight too."

Pauline's mother

"Be careful, otherwise these bad people may target you."

Pauline

"Now, I don't worry. I have to fight for Pola. Mom, I don't have time. I am going to the TV station right away."

Pauline gets up and leaves immediately.

Cut to:

169 : Int : Newsreader's cabin in a TV Station :Day

Pauline is in the newsreader's cabin in the TV station. The newsreader is a friend of Pauline.

Pauline

"David, I am well aware about Pola and his mission of saving the green earth. These bad people are portraying him as a villain and his animal contingent as rogue band of the lion man. The Government wants city dwellers to fight for them to destroy the environment and nature for their benefit. That is why they have distributed weapons and are urging for an effective fight. I want this perception of city dwellers to change. I need to address them on your TV channel. Kindly allow me as there is not much time left before this fight commences."

David

"But you have to be responsible for your statement and address on TV. We will not be held responsible for your statements on our TV."

Pauline

"I take full responsibility of my statement."

David [gives a paper to her]

"Then you need to sign these papers before your statement is put on air."

Pauline signs the papers and gives to him.

David

"Now you can sit and address your statement to the public."

David signals to the technicians, controlling the TV telecast operations. Pauline sits on the chair of the newsreader and starts addressing to the public, which can also be seen on a big TV screen kept beside the cabin.

[Voice of Pauline on TV]

"My name is Pauline and I am a friend of Pola, the lion man, who is branded as a villain by the bad people in our Government. Our Minister of Environment and Forest, instead of saving the environment and forest, is indulging in dishonesty by joining hands with industrialists in the name of building nation's economy. There are industrialists who create problems, to sell their products. Computer viruses are created to sell the anti virus pack. Industrialists first pollute air; water and environment to create fatal diseases like asthma, pneumonia, flu, cancer, etc and then produce medicines for cure. They promote uses of chemical fertilizer, chemical pesticides and other such poisonous products to pollute water that everyone including animals drink and fall ill due to fatal diseases like ulcer, cancer, etc. They die a painful death. These industrialists then sell purified water bottles to earn money. Pola is fighting not only for animal's cause but also for every living being including you and me."

"Bad people in the government want a battle between you and the animals for large scale death that suits them, as lesser number of citizens mean less complaints against the government. Pola's fight is your fight as well as mine. Pola does not want destructions. He wants that the ways and means be found to avoid pollution, to avoid erosion in our environment. He wants every one of us to follow the course in our everyday life that is environmentally friendly. He wants us to follow the biologically best and environmentally sound way of living to avoid every kind of pollution that kills every one of us including animals and plants. The fight, therefore, proposed between you and animals, and encouraged by the bad people in the government by distributing guns and weapons is not desirable at all. There is no reason for a fight. I would, therefore, urge every one of you to throw away the guns and weapons that have been given to you by the bad people in the government and refrain from coming out in the open on the Sunday morning as this fight is between the bad people in the government and Pola with his animal contingent. Animals want to live healthily and co-exist peacefully. They have the right to fight for that."

Cut to:
170: Ext: Downtown of the city : Day

People of this downtown city come out in the open with their guns and weapons. They are throwing their weapons at a place in the street.

1st man
"Pola is fighting for our health too. Why should we fight against him? He is our hero."

2nd man
"He has guts to fight against these bad people and is fighting for us."

3rd man
"Bad people were trying to fool us. Thanks to Pauline. She enlightened us."

4th man
"Bad people were misleading us. We are with Pola now as he is fighting for us."

People are coming in large number to throw their guns and weapons.

Cut to:
171: Ext: Overview of another location of the city : Day

People are thronging at a place to throw their guns and weapons. Some young people are shouting slogans.

Slogan [loud voice]
"Long live Pola. Bad people go to hell. Long live Pola. Bad people go to hell."

Cut to:

172: Int : Office of the Minister of Environment and Forest : Day

Mr Jackson Green, the Minister of Environment and Forest, is in a meeting with military commanders, many factory owners and industrialists.

Mr Jackson Green

"How do you propose to contain this situation? People of the city are not in a mood to fight against Pola and his animal contingent. They have thrown away guns and ammunitions that were distributed by us."

Military Commander

"Now we have no other option but to fight. My soldiers are ready to fight and I am going to place heavy artillery and canons before the entrance of this city."

Mr Jackson Green

"Because your soldiers have experience fighting Pola in the past, you need to take benefit of all his weaknesses. What about this Pauline?"

Military Commander

"We have checked. She is her acquaintance. She is his sympathizer."

Mr Jackson Green

"You need to ensure that we are winners in this fight otherwise it would prove precarious for us in the government."

Military Commander

"That is my duty to fight effectively against any dangerous elements."

Cut to:

173: Ext: Overview of a wide road near the jungle : Morning

Pola is leading the animal contingent comprising millions of animals. He is standing atop a tank, which is moving fast. There are many tanks moving parallel along Pola's tank. Animals are following this tank contingent from behind. They are walking very fast on the road and footsteps of animals are heard from a distance. Fast movements on the ground are billowing dust up into the sky.

Animals appear to be enthusiastic in their participation of this fight against the bad people.

Cut to:

174: Ext: Overview of a wide road near city's downtown : Morning

There are large number of artillery and canons placed on the road, ready to be fired. Behind the canon and artillery lineup, military soldiers in large number equipped with sophisticated weapons are seen amassed on a road leading to the city. The soldiers are extremely alert.

After a few minutes, animal contingent led by Pola is seen approaching this site. When the distance between both the rival factions remains about half a kilometer, Pola stops his tank, other tanks and the contingent of animals.

Pola [to the animal contingent]

"We can see that our enemies are waiting for our attacks. Therefore, our attack must be fierce in order to finish our enemy. We have no other alternative but to win against the bad people."

Pola closes his eyes to remember his ammunition box. Soon thereafter military autopilot helicopters and fighter jets equipped with bombs and missiles appear on the ground.

Pola [shouts to direct fighter jets, helicopters and animal contingent]

"Attack on our enemy and finish them."

Thereafter fighter jets and helicopters fly and pound on the enemy artillery and canon lineup. Pola atop his tank moves ahead and so also the other tanks and the animal contingent. A few moments later, both rivals are entangled in battle to kill each other. Since the military of bad people are not ready with air power, Pola's air power pounds them and inflict large casualty that breaks their guts to fight effectively. Pola's tanks bring havoc in the enemy camp as soldiers die like worms. To see large number of deaths of their fellow colleagues and friends, morale of soldiers fall to the lowest level. Instead of fighting, soldiers are running away from the site along with their guns and weapons. Animals chase them and kill them. The mayhem leaves thousand of soldiers dead and large number of artillery and canons destroyed. After about an hour, tanks, artilleries, canons, guns, weapons, pounding of fighter jets, helicopters and cries of dying soldiers fall silent.

Animals soon realize their victory over enemy. They dance in jubilation. Pola is taken on their shoulders to move around in sheer happiness.

Cut to:

175: Int : Office of the President : Day

A bronze plate bearing 'President' is hanging on a wooden door, which is very broad and artistically carved. A protocol escort is leading Pola with four representatives of animals consisting a lion, a tiger, a bear and a cat into the room of the President.

Cut to :

176: Int : Office room of the President : Day

The President's office is the highest seat of power, which is reflected well from its interior décor. The interior décor is classical with modern gadgets. It gives the feeling of a palatial interior. The office room of the President has a very large and elaborately decorated President's desk. There are nine chairs around this desk, one for the President and eight for the visitors with a desk placed between it. There is a large meeting table within this room, where twenty-five persons can sit on chairs for meeting, group discussions etc.

The President is sitting on his chair. He sees the visitors.

Protocol Escort

"He is Mr Pola with the representatives of animals of the forest."

The President

"I welcome Mr Pola with his friends. Please be seated."

Protocol escort leaves the room. Pola and four animal representatives sit on the chairs before the President's desk.

The President

"I regret of having placed the responsibility of the Ministry of Environment and Forest to a greedy and dishonest man. He has been wrongly briefing me contrary to the welfare of the environment and forest. I have ordered his arrest along with those industrialists who have been polluting soil, air and water. Though I know my responsibilities of saving the environment, I would like to know your concern and complaints."

Pola

"We are very happy Mr President to know that you are equally concerned about the environmental ailments. As you know, many living species are extinct now due to severe soil, air and water pollution and due to rampant killings. We wish that ways and means may be found to eliminate the existing pollutions and to avoid all kind of pollution by adopting such ways of living that nurture the nature of the earth so that peaceful co-existence of all living thing may prevail."

<u>The President</u>

"I fully agree with your concern. I shall personally be looking after the responsibilities of the Ministry of Environment and Forest. I shall ensure that studies are conducted to find ecologically excellent ways of living for creating a healthy and vibrant environment that allows peaceful co-existence of all living things on the earth."

<u>Pola</u>

"We are extremely grateful to you Sir, for your kind words and assurances. I would like to suggest that your Government must encourage scientists to invent 'Oxygen Emission Engines and Vehicles' to replace the existing 'Carbon Emission Engines and Vehicles' to effectively eliminate the air pollution and the global warming. "

<u>The President</u>

"This is a good suggestion, which would revolutionise the concept of engines and vehicles and make them environmentally friendly. I would certainly follow your suggestion and do everything possible to save the environment for peaceful co-existence of all living things on the earth."

All the members of the representative of animals appear to be satisfied with the assurance of the President. They are happy.

Cut to:

<u>177: Ext : Dense tropical forest : Day</u>

There is a fanfare of the animals in the forest to celebrate the win against the bad people. Every animal is dancing. Pola is the main attraction of this event where every animal dances with Pola to feel his affectionate hug and pat on back.

<u>Old tiger</u>

"This is a great day for us. Pola has not only won the battle against the bad people but has also won the hearts and minds of millions of city dwellers. He has appreciations from the President. The President is a great mind and soul for everyone. Pola is our hero. Pola is hero of everyone."

Every animal chants- "Pola is our hero. Pola is our hero." [Loud Voice]

Everyone is jubilant and laughing happily.

Fade out

Fade In

178: Int: Altar of a Grand Church : Day

There is a gathering in the church for the marriage ceremony of Pola and Pauline. Large numbers of animals and public figures have come to watch this ceremony. The father of this church is to carry out the rituals. Pola and Pauline are standing on the altar along with the father of the church and Pauline's mother.

Pauline's mother

"Father, today I am very happy that my daughter Pauline is to marry Pola, a public hero. Kindly perform rituals on this pious occasion."

Father moves forward and gives a ring each to Pola as well as Pauline.

Father

"Pola my child, if you love Pauline and are ready to make your wife, a life partner, then put this ring into her finger and kiss her. And you, Pauline, my child, if you love Pola and are ready to make him your husband and life partner, then put this ring into his finger and kiss him."

Pola

"I love her."

Pauline

"I love him the most."

Both come closer and put rings into each other's ring finger and then embrace each other before kissing.

Father

"Now I pronounce Pola and Pauline, husband and wife, to live together for ever. And this holiest ceremony as concluded."

Pauline's mother

"I am now the proudest mother-in-law of Pola, my lovely child."

Everyone present in the church to watch this ceremony gets up to clap in happiness and to shower his or her blessings to newly wed couple.

Fade out

Fade In

179: Ext: Garden : Day

After two years [on screen caption]

Pauline's mother, Pola, Pauline, and Praveen, the infant boy of Pola are in the garden for a picnic and relaxation. Praveen is a cute and lovable boy, who is fond of playing with his father, Pola. Pauline and Pauline's mother are sitting on the garden mat, whereas Pola has taken Praveen on his shoulder and is slowly running around in the garden to make Praveen happy. When he is afar, he stops to talk to his parents.

Pola

"Mom, dad, where are you? Are you listening?"

Voice of Kemu, the tiger [O.S]

"Yes, my child I can hear you."

Pola

"How are you mom? Dad?"

Voice of Kemu, the tiger [O.S]

"We are fine, son."

Voice of Kelly, the tigress [O.S]

"Pola, my child, it gives me pleasure to see you very happy within your family."

Pola

"Mom, how is my child Praveen?"

Voice of Kelly, the tigress [O.S]

"He is a cute darling. You are his proud father. You were just like him in your childhood. He would certainly become a public hero like you."

Voice of Kemu, the tiger [O.S]

"Thank you son, for making me a proud grand pa."

Voice of Kelly, the tigress [O.S]

"And making me a proud granny."

Pola

"Mom, how is God's accountant?"

Voice of Kelly, the tigress [O.S]

"He is very proud of you. You did carry out his assignments perfectly and now his balance sheet is in proper order. He has blessed you, your wife and your son for health and longevity."

Voice of Kemu, the tiger [O.S]

"In fact he is very impressed about your way of handling the whole affair to find incredible success in your mission of saving the earth."

Pola

"Mom and dad, convey my best regards to him."

Voice of Kemu, the tiger [O.S]

"Okay... son... sure.

Praveen is uneasy on Pola's shoulder, as Pola is stationary at one place. He would like Pola to run to have fun.

Pola

"Mom and dad, I would go now to play with Praveen."

Voice of Kelly, the tigress [O.S]

"Okay... my son, whenever you need us, call us."

Pola

"Thanks... mom... dad."

Pola carries Praveen on his shoulder and runs slowly, which amuses him and he laughs. Everyone of Pola's family is very happy to see Praveen laughing.

Fade Out:

The End

2

Terminal Condition
(Short Story)

Soon after the independence of India, an English magistrate, serving in Arunachal Pradesh, left for England. His Indian cook, Jai Kishan, also accompanied him to England to serve him there. Jai Kishan was a brilliant man. His English master did not live long after arrival in London. After his death, Jai Kishan found a job of an assistant in a financial institution in London, where he learnt all the business acumen of the financial dealings and how to make profits. Soon he started his own business, where he earned profit due to fluctuations in the hard currencies. He changed his name to Jackson Cook. He had a son, a grandson and a great grandson.

His daughter-in-law was against having a baby of her own to maintain her figure despite the desire of her husband and father-in-law. So Mr Jackson Cook brought an orphan infant from India who was finally adopted by his son as his grandson. He was named Rajen Cook. Unfortunately, his son Rabin Cook and daughter-in-law died in a road accident.

Rajen hardly got the affection from her adoptive parents but had the privilege of having good food, clothing, best schooling and other things as per his desire. He grew a shrewd businessman. Rajen married an Indian girl and had a son named Esben, whose health was not robust and needed constant medical care due to frequent sickness. Esben's mother had no affection for his ailing son and used to be busy with her kitty parties and high society friends. She too died in a road accident while driving drunk.

Later doctors diagnosed that Esben had Leukaemia and would not live more than a year or so. Rajen was reeling under shock to hear this bad news and was restless to save his son from the fatal disease. Rajen learnt from an Indian visitor of the same hospital where his son was hospitalised that there might be a cure available at the clinic of a herbal healer in Minjong in Arunachal Pradesh . Since there was no option other than this, Rajen flew to Itanagar with his ailing son. Rajen bought a jeep and drove to Minjong with his son. The road was potholed where rain water got filled. On his way to Minjong, he angered a young girl in Itanagar as his jeep splashed muddy water on her. They confronted each other rather angrily.

Rajen reached Minjong and found that the famous herbal healer and his family died when their boat capsized in a river while fleeing from their native Kingdom. He also learnt that a great granddaughter of the herbal healer was alive and lived in Itanagar. This information gave him some hope to find the cure for his son from the written records of the herbal healer. He returned to Itanagar and met the great granddaughter. She happened to be the same girl whom he had angered in Itanager enroute to Minjong. Her name was Lata. He tried to persuade her to help him to find the written records of the herbal healer in order to find out the remedy of his son's disease. Initially she was reluctant and refused to help him but later she agreed to help him after seeing his son's physical condition.

Finally she went to Minjong and stayed with Rajen and Esben. Their goal was to make a liveable shelter on the ruins of the ancestral house of Lata and find the written records of the remedies that her great grandfather might have left in the ruins before escaping. Her great grandfather and his family were under brutal attacks of assailants of the then coup leader, a military chief , who overthrew the local King and killed him. The queen escaped from them along with her infant Prince. She hurriedly came to the herbal healer and left her infant son and a box of diamond with him for safe custody before escaping from the chasing assailants. The assailants could, however, suspect that the herbal healer was helping the queen. They came to arrest the herbal healer who had, however, left his home along with his family, leaving the Prince in an orphanage in Itanager. He and his family members were trying to cross a river to leave the kingdom when their boat capsized in the river currents and everyone died. His great granddaughter was away from home and could escape death.

Rajen, Esben and Lata stayed in the dilapidated house of the herbal healer to find the cure against the ailment. The local goon of the area who was a big landholder and feudal lord threatened Lata of dire consequences if she found the diamond box left by the queen and handed it over to the magistrate of Itanagar. He wanted her to share it between them.

Ultimately Rajen was able to find the cure of his son's ailment. It was also found out that Rajen was the infant Prince left with the orphanage and taken to England by Mr Jackson Cook. The magistrate of Itanagar was the custodian of the princely estate and the Palace left by the King, his father. After due verification, the magistrate handed over the keys of the Palace as well as the documents of the huge princely estate to Rajen. He was very happy to find the cure of his son's ailment and his root in Minjong.

When Esben was cured, Lata felt that her duty towards Esben was over. She prepared to leave for Itanagar to find a job for herself. Esben was, however, restless to know that he would not be able to live with Lata, who loved him as his mother. Rajen also felt that Lata's association had been extremely fulfilling and that without her he would be lost. He realised that he loved her. Thereafter, both Rajen and Esben rushed to Lata who was waiting for a bus at the bus station of Minjong. Esben told her that he could not live without her as he got motherly affection from her. Rajen pleaded that though his son had recovered from the terminal condition she should not leave him as he himself had fallen in a terminal condition because of his desire for her. He loved her and would like to live with her forever.

Lata replied that while she had no problem living with Rajen and becoming Esben's mother, she could not agree to go with them unless her relation with Rajen was solemnised. Rajen agreed immediately. All the three came back to the Palace. Rajen married Lata and all the three made a happy family.

XXXXXXXXXX

Terminal Condition
(Screenplay)

FADE IN

1: EXT : Cook Mansion at Stratham Hill in London: DAY

Stratham Hill: London (On screen caption)

(V.O)

"Mr Jackson Cook, actually an anglicised version of an Indian name Mr Jai Kishan Cook, has built a Palatial Cook Mansion. He is the eldest member of the family and his business skill was the main reason for the rise of a grass-root man upto the level of celebrity. He was originally an Indian cook brought to England in 1947 by an English magistrate, who was District Collector for two years in north-eastern region during the last leg of his fifteen years' tenure in British colonial rule in India. His master died soon after arrival in England, and thus Mr Jai Kishan Cook was free to choose his path. He chose Christianity, British lifestyle and a job in a financial investment company. Soon after learning the tricks of the trade he started his own independent business and his sole hard work led to a successful empire. His family had all good things of the world, a grand business of finance investment for ripping the benefits of the fluctuations in rate of exchange of hard currencies and a large contingent of servants to their beck and call."

"Though he has a grandson and a great grandson, he could not resist marrying a very young and beautiful girl in his retired life after the successive deaths of his two wives one Indian and another English. His only son, Rabin Cook from his first wife and daughter-in-law died in a road accident. His daughter-in-law was against having a baby of her own as she was adamant to preserve her beautiful figure despite the desire of her husband and father-in-law. Mr Jackson Cook, while leaving India brought an orphan with him out of pity, who was finally adopted by his son and was called Rajen Cook."

"Rajen barely received any affection from his mother but had the privilege of best food, clothing, schooling and other things as per his desire. He grew into a shrewd businessman and married an Indian girl and has a son, Esben, who suffers from ill health and needs constant medical attention. Rajen remains upset about an unconcerned attitude of his wife towards her ailing son in quest of a so-called highest-class social recognition. She does not value the Indian tradition and is anglicised".

Cut to:
<u>2: INT : BED ROOM OF MR RAJEN : MORNING</u>

Mr Rajen and his wife Lina are sleeping on their bed. It is early in the morning and sunrays are coming in from the windows. The wall clock strikes eight, which is why they wake up.

<u>Rajen(gets up and looks at his wrist watch)</u>
"Oh! My God.... it is eight now!"

<u>Lina (his wife also gets up)</u>
"Oh! I am late and why didn't you wake me up early?"

<u>Rajen (glares at his wife)</u>
"What? What did you say? You are going nowhere. Esben wants you to spend time with him. So you shall stay at home today with Esben."

<u>Lina</u>
"I am very busy today asI have to go to the race-course and I also have other appointments. It won't be possible for me to stay at home."

<u>Rajen</u>
"You give the same old excuses everytime. What type of a mother are you that you can't even spare a day for our ailing son."

<u>Lina</u>
"I am a mother, not a governess. This house has many governesses to look after him. Why should I sit at home with him unnecessarily? I am not going to ruin my social life and career for this frail boy."

She exits the room and enters into the bathroom. Rajen is very unhappy and goes to the other bathroom.

By the time Rajen could come out of the bathroom, he sees Lina leaving the room. He is upset but does not stop her. A servant knocks at the door. Rajen beckons and the servant comes inside the bedroom.

<u>Rajen</u>
"Yes, Why are you here?"

<u>Servant</u>
"Grand pa is looking for you at breakfast table. Today you are late, Sir."

Rajen
"That is true. Are Esben and Lina on the table?"

Servant
"No Sir, Madam has left without having breakfast as she was in hurry, but Esben is on the table."

Rajen (wearing his official suit)
"I will come in a minute."

The servant leaves the room. Rajen sprays a dash of perfume on himself.

Cut to:
3: INT : DINING ROOM: DAY

Grand pa, his new wife and Esben were sitting at the dining table. Rajen enters the dining room with a smile.

Rajen
"Good morning everybody."

Everyone present on the dining table reciprocates by saying, "Good morning."

Grand pa

"How are you, today? You are late."

Rajen

"Yes, Grand pa. Last night I came home late from office."

Grand pa
"Is there some problem between you and Lina ? She was very disturbed and did not have her breakfast."

Rajen
"No, Grand pa, I just wanted her to spend time with Esben today, but she did not appreciate."

Grand pa
"How is the business?"

Rajen
"Business is going good Grand pa. Yesterday, I.R.A terrorists had bombed the building of share market and many big stores. They have threatened to bomb the area in coming days. This have led to a fall of prices in share market plus the value of Pound sterling. The Government is gearing to deal with the probable threat, and we

expect that normalcy would return in a month or so. Today I have to withdraw funds in US dollar to buy Pound sterling so that I can invest in shares. I hope when normalcy returns, I would be able to rip the benefit of surging stock share market and Pound sterling."

Grand pa

"That is quite brilliant. You are managing the family business very well. Well done, my boy!"

Esben

"I am very upset. Nobody cares for me, whether mummy or papa. Though I am sick, mummy has gone out and now papa is also going. No one likes me."

Rajen

"That is not true, my son. I am going to the office just to return quickly after briefing my managers. "

Rajen hugs Esben and makes him seat on his lap. Esben appears to be assured and contented.

Grand pa

"Lina has unnecessarily involved herself socially..."

They proceed with their breakfast.

Cut to:

4: EXT: COOK MANSION : DAY

Rajen takes out his car from the garage and drives to his office. He is seen driving his car on the road.

Cut to:

5: INT: OFFICE OF COOK INVESTMENTS, LONDON : DAY

A wall mounted bronze plate reads as 'Cook Finance Investment Company, London'. Rajen climbs the stairs and walks into the hallway of the main office. All the employees greet nim 'Good morning'. He then enters his room.

Cut to:

6: INT: OFFICE ROOM OF RAJEN:DAY

Rajen enters into his room and sits on his chair. He picks up few papers and looks at those. A few minutes later his manager enters into the room.

Rajen

"Yes, Rana. What is the matter?"

Rana

"Sir, the Belgian currency has fallen by 15 per cent against the US dollar as CIS countries have stopped importing pork and beef products from Belgium."

Rajen

"That is a good news. But what is the reason for the ban?"

Rana

"A surpise check of the meat stock done by the 'Food and Nutrition Department' of Moscow reveals that the meat was infected with bacteria. As this news spreads, other CIS countries slap an import ban against importing of meat from Belgium. The Belgian Government, however, is taking all the measures to clear the doubts on their products and their Commerce Minister is going on immediate visits to these CIS countries in order to get the import bans lifted for their pork and beef products . I hope normalcy would return in a month or two."

Rajen

"Buy Belgian currency worth ten million dollars, and sell it for profit when it regains its normal position against US dollars."

His cellular phone rings and he picks up his handset to listen.

Rajen

" Hello."

The incoming sound from the cell phone is audible.

"Sir, Esben has fallen unconscious. Kindly come quickly." (A servant from Cook mansion was speaking on the cell phone.)

Rajen

"When did it happen? Did you call an ambulance?"

"Yes, Sir. I have called the ambulance. He has been unconsicious for the last five minutes." The servant replies on the cell phone.

Rajen

"Take him to the hospital. I am reaching there."

He puts off his cell phone. He seems in extreme hurry.

Rajen

"Rana, my son has fallen unconscious and I have to rush to hospital. Please take care of everything here."

He gets up from the chair and leaves the room.

Cut to:

7: ENT: HOSPITAL PREMISES : DAY

Rajen is approaching towards the Intensive care unit of the hospital. His Grand pa and the servant are waiting outside the ICU ward. They all enter into the ICU ward.

Cut to:

8: ENT : ICU WARD OF HOSPITAL : DAY

Rajen, his grand pa and the servant could see Esben lying on a bed behind the glass screen separating viewers from the patient's ward. It is seen that oxygen and glucose transfusion are being administered. After monitoring the health of Esben, the doctor comes out of the ward to meet Rajen.

Doctor

"Mr Rajen we were treating the weak immune system of your child but today's sudden unconsciousness is the cause of concern for us. We have called various specialists for differential diagnosis of your child's ailment."

Rajen

"What do you think?"

Doctor

"I cannot predict. But some times these kind of symptoms appear initially in patient's with Leukaemia."

Rajen

"What ? Leukaemia ! Cancer !!"

Doctor

"But you don't worry? We will know finally after pathological tests. May god bless him with a long life."

Rajen

"Doctor, please do everything which is necessary to cure my child. My only child."

Doctor

"Don't worry; we will do everything possible to make him well. Please wait outside."

Rajen

"Thank you, Doctor. I shall be highly grateful."

Rajen, his Grand pa and the servant come out of the ICU ward.

Grand pa and the servant sit on the chairs outside the ICU ward. Rajen walks a little farther and calls up his wife.

Rajen

"Hello, Lina...Rajen speaking. Esben has fallen unconscious and is at present in the hospital. I am calling from the hospital. Please come quickly."

Lina can be heard from the cell phone.

Lina (Loud voice from cell phone)

"I am at a gala party. I can't come now."

Rajen

"What kind of mother you are? Your son is unconscious but you are more bothered about your party. This is horrible."

Lina(Loud voice from cell phone)

"Can you understand my situation?"

Rajen(angrily)

"Go to hell you and your situations. The doctor has doubts about his ailment as leukaemia. Your son may die but you enjoy your party. "

Lina (Loud voice from cell phone)

"What? Cancer! I am coming."

Rajen disconnects the cell phone.

Cut to:

9: INT : BANQUET HALL OF A HOTEL

A gala party is going on in the banquet hall of a hotel and the party is meant for the ladies only. A light music is on and almost every lady is holding her glass of drink and chatting. Very few are dancing. Lina looks drunk and goes to her host friend, Irina.

Lina

"Irina, I have to go now."

Irina

"Why now? Party is yet to finish."

Lina

"Actually my son has fallen sick and is in hospital. I am going to him."

Irina

"Would you be able to drive your car now?"

Lina

"Don't worry. I shall take care of myself. I can drive."

Irina

"All right, Lina. Take care. Bye".

Lina leaves the party in drunken state and exits the banquet hall.

Cut to:

10: EXT : HOTEL'S OPEN COMPOUND: DAY

Lina in drunken state comes to her car and somehow is able to put herself on the driving seat of the car. She shuts the door and starts the car. She drives away from there in a high speed.

Cut to:

11: EXT : ROAD : DAY

Lina is driving her car on the road with a high speed but incoherently.

Cut to :

12: EXT : CROSS SECTION OF ROAD : DAY

The siren of a Traffic police car and an ambulance is heard. On the cross section of the roads a massive accident is seen. A lorry with heavy containers has met head on collision with the car of Lina. Ambulance personnel are busy retrieving the body of Lina from the scrap remains of her car. One traffic policeman is busy collecting the personal belongings of Lina from the car. The scene is busy and noisy because all the rescue personnel are talking on their wirelss phones.

Cut to:

13: ENT: HOSPITAL :DAY

Rajen is awaiting for his wife desperately and looking at the entrance door in hope of her arrival. His cellular phone rings. He puts the phone on to listen.

Rajen

"Hello ..."

(Loud voice from cell phone)

"Hello! May I speak to Mr Rajen Cook please?"

Rajen
"Yes, Rajen speaking..."

(Loud voice from cell phone)
"Sir, this is traffic police sergeant Thomas Hardy speaking."

Rajen
"Yes, Mr Thomas Hardy. Please go on."

(Loud voice from cell phone)
"Your wife, Mrs Lina Cook, has died in a severe road accident at 12.25 p.m She was in drunken state while driving her car."

Rajen
"What?!! "

(Loud voice from cell phone)
"Yes, Sir. This is true. We would like to have you here in Ald-gate police station for completing all the formalities before we could hand over her dead body to you. Kindly present yourself."

Rajen
"All right. I will..."

Cut to:
14: EXT: CEMETRY: DAY

All the relatives, near and dear ones including friends & servants, of Lina & Rajen are present at the burial ground where a priest is doing the religious formalities and reciting the holy bible while spraying holy water on the coffin of Lina, which is beautifully made and covered with flowers. Everyone present at the burial ground is mournful.

After a while, Lina's coffin is placed in the grave with the help of ropes tied on both side of the coffin. Everyone present, including Rajen and Grand pa, pours handful of earth on the coffin before the burial.

Cut to:
15: INT : INTENSIVE CARE UNIT OF HOSPITAL: DAY

Esben is conscious and is bitterly weeping on his father's lap on the hospital bed. He calls out for his mother. Rajen is trying to console him by patting on his back gently. After a while Esben becomes normal.

Just then the doctor enters into the room.

Doctor

"Mr Cook, I would like to speak to you. Could you come out of the room, please?"

Rajen

"Yes, Doctor. (to Esben) Son, I will just come back in a minute."

Rajen and the doctor exit from the room.

Cut to:

16: INT: OUTSIDE ICU :DAY

Doctor

"Mr Cook, you son's reports have come and the matter is very serious."

Rajen

"What are the results? What is the diagnosis?"

Doctor

"We were correct to doubt his ailment as Leukaemia."

Rajen

"Cancer! How can it be possible? He is just a small boy."

Doctor

"Sorry, but this is the truth. He is in the third stage. Unfortunately it is known only in this stage when it is quite late and we are helpless."

Rajen

"Do you suggest that there is no cure and my child will die?"

Doctor

"We would be treating him symptomatically and would keep him well."

Rajen

"But for how long?"

Doctor

"May be a year and a half or so…"

Rajen

"Then he will die. You suggest…"

Doctor

"You have to be strong Mr Cook. We are helpless."

Rajen

"It means Esben has to stay in the ICU till his death. No one can save him."

Doctor
"Miracles do happen Mr Cook. Let us pray for his recovery."

Cut to:
17: INT: HOSPITAL'S LOBBY : DAY

Rajen and his Grand pa are seen in the reception area. A female receptionist is seen behind the table.

Rajen
"Where is Esben? He was on bed number 11."

Receptionist
"Sir, Esben has been taken to Intensive Care Unit as his condition had worsened. He would be brought soon. Kindly have a seat in the lobby and wait for a while. You would be able to see him soon."

Rajen
"Thank you..."

Rajen and his Grand pa sit on two arms chairs kept in the lobby which is just opposite to the desk of reception. They have a grim look on their faces.

A Chinese looking couple come to the lobby and sit nearby. Compared to the man, the wife is young.

Man(to his wife)
"My darling, do you know that this is one of the biggest private hospitals with every modern facility. Only people who are rich enough can receive medical treatment here. I am an old resident of England with no dearth of money, that is why I am registered here for medical treatment. You will deliver my child here in this top hospital."

That man appears to be talkative, whereas his wife seems nonchalant and ill bred. He is laughing in a funny way. Just then a nurse comes to the lobby looking for his wife.

Nurse
"Mrs Harsukh Lal . You kindly come with me."

Mrs Harsukh Lal gets up to go with her.

Man
"Sister, can I also come?"

Nurse
"Mr Harsukh Lal. You are not pregnant. So you sit here and wait for your wife."

The nurse and Mrs Harsukh Lal leave the lobby. Rajen could not help but smile at the conversation between Mr Harsukh Lal and the nurse. Seeing Rajen smile, Mr Harsukh Lal feels awkward.

Mr Harsukh Lal
"The nurse is very naughty."

Rajen kept quiet but Harsukh Lal did not bother and continued with his talk.

Mr Harsukh Lal
"Are you from India?"

Rajen
"No, I am an English national."

Mr Harsukh Lal
"But your physical features are like mine."

Rajen
"Yes, my parents were Indian but I was brought up by my grandfather." (He indicates towards his grandfather, seated next to him in the lobby.)

Mr Harsukh Lal
"Have you been brought from an orphanage?"

Rajen
"Yes, that is a fact. Do you have any objection to that?"

Mr Harsukh Lal
"No...no...no. Why should I have such an objection? In fact that is very fine." (He laughs)

Mr Harsukh Lal keeps quiet for a moment but again starts speaking, being a talkative man.

Mr Harsukh Lal
"Are you here for some medical treatment?"

Rajen
"Yes."

Mr Harsukh Lal
"What has happened ...and to whom? Is your wife pregnant like mine? Is she going to deliver today?"

Rajen
"My son is sick."

Mr Harsukh Lal
"Sorry...what has happened to him? What ailment?"

Rajen
"He is suffering from Leukaemia."

Mr Harsukh Lal
"What kind of ailment is that ? I have not yet heard about it. I am sure, he will be all right soon."

Rajen
"No, he will not be fine. My dear Sir, my son will die soon." (Rajen blurted in frustration because of unncessary grilling by Mr Harsukh Lal.)

Mr Harsukh Lal
"Don't speak bad about him. There are no disease that cannot be cured in this reputed hospital. Don't lose hope; your son will be all right soon."

Rajen
"No, doctors are helpless. The doctors of this hospital have confirmed that my son would not be able to live more than a year and a half or so."

Mr Harsukh Lal
"No, they should not say like that. They are not God. By the way, what has actually happend to your son?"

Rajen
"He is suffering from a kind of blood disease ...that is called leukaemia..."

Mr Harsukh Lal
"I think this disease can be cured. It may be 'Likumia' in English but it is called something else in Hindi in my native place."

Rajen
"It is also called cancer."

Mr Harsukh Lal
"It was also an incurable blood disease intially. It was called 'Kura karkat' disease in my native place and the people infected with this disease were considered a trash to be buried soon. Later a herbal healer of my village had found out a cure of this disease and all the patients suffering from 'Kura karkat' were cured."

Rajen
"What? What did you say?"

Grandpa
"What are you saying? Is it true?"

Mr Harsukh Lal
"Yes, if it is the same blood disease that we call 'Kura karkat', then it is curable. I doubt if there is any other incurable blood disease other than 'Kura karkat'. I think you should visit that herbal healer of my native place."

Rajen
"If that ensures certain recovery from this disease, then I will certainly go there for the longivity of my son. Tell me...where do I have to go...?"

Mr Harsukh Lal
"I am from Arunachal Pradesh, India. My native place is known as Minjong, which is near the Yangon border. Now I don't have anyone there. Mr Chandrakant Sangla was the famous herbal healer of that area. He used to treat patients at his herbal clinic in Minjong. There was a mud road between Itanagar and Minjong back when I was there, i.e 25 years back. Minjong is 358 kilometres away from Itanagar. I am sure if you take your son there, his health will improve and he will go on to live a long life."

Rajen
"I am extremely grateful to you for providing me a ray of hope. Thank you."

Two nurses bring Esben on a stretcher and take him to the ward where he is lodged for treatment. Rajen and Grandpa get up from their chairs and follow Esben to the ward.

Mr Harsukh Lal
"May god bless your son."

Cut to:
18: INT: BREAKFAST TABLE: DAY

Rajen and Grandpa are having their breakfast in the morning.

Grandpa
"So...you have decided to go to India."

Rajen

Grandpa
"Do you think ...we should believe in that rustic fellow?"

Rajen
"He could have no selfish motive. He was just being concern and helpful. Moreover, what option do we have? We have no choice but

to listen to him. It is better to try something than to wait helplessly and see Esben die."

<u>Grandpa</u>

"Yes, you are right."

<u>Rajen</u>

"Even if nothing comes out of this, it would at least give a solace to reconcile that I tried my best to save my child. Just sitting and waiting leads us to what doctors have predicted."

<u>Grandpa</u>

"That is right. But in your absence, the family business will suffer."

<u>Rajen</u>

"What is left in my life except Esben. If I am not able to do something and save my child's life then this money or business is not worthy enough."

<u>Grandpa</u>

"But money has its own importance."

<u>Rajen</u>

"You are here and we will be in contact on our mobile phone. I will talk to the manager every day. I am sure Rana would be able to handle the business well in my absence."

<u>Grandpa</u>

"When are you going?"

<u>Rajen</u>

"I am going tomorrow."

<u>Grandpa</u>

"What is the itinerary?"

<u>Rajen</u>

"I will fly from London to Itanagar via Kolkata. And once I reach their I will hire a mountain jeep for my journey to Minjong. It will have a comfortable stretcher for Esben to sleep well."

<u>Grandpa</u>

"How will you get the mountain jeep?"

<u>Rajen</u>

"I have spoken to a car dealer in Itanager. He has agreed to make all the arrangments of my journey after Itanager."

<u>Grandpa</u>

"Make sure you take sufficient money with you to meet the requirement in case of a longer stay."

Rajen

"Yes, I am taking twenty five thousand pound sterling with me."

Grandpa

"Take good care of yourself and Esben. I will be calling you every day. You and Esben are all I have and you both are my life."

Rajen

"Don't worry Grandpa. I hope miracle would happen and my Esben would be all right."

Cut to:

19: ENT: HOSPITAL, DOCTOR'S CABIN : DAY

Rajen has come to the hospital to take Esben to India. The doctor is not very happy with his decision.

Doctor

"Mr Cook, it would not be advisable. Why should you go to a remote place? If Esben's condition deteriorates, what will you do to get medical help? Think twice before you go there."

Rajen

"One thing I know that my son is to die within a year. He can't be saved. I am going to find a cure for his ailment. If I am successful in my mission then my Esben will be cured otherwise even if he dies a few months earlier, does not make much difference."

Doctor

"Since you are very sure about your mission, may god help you in finding the remedy of this disease. In case you are successful, kindly let us know to enable others to benefit."

Rajen

"Yes, Doctor. I will."

Doctor

"So now you can take Esben from his ward. Please do not forget to collect four types of medicine which would be useful in emergency. I hope all the formalities are ready by now."

Rajen

"So I will take your leave, Doctor."

Doctor

"Thank you Mr Cook. Wish you all the best."

Rajen gets up from the chair and exits from the cabin.

Cut to:

20: ENT: HEATHROW AIRPORT, LONDON : DAY

Rajen is slowly moving towards the checking area, near the counter of Terminal-2 of Heathrow airport. Esben is on a wheelchair. Rajen is pushing the wheelchair and at the same time pulling the rolling suitcase. His grandpa is waving his hand far behind a screen separating passengers from onlookers at the airport, who had come to see-off the passengers.

Esben

"Papa, how is this place? Arunachal Pradesh..."

Rajen

"Son...I have no idea. Let us explore it. There may be scenic natural beauty."

Esben

"How long will we stay there?"

Rajen

"Till the time you fully recover from your sickness."

There is an announcement from the microphones installed at the airport.

(Loud voice from microphones)

"Attention please ! Passengers travelling to Delhi, Kolkata and Dhaka by British Airways' may proceed to the gate number 4."

Esben

"Where will we go papa ?"

Rajen

"We will go up to Kolkata first. Thereafter, we will take the local flight to reach Itanagar. From Itanagar, we will travel in a jeep to reach Minjong."

Esben is calm. They both move towards the check-in counter.

Cut to :

21: EXT: ITANAGER AIRPORT ; DAY

Itanagar has a small airport as it receives very few flights daily. A flight has landed and passengers' staircase has been added against the entrance door of the aircraft. Passengers are coming down through the stairs. Rajen is also seen coming down, while holding Esben in his arms. At the end of the staircase, one airport staff is standing with a wheelchair. He helps Rajen to make Esben sit on the wheelchair. Loaders are seen loading luggages of the passengers in a big trolley from the craft. Passengers are taking their luggage from the loader's trolley and keeping them in their own trolley. Rajen also takes out his luggage and keeps in one trolley. One man approaches him.

<u>Tirath Gulati</u>
"You are Mr Rajen Cook and he is your son, Esben. Isn't it ?"

<u>Rajen</u>
"Yes, you are right."

<u>Tirath Gulati</u>
"I am Tirath Gulati. Your 'Tata Sumo' jeep is standing outside. As per your booking we have arranged the jeep, removed its backseats and instead fitted a sofa-cum-bed for you and your son."

<u>Rajen</u>
"Should I pay you right away?"

<u>Tirath Gulati</u>
"No Sir, I am not in a hurry. Let me push your trolley and you can push Esben's wheelchair. You are our guest. You need a guide and I am here for you. First you come to my office, make yourself comfortable, take rest and then you can decide on your further course of journey."

Tirath Gulati is seen pushing the luggage trolley and Rajen is seen pushing Esben's wheelchair. They leave the airport.

Cut to:
<u>22: ENT : OFFICE OF TIRATH GULATI:DAY</u>

Tirath Gulati is handing some documents to Rajen, and Rajen in turn gives him some money which Gulati accepts. A servant comes in with a tray- cups and saucer and a tea kettle.

<u>Rajen</u>
"Thank you, Mr Gulati. Please count the money."

<u>Tirath Gulati</u>
"Since you have counted and given it to me, I don't need to count."

<u>Rajen (Accepts tea from the servant and sips)</u>
"Thank you for the tea. My son is wating in the car, I better hurry up."

<u>Tirath Gulati</u> (While handing over a road map)
"This is the road map which will help you to reach Minjong. I will leave you at the periphery of this town."

<u>Rajen</u>

"Thank you. I am very grateful to you for all the help that you have extended."

<u>Tirath Gulati</u>

"I am privileged to serve you, Sir."

Both exit from the office.

Cut to:

<u>23: EXT: ITANAGAR ROAD : DAY</u>

There are many pot holes on the road of Itanagar and it was waterlogged due to rain. Rajen is driving the jeep and Tirath Gulati is guiding him through the route to get out of the town.

<u>Tirath Gulati</u>

"Sir, now take the left twin, which is shortcut to get out of the town.

Rajen turns his jeep on the left side at a high speed and splashes muddy water on a woman. She shouts in rage as her cloth gets wet and dirty.

<u>Girl</u>

"Are you blind? hopeless man. Can't you see I am walking on this road?"

Rajen stops his jeep and looks behind to see the woman. She is a beautiful woman of about twenty five years. She approaches towards the jeep in rage.

<u>Tirath Gulati</u>

"Why did you stop the vehicle. Let us get out of this place, otherwise she will make a big drama."

Rajen appears to be apologetic. Tirath Gulati gets out of the jeep and goes towards the woman. He tries to calm her.

<u>Tirath Gulati</u> (To that woman)

"Please don't mind. It was not his fault. The waterlogged pot holes on the road could not be avoided."

<u>Woman</u>

"He has spoilt my clothes. Is he blind?"

<u>Tirath Gulati</u>

"He is a big man from London. He does not know about this place."

<u>Woman</u>

"I don't care whether he is from London or America. But he does look blind."

Rajen takes out a five hundred Rupee note and calls Mr Gulati.

Rajen

"Mr Gulati, please hand over this money to her so that she can dryclean her clothes."

The woman does not like Rajen's offer of money for drycleaning her clothes. She takes it as an offence. She comes to Rajen angrily.

Woman(She takes the note from Rajen's hand and throws it on his face)

"You appear to be very proud of your wealth. Instead of an apology, you are offering me money. Do you think that everything can be purchased and everyone is saleable?"

Rajen is quiet and very annoyed. His face is all red with fury.

Woman

"He must apologise."

Tirath Gulati

"I apologise for him. It was my mistake as I was guiding him on the road. I should not have come to this road."

Woman

"No, this wealthy bigheaded fellow from London should apologise. He has offered me the money not you."

Rajen

"This road is meant for motor vehicles. If road conditions are bad and your dress is spoilt due to that, then you should call for an apology from the local administration and not me. I felt bad about your dress so I offered you the money. And you instead of accepting the money behaved very rudely and called me a wealthy big headed fellow from London. Yes, I have a fortune of hundred million dollars, with many servants like you at my disposal. Mind it. "

Rajen gets back into the jeep on the road and Gulati also follows him. Esben is unaware of all this as he is asleep in the rear section of the jeep.

Woman

"Hotheaded rascal, wealthy, proud, idiot, scoundrel."

Cut to:

24 EXT: ROAD LEADING TO MINJONG: DAY

Rajen is driving the jeep. Esben is sitting beside Rajen.

Esben

"How far is that place?"

Rajen

"Son, we have crossed Gasigaon Pasighat. We have to go about a hundred kilometres."

Esben

"Papa, I am hungry now."

Rajen (Gives Esben a packet of potato chips)

"Eat this. We will have our lunch when we reach the destination."

Esben happily eats the chips. After some time a milestone is visible having the sign 'Minjong 2 Kilometres'.

Cut to:

25: EXT: A ROAD SIDE FOOD STALL (DHABA): DAY

Rajen stops his jeep near a roadside kiosk . He gets down from the jeep and goes to the kiosk to buy something. Esben looks at his father from his seat in the jeep.

Kiosk Owner

"Can I help you, Sir?"

Rajen

"Give me two bottles of Coke and two vegetable sandwiches."

Kiosk Owner (To his servant)

"Ramu, give two bottles of coke and two vegetable sandwiches."

Rajen

"My dear friend, can you tell me as to how far is the clinic of Dr Chandrakant Sangla?"

Kiosk Owner

"Sir, after reaching Minjong you have to further go about four kilometres through bumpy road within the town to reach his clinic. Do you have to go there?"

Rajen

"Yes."

Kiosk Owner

"You appear to be a new person in this area. It would be difficult for you to reach there as it is a deserted place. Is there anyone who guide you to that place?"

<u>Rajen</u>
"No, can you send someone with me to be my guide? I will reward him."

<u>Kiosk Owner</u> (To his servant)
"Ramu, please go with this gentleman and guide him to reach the clinic of Dr Sangla."

<u>Kiosk Owner</u> (To Rajen)

"Sir, kindly give him a hundred rupee note after reaching your destination."

<u>Rajen</u>
"I am grateful to you. Thank you."

Ramu gives coke bottles and sandwitches to Rajen. Rajen pays up for the food items. Ramu and Rajen approach the jeep parked at a distance. Ramu sits beside Esben. Rajen takes his seat and starts his car. His car is seen going ahead.

Cut to:
<u>26: EXT : CHANDRAKANT'S CHIKITSASHALA :DAY</u>

Rajen stops his car just outside the boundary of the clinic of Chandrakant Sangla, an old dilapidated building in a sprawling one acre land, demarcated by a herbal hedge and a metal gate. This gate was locked. Above the gate, there is a metallic name plate with the inscription of 'Chandrakant Sangla's clinic'. The building appears to be deserted.

<u>Rajen</u>
"Ramu, do you know whether Doctor Sangla lives here?"

<u>Ramu</u>
"I have no idea as to who actually lives here?"

Just then a bicycle rider is seen approaching towards them from the opposite side.

<u>Ramu</u>
"My dear friend, can you tell me if this is where Dr Sangla lives?"

<u>Bicycle Rider</u>
"Sorry, I have no idea. You may enquire about it from the school which is located just fifty metres from here."

<u>Rajen</u>
"Thank you, my friend."

The bicycle rider goes away. Rajen also moves his jeep ahead on a pebbled road towards school.

Rajen
"Ramu, this pebbled road is very bad. In case the tyres puncture who would repair ? Is there a garage nearby?"

Ramu
"I am not very familiar with this area. There is a motor garage behind our shop."

Rajen looks worried because of the bad road. He drives his jeep carefully.

Cut to:
27: EXT : PRIMARY SCHOOL, MINJONG: DAY

Rajen stops his car just outside the boundary of the school. It is recess time in the school. The students come outside of the school gate to see a jeep, as they have seen a jeep after a long time. A teacher also approaches Rajen.

Ramu
"Sir, we want to meet Dr Chandrakant Sangla?"

Teacher (Laughs)
"You can meet him in heaven. He has died about twentyfive years ago."

Rajen
"Who runs his clinic? There must be someone who runs his clinic. How did he die?"

Techer
"He and his family members were murdered. They were drowned into the Toonga river."

Rajen
"Who was the culprit? Is anyone alive in his family?"

Teacher
"I am not aware of the reasons of this brutal killing. No one knows about the assailant. His granddaughter, Lata is the only family member who is alive, she stays in a ladies' hostel in Itanagar. She works there. His clinic has been closed for the last twenty five years."

Esben is disappointed and distressed.

Rajen (Tries to boost his son's morale)
"Don't worry, my son. Though the doctor has died, he must have written down about his cure somewhere. I need to find that out. It must be within the four walls of his clinic. I need to find out his granddaughter. May be she could help us in finding the method of curing the illness. Thereafter I am sure you would be perfectly all right."

Ramu
"Sir, we should return to Itanagar. It would be night when we reach there."

Rajen
"You are right. We shall to go back. Please sit. I will drop you at your shop."

Ramu sits in the jeep and Rajen moves his jeep to return on the road to go to Itanagar.

Cut to:
28: EXT : A STREET IN ITANAGAR IN FRONT OF LADIES HOSTEL: EVENING

It is raining. Rajen and Esben are in the jeep. Rajen has stopped the jeep in front of the building of ladies hostel. He gets out of the jeep. The ladies hostel has a big compound with high walls and a metal gate, which is closed and a security guard is sitting on a chair in a metallic cubicle in front of the door. Rajen goes to the security guard. He is fully drenched.

Rajen
"Brother, I need to meet Lata. Is she in the hostel now?"

Security Guard
"Why do you want to meet her? Who are you?"

Rajen
"I am her brother-in law."

Security Guard
"And who is this boy?"

Rajen
"He is my son. Is Lata in ?"

Security Guard (Opens the gate)
"She is in room no.7 on first floor."

Rajen goes back to his car and drives on within the compound. He takes Esben out of the jeep alongwith a suitcase. Both are drenched. They run towards the verandah of the ladies hostel.

Cut to:

29: INT : CORRIDOR BEFORE ROOM NO. 7 IN THE HOSTEL

Rajen and Esben are wet and are shivering due to cold. Rajen is standing in front of the door number seven. He rings the doorbell. A moment later the door is open and Lata is standing before them. Rajen is taken aback to see the same girl whom he saw on a road in Minjong and engaged in a verbal dual.

Rajen (Checks the door number again)
"It appears that I am at a wrong place. Actually I wanted to meet Lata."

Lata
"I am Lata ".

Rajen
"You ! Lata?

Lata
"Yes, I am Lata. Do you have a problem?"

Rajen
"No, not at all. I am looking for the grandchild of Doctor Chandrakant Sangla."

Lata
"Yes, of course I am the grandchild of Doctor Chandrakant Sangla."

Rajen
"Then I am in a big problem."

Esben starts sneezing and his condition suddenly worsens.

Lata
"This child is shivering. Why are you out in the rain with him?"

Rajen tries to enter her room with Esben, when Lata stops him.

Lata
"You please stay outside. I will wipe the child and dry to save from cold. I do not allow outsiders in my room."

Lata takes Esben inside the room and wraps him with a dry towel. When she sees that Rajen is peeping in, she closes the door.

Cut to:

<u>30: INT : CORRIDOR IN FRONT OF ROOM NO. 7 OF LADIES HOSTEL</u>

Rajen is drenched and is strolling in the hallway for sometime and at the end sits on the floor due to tiredness. He looks worried.

Cut to:

<u>31 : INT : HOSTEL ROOM OF LATA</u>

Lata helps Esben to remove the wet clothes. She wraps him in a dry towel and helps him sit on the bed. Esben's face is turning red due to fever. Though he is awake, he looks very sick and fragile. Lata touches his forehead and finds it unusually hot.

<u>Lata</u>

"What is your name?"

<u>Esben</u>

"Esben."

<u>Lata</u>

"You are having a high fever. I will give you Tulsi kahwa. You will be all right."

Lata leaves Esben for few minutes. Esben tries to keep his eyes wide open as he feels extremely sleepy. Lata comes back with a glass of Tulsi kahwa.

<u>Lata</u>

"Esben, take this kahwa and your fever would come down."

But Esben's eyes are closed and he becomes unconscious. She checks his pulse and finds it unusually fast. Esben's body temperature is also very high. She is worried due to his sudden deterioration.

Cut to:

<u>32: INT : CORRIDOR IN FRONT OF ROOM NO.7 OF LADIES HOSTEL</u>

Lata, panic-stricken, opens the door and calls Rajen.

<u>Lata</u>

"Hello, your son has fallen unconscious. Please come and see. I don't know what has happened?"

Rajen comes inside the room. Lata closes the door.

Cut to:
33:INT : HOSTEL ROOM OF LATA

Rajen checks Esben's wrist and feels the pulse. He rushes out of the room and speaks up before leaving.

Rajen
"I will just be back with the needed medicines."

Lata is in a state of distress with all that has happened.

Cut to:
34: EXT : A STREET IN ITANAGER IN FRONT OF LADIES HOSTEL: EVENING

Rajen geta into his jeep and collects a bag. He closes the door and then rushes back to the hostel.

Cut to:
35:INT : HOSTEL ROOM OF LATA

Rajen enters into Lata's room which is not bolted from inside. He has a bag. He takes out a small pack of medicine, a liquid syrup, and puts it in a dropper. He opens the mouth of unconscious Esben and puts the medicine drops in his mouth. He takes out another vial of injection and a disposable syringe. He takes the medicine in the syringe and ties the upper part of Esben's hand to inject it as an intravenous. He injects it and after that unties the upper part of the hand. Lata, in a state of shock, is looking at Rajen.

Lata
"What has happened to your child? Why do you inject him?"

Rajen
"I am from London and very wealthy but my son is dying. I am not able to save him despite of my huge wealth. He is suffering from Leukaemia. His condition is deteriorating day by day. He can succumb to his ailment at any time. He will die soon."

Lata
"Oh, but what help can I offer?"

Rajen
"Someone told me that your grand pa Dr Chandrakant Sangla had found out the remedy of this ailment. Actually this disease is locally termed as 'Kura karkat', which in fact is the synonym of cancer. I

have come with a hope that I shall be able to meet Dr Sangla and my son will recover from this disease. But I am told that Dr Sangla and his family members were killed by drowning in the 'Toonga' river and his clinic is closed. And you are the only next of kin."

Lata

"What do you expect from me?"

Rajen

"I need your help. I am sure your grand pa must have written about the new medicine. I think, if am able to lay my hands on those papers, I shall be able to treat my son. I need your help in searching those papers. It would save my child."

Lata

"I have a job, that too temporary. I can't go anywhere. Even if I help you in finding those papers, what is the guarantee that it has not yet been destroyed? I do not want to lose my job for a cause that is not sure to be fulfilled."

Rajen

"I shall compensate you. I would pay any amount that you ask."

Lata (Angrily)

"What do you think of yourself? You cannot buy anyone and everyone. Not me at least. Go away from here. I shall not go anywhere for you."

Rajen

"Sorry, I didn't mean to hurt you. I am desperate to save my son. A very little time is left for him."

Lata (Angrily)

"Every rich man has similar negative traits. You can easily bury the poor for your business. I will not go with you. Just go from here when your son wakes up."

Rajen

"Now it is night and my son is sick. Please allow us to stay here tonight."

Lata

"I have only one room. Where will you stay? You have to go..."

Rajen

"I can sleep on the couch. I will have to wake up frequently to look after my child. I shall be grateful if you bear the discomfort as my son is also sleeping on your bed. I promise I will leave in the morning. Please do not throw me out in this rain."

Lata

"People will know about my having lived in the same room with a stranger. I cannot bear this stigma."

Rajen

"You are not alone. You are with a father and son. But why do you worry about others? Your conscious should be clear and bold."

Lata (After a pause)

"You will just leave at the dawn."

Rajen

"Can I have a towel? I am drenched."

Lata

"No, I do not have an extra towel."

Rajen

"All right my clothes would dry in the body itself."

Lata

"Can't you go and sleep in your jeep?"

Rajen

"Please don't force me to sleep in the jeep. It is raining and I will have to take care of my child in the night. I do not need any towel or anything. Please allow me to stay here in your room with my child tonight."

Lata

"I will go and sleep now but you will not move from the couch."

Rajen

"Yes, fine.

Rajen sits on the sofa and Lata sleeps on the bed beside Esben.

Cut to:

36: EXT: WOMEN'S HOSTEL : NIGHT

It is pitch dark and raining. Thunderclaps can be heard and flashes of lightning could be seen.

Cut to:

37: INT : HOSTEL ROOM OF LATA

It is midnight. Lata and Esben are fast asleep on the bed, whereas Rajen is sleeping on.the couch due to exertion. At times his snoring sound is also heard. Esben is coming to consciousness and he is murmuring ...'mom'...'mom'. He is trying to open his eyes and is moving his hands to touch and feel the bed. He touches Lata and she awakes. Rajen is still fast asleep on the couch. Lata stares at Rajen for some time and thereafter touches Esben's body to wake him up.

<u>Lata</u>
"Son, how are you? Are you feeling better?"

Esben is now fully awake. He feels assured to find Lata near him."

<u>Esben</u>
"Where is my dad?"

<u>Lata</u>
"He is tired. He is sleeping on the couch. How are you feeling now?"

<u>Esben</u>
"I am fine."

<u>Lata</u>
"You had fallen unconscious. You were calling for your mother in the sleep. Why didn't your mother come with you?"

<u>Esben</u>
"My mother is no more."

<u>Lata</u>
"Oh, what happened to her?"

<u>Esben</u>
"She died in a car accident."

<u>Lata</u>
"Oh, ...don't worry, you have a loving father."

<u>Esben</u>
"Yes ...but..."

<u>Lata</u>
"What...?"

<u>Esben</u>
"Nothing..."

<u>Lata</u>
"There is something. Tell me...what is it?"

<u>Esben</u>
"Papa loves me very much. I have blood cancer and I will die within six months. Dad is desperate to save me but God does not want.

Doctor Sangla is no more and my death is sure. I want to live with my Dad but what to do now I have to die."

<u>Lata</u>

"Don't worry...you will be all right."

<u>Esben</u>

"Aunty...I know ...my death is near."

<u>Lala</u>

"I will find a cure and you will not die. You are a good boy."

<u>Esben</u>

"Aunty, you are very kind. My mother never said like that. She used to be busy with her friends and parties. My dad is my only friend."

<u>Lata</u>

" Now I am also going to be your friend. Do not worry. Please sleep it is just midnight."

<u>Esben</u>

" Please put off the light. I cannot sleep."

Lata gets up from the bed and puts off the light. It is totally dark. Lata sleeps on the bed.

Cut to:

<u>38: EXT: WOMEN'S HOSTEL :MORNING</u>

It is early morning and birds are chirping in the trees.

Cut to:

<u>39: INT: HOSTEL ROOM OF LATA</u>

Rajen wakes up when a alarm clock rings. He is startled. He gets up from the couch and looks his wrist watch. It is six o'clock in the morning. He sees Lata packing her suitcase as if she has to travel somewhere. Esben is also awake. Esben starts laughing when he sees his father being startled due to the alarm of the table clock.

<u>Esben</u>

" Dad, it is morning. No more sleep now."

<u>Rajen</u>

"How are you, my son? It is six o'clock. Let us go now."

<u>Esben</u>

"I am fine Dad."

Rajen

"Lata, I am thankful. (To Esben) Say thanks to Lata aunty for allowing us to stay here."

Esben

"Thank you, aunty. You are kind."

Rajen

"Esben, now get up. Let us go."

Esben

"Aunty will also go with us. Isn't it aunty?"

Lata smiles and nods in affirmation.

Rajen

"Son, you have done wonder. (To Lata) Lata, I am grateful."

Lata

"Do not ever show your money power. I hate it."

Rajen

"I promise I will never dare."

Lata appears assured. Rajen and Esben are happy.

Cut to:

40: EXT : CHANDRAKANT'S CHIKITSASHALA :DAY

The tyre of Rajen's jeep is punctured. Rajen and Lata are pushing the jeep on a road of Minjong. They have brought the jeep before the clinic of Dr Chandrakant Sangla. Both are tired and they sit on the ground to relax. Esben is sitting on the front seat of the jeep.

Doctor Sangla's clinic is located in an old building with the roof made of straw and burnt earthen tiles. The building is situated on a land measuring more than an acre, which has a brick fence on its periphery. There is a metal gate to enter into the boundary of the building with a metallic board having inscription as ' Dr Chandrakant Sangla's clinic'.

Rajen

"This is a new jeep that I purchased from Itanagar. It is amazing that tyre has got puncture so soon."

Lata

" The roads are bad. The tyres cannot help."

Rajen

"We are lucky that it has burst just near the clinic."

Lata
"I am tired of pushing your jeep."

Rajen
"I am very sorry."

Esben offers drinking water bottles to enable them to quench the thirst.

Esben
"Both of you seems to be thirsty. Please take the water bottles."

Lata (Holding the water bottles)
"Thank you. I am really thirsty."

Lata drinks water and gives one of the bottles to Rajen. He also drinks the water."

Esben
"Aunty, the metallic gate has got a lock. Do you have the key?"

Lata
"Yes, I have the key. This is my home that was built by my grand pa."

Lata gets up and opens the lock of the metallic gate. Rajen takes Esben in his arms and Lata takes the luggage from the jeep and enters into the compound of the house.

Cut to:
41: INT: A BEDROOM OF SANGLA'S HOUSE: DAY

Dr Sangla's house is in a dilapidated condition that requires thorough cleaning and dusting. Only one room and the kitchen is in a usable condition. The room can be used as a bedroom. The kitchen has got fire wood for cooking. Rajen, Esben and Lata enter into the room. The dirty condition of the room amkes everyone uneasy. Rajen pulls two chairs in the room, cleans them and maks Esben sit on one of the chairs and he sits on the other chair. Lata does not like Rajen relaxing on a chair.

Lata
" Mr Rich and Wealthy, you can not afford to sit and relax. We need to make this room livable. We have to make all the arrangements before today evening for our comfortable stay here.

Rajen
" Let us find someone who can help us. Can we not find servants here?"

Lata
"The population is small here. Most of the people are engaged fruitfully in their fields. No one likes to become servants. It is something they consider lowly."

Rajen
" Why should there be people who do not work against payment? I am in problem now."

Lata
"Mr Rich and Wealthy, you will have to become a servant now."

Rajen
" When you are there to help me, I need not worry."

Lata
"I am also not your servant. You have to behave well otherwise..."

Rajen
"Sorry, I was kidding..."

Lata
"I do not like this kind of things. Please be serious..."

Rajen
"As you wish..."

Esben
"Dad, stop kidding and work now."

Rajen
"Yes my son, I will..."

Rajen gets up from his chair and picks up a broom to clean the house.

Cut to:
42:INT: KITCHEN OF SANGLA'S HOUSE: DAY

Lata is sitting on the ground and cleaning the leafy vegetable for cooking. Esben is sitting on a chair.

Esben
"Aunty, what is the name of this leafy vegetable?"

Lata
"This is a wild type of leafy vegetable. This is called 'Bathua Saag'."

Esben
"Why is it termed as wild?"

<u>Lata</u>
"It is very common and grows everywhere. Cattles like to eat it very much."

<u>Esben</u>
"Is it safe for human?"

<u>Lata</u>
"Though the villagers do not prefer to eat it, I find it very tasty. My grand pa used to tell us that it purifies the blood and reduces obesity. It is very healthy."

<u>Esben</u>
"It has got medicinal value."

Just then Rajen enters into the room with a polythene bag in his hand. He is tired.

<u>Lata</u>
"Did you get everything that I have told you? Why did you take so much time to return?"

<u>Rajen</u>
"You said that the grocery shop was nearby but it was quite far...about two miles. I am exhausted."

<u>Lata</u>
"In villages a mile or two are not a distance. Did you get everything?"

<u>Rajen</u>
"Yes, I have got everything. I will have to buy a horse for the day-to-day chores, walking on pebbled road is very difficult. I am tired."

<u>Lata</u>
"You cannot afford to be tired. You do not have to ride a horse now, just help me in cooking."

<u>Rajen</u>
"Okay, please tell me...what should I do?"

<u>Lata</u>
"Use the handpump and bring me a bucket of water. Then take the rice grains and pulses in two different utensils and wash them properly. I am going to arrange the fire for cooking."

Rajen takes out two utensils and puts the rice and pulses in them from the polythene bag, whereas Lata is trying to light the oven.

Cut to:

<u>43:INT : BEDROOM OF SANGLA'S HOUSE: NIGHT</u>

There is only two single beds in the room. Lata is spreading the bed sheets. She puts Esben on one bed and sits on the other. Rajen sits on Esben's bed.

<u>Lata</u>

"This room can accommodate me and Esben. You will, therefore, sleep outside in your jeep."

<u>Rajen</u>

"So...no possibility of my staying here."

<u>Lata</u>

"No."

<u>Rajen</u>

"As you wish..."

Rajen gets up and takes a blanket with him. He exits from the room. Esben and Lata lay on the beds and cover themselves with blanket to sleep.

Cut to:

<u>44: INT: RAJEN'S JEEP: MIDNIGHT</u>

Rajen is sleeping in the backside of his jeep and has covered himself with a blanket. His sleep is disturbed due to severe cold. He is almost shivering. He gets up.

<u>Rajen (to himself)</u>

"It is very cold here. If I sleep out here for two days, I shall die."

He gets out of the jeep.

Cut to:

<u>45: EXT: SANGLA'S HOUSE: NIGHT</u>

Rajen walks towards the house, where Lata and Esben are sleeping. He knocks at the door and says 'Please open the door...please open the door.'

After a few knocks, the door is opened. Lata is on the door.

<u>Lata</u>

"What is it?"

Rajen

"It is very cold out here. I am shivering. Please allow me to sleep inside the house. it will be a great favour, otherwise I shall die in two days."

Lata

"How can you sleep inside the house?"

Rajen

"It is extremely cold outside. Please allow me, I shall die otherwise. Please believe me."

Lata

"People would talk rubbish, if they come to know that I am sleeping in the same room with a stranger."

Rajen

"People will never come to know. Please do not kill me in this cold."

Lata

"Okay. Come in and sleep on Esben's bed."

Rajen

"Thank you. I am grateful."

Rajen enters into the room and Lata closes the door.

Cut to:

46: EXT: SANGLA'S HOUSE: MORNING

It is early morning and the sun is shining on the horizon. The birds are chirping outside. The house appears to be neat and clean now. Rajen's jeep is seen parked outside the house.

Cut to:

47: INT: BEDROOM OF SANGLA'S HOUSE: MORNING

Rajen and Esben are sleeping on the same bed. The window of the room is open and sun-light is coming in the room. Lata makes tea and brings it in a tray towards Rajen and Esben. She tries to wake Rajen up.

Lata

"Mr Rich and Wealthy get up. Bed tea is ready."

Rajen gets up lazily and straightens his limbs.

Rajen

"Is it already morning, I still feel sleepy."

Lata
"You appear to be carefree, don't you remember your mission?"

Rajen
"I do remember. Thank you for reminding me and also for the bed tea."

Rajen takes a sip of the tea and finds it very tasty.

Rajen
"The tea is fantastic. Thank you."

Lata
"Please wake up Esben also."

Rajen
"Let him sleep for a while. Yesterday he got very tired. Now where is our toilet? I am now feeling the punch in my stomach."

Lata
"Do not expect a toilet here. Go to the bushes and relieve yourself. There is a pond nearby. That would help you to clean and bathe.

Rajen
"Oh God, this is a big problem."

Lata
"Mr Rich and Wealthy, today is just the first day. Many more problems are ahead but remember your mission."

Rajen
"Oh, I can not control myself. I have to rush."

Rajen takes a towel and runs away from there.

Cut to:
48: INT: KITCHEN : DAY

Lata is in the kitchen. She is making breakfast. Rajen enters into the kitchen. He is fresh after bathing.

Lata
"Have you taken a bath?"

Rajen
"Yes, but the water was very cold. I was shivering. I might catch cold. I have been snizzing quite a few times."

Lata
"Those who are rich and wealthy get caught with health problems. I have taken bath early in the morning but I am fine."

Rajen
"I need a cup of warm tea. I am still shivering."

Lata
"No, just take your breakfast and drink cold water. If you take hot tea, you will certianly get cough and cold."

Rajen
"You have good knowledge about health."

Lata
"I am the grandchild of a doctor and not a rich man."

Lata hands over the breakfast plate to Rajen. He is happy to see the delicious breakfast. He starts eating happily. Lata watches him.

Cut to:
49: INT : BEDROOM : DAY

Rajen is sitting on Esben's bed. He belches after a heavy breakfast. Just then the mobile phone in the pocket of his shirt rings. He gets up from the bed and answers the call.

Rajen
" Hello, Rajen here."

The sound from the ear piece of his mobile phone is quite loud and can be heard. The sound is identifiable. His grandpa was on the line.

Grandpa's sound from the ear piece of mobile phone: "Hello, Rajen, how are you and Esben? Where are you?"

Rajen
"Grandpa, I have reached my destination. I am yet to find the cure of Esben's ailment. We both are all right."

Grandpa's sound from the ear piece of mobile phone: "Your absence has affected the business very badly. When will you return home?"

Rajen
" Grandpa, you cannot expect me to come back without the completion of my mission. It has only been a day that I am here. You are an expert in business, you can also supervise."

Grandpa's sound from the ear piece of mobile phone : " I I have been away from the family business for too long. That is why I need you."

Rajen

" Grandpa, I cannot come until I have completed my mission. You may inform Rana to call me to get instructions from me, if he needs."

Grandpa's sound from the ear piece of mobile phone : "He is just standing here. Talk to him..."

Rana's sound from the ear piece of mobile phone: "Hello, how are you sir?"

Rajen

"I am fine. Tell me, what is the problem?"

Rana's sound from the ear piece of mobile phone: "Sir, Euro is showing stronger possibility against individual currencies and I am afraid we can lose heavily as our holding is in US dollars."

Rajen

"What is the condition of Euro against US$?"

Rana's sound from the ear piece of mobile phone: "Euro is steadily getting stronger against the US$. Should we convert our money holdings in Euro only?"

Rajen

"Yes...do that. The surge in Euro may continue. I think USA would allow the US$ to slide to promote its export to Europe. Buy the Euro, I am sure, it would be stronger and then we would make profit. What do you think?"

Rana's sound from the ear piece of mobile phon: "I think you are correct, Sir. Your judgements have always been correct."

Rajen

"OK, then do this and keep me informed."

Rana's sound from the ear piece of mobile phone: " Sure Sir, I will. Thank you and goodbye."

Rajen puts off his moble. Lata is standing behind him and listening to his conversation carefully.

Lata

"So, you are still in London and in command of your business."

Rajen

"What to do? I am a person with enormous responsibilities."

Lata

"You are an expert businessman."

<u>Rajen</u>
"How do you say so?"

<u>Lata</u>
"I have sensed the business acumen that you have shown in your conversation with your Manager.

<u>Rajen</u>
"Thank you for the compliment."

<u>Lata</u>
"Now let Esben awake. Help him freshen up."

Esben is sleeping on the bed. Rajen touches his body and shakes him. But he finds that his body is very hot due to fever. Despite Rajen's pat, Esben does not wake up. Rajen is alarmed.

<u>Rajen</u>
"He has fever and is unconscious. Kindly massage his hands and feet with hot oil. I will inject him."

<u>Lata</u>
"What kind of a father are you? You did not sense his illness despite sleeping with him on the same bed."

Rajen does not care what Lata says. He takes out a box . He opens it and takes out the injection and syringe. He then injects intravenously. He also administers medicine into his mouth with the help of a dropper. Then he prays to God for Esben's well being.

<u>Lata</u>
"What kind of medicine is this? When do you expect Esben to be conscious?"

<u>Rajen</u>
"This medicine takes care of his high fever and unconsciousness. But this is not the remedy. As long as his body has the stamina, this medicine would be effective and the moment his health deteriorates, the medicine would not work. I wish to find a cure before such a situation."

<u>Lata</u>
"When will he be conscious?"

<u>Rajen</u>
"It may take five to six hours."

Lata is busy massaging Esben's palm and feet with hot oil.

<u>Rajen</u>

"Lata, please take me to your grandpa's clinic. I am sure your grandpa has left the prescription of the medicine that he discovered."

<u>Lata</u>

"How can you leave Esben like that."

<u>Rajen</u>

"We cannot do much as he would be conscious only after six hours. We have to find the cure."

<u>Lata</u>

"Grandpa's clinic was in the basement."

<u>Rajen</u>

"Is there a basement here?"

<u>Lata</u>

"Yes, but in a dilapidated condition..."

<u>Rajen</u>

"Let us go there."

Rajen and Lata exit from the room.

Cut to:

<u>50: EXT: SURROUNDINGS OF SANGLA'S HOUSE: DAY</u>

Lata and Rajen are standing behind Doctor Sangla's house. Lata inspects the area carefully and then she moves the bushes and dry branches fallen from trees. Suddenly a wooden door is visible behind it.

<u>Lata</u>

"We have to clear this area as it is blocking our route to the basement."

<u>Rajen</u>

"Thank you, I shall do that."

Thereafter, Rajen removes the branches and clears the bushes. Lata also helps him.

Cut to:

<u>51: INT : BASEMENT OF SANGLA'S HOUSE: DAY</u>

Rajen and Lata are in basement. A ray of light is coming in from a window. Rajen opens another window and the basement room is amply lit. They both clean the room infested by cobweb. Rajen is cleaning the room with a broom.

<u>Rajen</u>
"Lata, can you tell me where your grandpa used to keep things?"

<u>Lata</u>
"I have no idea as I was very small then. We need to scan the whole area."

<u>Rajen</u>
"Okay...no shortcuts."

Rajen as well as Lata move each and everything of the room to find details or documents about the medicine. Rajen finds a big metal box under a wooden cot. He takes out the box. This metal box is closed with a rusted lock. Rajen uses a stone to hit the lock. After a few stroke of hammering, the lock gives away. He opens the box and finds many small bottles filled with medicine. He also finds a notepad at the bottom of the box. He takes it out and tries to read.

<u>Rajen</u>
"Your grandpa has written something in Hindi. Can you read it for me please?"

<u>Lata (</u>takes the notepad from Rajen and carefully examines it)
"This notepad is not complete. It is halftorn. Where is the other half of this notepad?"

<u>Rajen</u>
"We will find that later. Please read it."

<u>Lata</u>
"This notepad has details of a medicine named 'Raktim'.

<u>Rajen</u>
"Please read it elaborately."

<u>Lata</u>
"It says, I have found a medicine titled 'Raktim' that helps the cancer patients to recover from weak health. Though Raktim does not root out cancer but helps build a strong stamina to face the severe effects of 'Arunim', the actual medicine for cancer. A person having fragile health cannot bear the cleansing action and effects of 'Arunim' and may die. Hence Raktim may be given to a cancer patient for at least three months. The patient should gulp the Raktim-paste with cow milk four times a day. He should not eat cereals such as rice, pulse, wheat, etc. He should take leafy vegetables such as Brahmni, spinach, chaulai, wild bathua, bitter helancha and seasonal fruits and milk, only."

Rajen

"This is the first medicine. How to make this medicine? How can we distinguish?"

Lata

"The second chapter has details of its preparation. It says 'now I am writing about Raktim. This is a medicinal herb, which grows in and around the Minjong hill. The leaves of this are reddish and prickly. I believe nobody knew its medicinal properties. This herb is not eaten by humans nor herbivorous animals because of its prickliness and extremely bitter taste. I will write the details of 'Arunim' in the next chapters."

Rajen

"Please read the next chapter..."

Lata flips the page to read the next chapter but to her surprise the next chapter is not there. She has read the last page of the notepad.

Lata

"The next chapter is not here. This notepad is halfway torn."

Rajen

"What to do now?"

Lata

"We will try to search the next pad. At least we have found something that would stop Esben's health from declining. It would build his stamina that would enhance his longevity. Let us find 'Raktim' first and let Esben take this medicine for three months before 'Arunim' could be given. In fact we have three months time to look for the details of 'Arunim'."

Rajen

"You are right. Let us find the herb 'Rakitim' today. From tomorrow we have no other work but to search for 'Arunim'."

Lata

"Tomorrow you have to go to the village and buy a cow, otherwise the medicine cannot be given. We also have to grow the suggested vegetables in the kitchen garden. They are going to be the staple food of Esben hereafter."

Rajen

"Can we not buy milk instead of a cow?"

Lata

"It would be adulterated. We need pure milk. Hence, the cow is necessary."

Rajen

"Okay, let us go and find the Raktim."

Lata

"Yes, by now Esben might have come to senses. Let us go."

Both exit from the basement.

Cut to:

52: EXT : SANGLA'S HOUSE : MORNING

Rajen and Lata are busy clearing the weeds and wild grass in the backyard to make the area suitable for kitchen garden. Both are tired but they keep working and sow seeds of leafy vegetables. Esben is sitting on a chair inside and watching them just outside.

Esben

"Dad, how long would you take?"

Rajen

"I want to clear up some more area to sow vegetables."

Esben

"Leave it for tomorrow."

Lata

"All right. Let us leave it for tomorrow. Now you can go to the village to buy a cow."

Rajen

"Where should I go?"

Lata

"There are some families in the nearby village who are engaged in the trading of cows. After having lunch, you can go to them."

Rajen

"Okay."

Lata

"The lunch is ready. Let us have our lunch. Thereafter you may go..."

Rajen and Lata wind up their machines and tools.

Cut to:

53: EXT: SANGLA'S HOUSE: EVENING

Esben is sitting on his wheelchair just outside the house. There is a big tree in front of the house. Lata has tied a long rope around a branch to make a swinging plate for oscillation. Esben is watching Lata. She is having fun while swinging from the branch of the tree.

Esben

"Aunty, I would also like to swing."

Lata stops swinging and comes to Esben.

Lata

"Yes, you can also have fun. Come... I will help you."

Lata takes Esben in her arms and helps him to sit on the hanging plate for oscillation. She pushes the hanging plate. Esben is very happy to swing. He is enjoying himself.

Esben

"Aunty, you are fantastic. I love your company."

Lata

"Why ?"

Esben

"At home everyone would be busy with their business. No one had time for me. No one played with me like you, you are fantastic. I was lonely at home. As you are with me, I am very happy now."

Lata

"You will get well soon. You would go to school and have many friends. Then you will not feel like that."

Esben

"When will dad be back? Will he find a cow today?"

Just then Rajen is seen coming towards them with a cow and a calf. He is holding the ropes tied around the neck of the cow and the calf. There is also a sack on the back of the cow.

Lata

"Look...your dad has got a cow and a calf for you. You will have pure milk now."

Rajen reaches the place where Lata and Esben are present.

Esben

"Dad, will this cow give milk from today."

Rajen

"I believe that is what she will do for you."

Lata

"How much did you pay?"

Rajen

"This is the costliest cow available in the village market. Buying a cow is a unique experience for me. I am told that she would give at least ten kilo of milk every day, if she is properly fed. I have also bought some fruits and vegetables from the local market for Esben."

Lata

"I can say that the seller was honest with you. The cow indeed is very healthy and I am sure, she would justify her worth."

Rajen

"I am happy to know that I have not been cheated."

Lata

"People of this area are not like the ones you might have come across in other places. They are mostly honest."

Rajen laughs at the sarcastic remark of Lata.

Cut to:

54: EXT: SANGLA'S HOUSE: MORNING

The sun is brigthtly shining through the horizon. Lata is watering the vegetable plants of the kitchen garden. The cow and the calf are tied with a pole in front of the house. Just then Rajen emerges from the back of the house.

Rajen

"We can pluck these vegetables for our use, may be after a week."

Lata

"Did you find anything in the basement?"

Rajen

"I have searched every inch of the basement since six o'clock in the morning. I have not found the next portion of the notepad having details of 'Arunim'. I do not know what to do now?"

Lata

"You have to search the entire area of the house. That part of the information is very necessary, otherwise Esben's total recovery would be difficult."

<u>Rajen</u>
"That is my mission. I am happy that Raktim would help build Esben's health for time being."

Just then four strangers enter into the compound of the house. All four men have bamboo sticks in their hands. Lata is very annoyed to see them.

<u>Lata</u>
"Mr Narsingh, why have you come here?"

<u>Narsingh</u>
"When did you return? And who is this gentleman?"

<u>Lata</u>
"Just two days, and he is my distant relative."

<u>Narsingh</u>
"Do you have any information about those diamonds?"

<u>Rajen</u> (to Lata)
"Who are these people?"

<u>Lata</u>
"They are the kinsfolk of the military commander of the king, who used to rule this area. They are the most wealthy family and big landholders of this area but their desire to have more and more wealth has never faded. Their grandfathers killed my grandpa and his entire family by drowning them in the Toonga River. They are still in search of a diamond box."

<u>Narsingh</u>
"You have the wrong information that our grandfathers killed your grandpa and family. They died because of the attack by crocodiles on the boat by which they were trying to cross the river. They fell into the river and were killed by the crocodiles. Our enemies have misled you."

<u>Lata</u>
"I know the truth. If I get the diamond box, I would surely deposit it with the treasury of the Government. I will never give it to you."

<u>Narsingh</u>
"That would be a foolish step on your part. If we share it half-half, then it would be beneficial for both of us. I will find a good house and a suitable groom for you. You are the daughter of our village. These diamonds would immensely help me in solmenising your marriage with pomp and glare."

<u>Lata</u>
"I don't need a well wisher like you. Now you can go away."

Rajen is wearing a chain with locket. It is visible as the top button of his shirt is open. A man standing beside Narsingh is looking at the chain carefully.

<u>The man beside Narsingh</u>
"Where did get this locket?"

<u>Rajen</u>
"I have purchased it from London."

<u>Narsingh</u>
"London? Are you from London?"

<u>Lata</u>
" No. He had gone there for a business."

Rajen is uneasy to see that Lata is blatently lying to them.

<u>Narsingh</u>
"But the marks that this locket bears is of the royal mark of the kingdom that existed here. This is a locket that was used by the royalties or kings of this area."

<u>Rajen</u>
"There is a particular area in London where antique items as well as replicas of royal items are sold. I have purchased it from there."

<u>Narsingh</u>
"Lata, we will come again. If you find the diamond box, I will reward you. If you hand it over to the Government, I will kill you. So, use your head and do not go insane."

<u>Lata</u>
" The diamond box has not been found so far, I doubt whether it would be found."

<u>Narsingh</u>
"Time changes very fast. There is every possibility to find it. (To his men) Let us go."

Narsingh and his men go away from there. Thereafter, Lata stares at Rajen's locket.

<u>Lata</u>
"Did you realy buy it from London?"

<u>Rajen</u>
" Yes, but who were thess men?"

Lata
"He is a wealthy person of this area. Forget about him. Let me wake up Esben and give him the medicine along with milk and fruits."

Rajen
"Is Esben still sleeping?"

Lata
" Yes, he was feeling exhausted."

They enter into the house.

Cut to:
55: INT: BEDROOM OF SANGLA'S HOUSE:NIGHT

Rajen, Esben and Lata are sleeping in the bedroom. Rajen and Esben are sleeping on one bed whereas Lata is sleeping on the other bed. It is midnight but the bedroom is dimly lit because of the moon light coming in from windows. Esben is unable to sleep. While lying on bed he is trying to see out of the window. Lata also moves while sleeping and her sleep is disturbed. She wakes up and sees Esben awake. She is surprised to see him awake and calm.

Lata(slow voice)
"Esben, Are you awake?"

Esben
" Yes, aunty."

Lata
"How long have you been awake?"

Esben
" For quite some time. May be more than an hour."

Lata
"I will sing you a lullaby."

Lata starts singing.

Esben
"Aunty, you are singing."

Lata
"It has a story also. Please listen..."

Lata starts singing and Esben is quietly listening. Rajen's sleep is disturbed despite of Lata's soft and low voice. He does not move but quietly listens her song. He watches her glowing face in the dim moon light and finds it very innocent and lovable. After some time Esben feels sleepy and his eyes gradually droops. Esben falls sleep. When Lata finds him fast asleep, she stops singing. She takes a stock of the surrounding. Rajen closes his eyes as if he is fast asleep. Lata is assured. She also sleeps.

Cut to:

56: EXT: SANGLA'S HOUSE: MORNING

Esben sitting on his wheelchair watches Lata watering the kitchen garden. He appears to be healthier. Rajen is trying to massage the body of the cow. He is serving fodder, water and oil cakes to the cow as well as her calf.

Esben

"Aunty, I want to work in the kitchen garden with you. Can I join you?"

Lata

" My dear, you would be able to do everything. Just wait till the time you are fully recovered from the ailment. How are you feeling now after taking the medicine for two weeks?"

Esben

"I am much better now."

Rajen's cellphone rings. He picks it up.

Rajen

"Hello...Hello."

He cuts the call, as he ca not hear anything.

Rajen

"Bad connection..."

Lata

"Go and milk the cow. I have to give Esben his medicine."

Rajen takes a bucket with him to collect the milk. The calf is sucking milk from the udder of the cow. After some time he moves and tie calf away with a pole in front of the house. Thereafter, he starts milking the cow.

Esben

"Dad, you have learnt to milk a cow."

Rajen

"It is the necessity that makes you learn."

The cow is not feeling comfortable with the style of milking by Rajen. She moves ahead and kicks with her two hind legs. Thus Rajen is imbalanced and his cellphone in front pocket of his shirt falls in the bucket of milk. Rajen too falls on the ground but is able to save the milk from falling on the ground. Lata rushes to help him. She takes the milk-bucket from him and takes out the cellphone.

Lata

"What happened? Are you hurt? Why did cow kick her hind legs? Did you pinch her?"

Rajen

"I was gently milking her. I do not know as to why she kicked me? I have a mild sprain in my back."

Lata

"Go and take rest. The milk is saved but your cellphone may go out of order."

Rajen

"Oh God".

He takes the cellphone in his hand and tries to wipe out the milk. He dials a number but it does not function.

Rajen

" What to do? It is out of order. How will I contact London?"

Lata

"Don't you think, it is fine that no one will disturb you any more?"

Rajen walks back to the house limping. Lata also follows him with the bucket of milk.

Lata

"I will massage your back with hot oil. Do not worry, you will soon be all right."

Cut to:

57: INT: BEDROOM OF SANGLA'S HOUSE: DAY

Rajen is lying on the bed. Esben is sitting on his wheelchair. Lata is giving him medicine and a glass of milk.

Lata

"Esben, take this medicine."

Esben

"I really do not like this medicine. It is horribly bitter."

<u>Lata</u>
"But it will cure you. Gulp quickly and drink the milk. Do not keep it for long on your tongue."

Esben gulps the medicine and drinks the milk. Lata also gives a glass of milk to Rajen.

<u>Lata</u>
"After the hot oil massage, take this hot milk. You will be relieved of your backache."

<u>Rajen</u>
"I don't take milk."

<u>Lata</u>
"No, excuses now, just take the glass of milk and drink."

<u>Rajen</u>
" You just sound like my mom."

<u>Lata</u>
"Esben, then you drink this glass of milk."

<u>Esben</u>
"No aunty, not any more."

<u>Lata</u>
"You have eaten very little. Just take this glass of milk."

<u>Esben</u>
"No aunty, please. Not again."

<u>Lata</u>
"You must be obedient to your grandmother."

<u>Esben</u>
" Who is my grandmother here? You?"

<u>Lata</u>
"Yes, I sound like mom to your dad."

<u>Rajen</u>
"Sorry, I didn't mean it. Okay I will drink the milk."

<u>Esben</u>
"Aunty, you can surely set my dad right. He is not an innocent guy."

<u>Rajen</u>
"Esben, your dad is an innocent guy."

<u>Esben</u>
"No, not to my aunty."

Lata

"Esben is right. You need to be straightened."

She speaks in a humorous tone and everyone roars in laughter.

Cut to:

58: EXT: A WIDE LANDSCAPE OF MINJONG : MORNING

It is morning and the breezes are mildly blowing. The sun is steadily rising above the sky. The weather is pleasant. In a vast green and beautiful landscape Lata is strolling while pushing Esben's wheelchair. Esben is happy to see the scenic beauty of the surrounding. Within this landscape, there are orchards of various fruits which stuns Esben.

Esben

"The beauty of this place is breathtaking."

Lata

"Is London not so beautiful?"

Esben

"London is also beautiful. But London is a city with lot of noise where everyone is running. No one has time to stop and see the breathtaking beauty of nature. This place is very peaceful and beautiful. I love you and I love this place. Aunty you are great."

Lata

"You are a good boy."

Lata and Esben are moving through a sandy road. Esben sees the birds flying in the sky. He watches them attentively. He is quiet.

Lata

"Esben, what are you thinking?"

Esben

" The birds flying in the sky are very joyful and fortunate. They are flying with their wings."

Lata

" That is true."

Esben

"In this life, perhaps...I may not be able to walk on my legs."

Lata

"Do not be sad my son. You will soon be walking and running on your legs."

<u>Esben</u>
"Do not give me false hope."

<u>Lata</u>
"You must think positive. Positive thinking gives good feelings to the body and mind. It recovers you from your weaknesses and ailments. Are you not feeling well after the medication of Raktim for three weeks."

<u>Esben</u>
"I am certainly better. I do not feel any pain. But would it continue? Would I fully recover? Perhaps not."

<u>Lata</u>
"You must think positive and you will be perfectly all right."

<u>Esben</u>
"Aunty, you are a good person. You always think good for others."

Lata and Esben are quietly moving on the road. A fowler is seen pulling a cart with a parrot. The parrot is restless in a small cage, and makes noise to get freed from the cage. The fowler moves ahead of them and the parrot catches Esben's attention.

<u>Esben</u>
"Mr fowler, please wait. Wait for a minute."

The fowler stops his cart.

<u>Esben</u>
"Would you kindly sell your parrot to me."

<u>Fowler</u>
"Yes, for a hundred rupees."

Esben takes out a hundred rupee note from his pocket and hands it over to the fowler. The fowler gives his cage with the parrot to Esben. Esben opens the cage and frees the parrot in the open sky. The parrot flies away happily into the sky. The fowler goes away from there.

<u>Lata</u>
"Why did you free the parrot?"

<u>Esben</u>
"No one likes captivity. I am captive to my wheelchair. I just helped a parrot to be free. To be happy."

<u>Lata</u>
"You are a kindhearted boy. The parrot will bless you. You will soon be fine."

Esben and Lata see the parrot flying and going deep into the sky.

Cut to:

59: INT: BEDROOM OF SANGLA'S HOUSE: DAY

Esben is sitting on his wheelchair and he is trying to get out from the chair and walk without any help. He tumbles. Rajen is standing near him and provides his hand to make him stand.

Lata

"Esben, if you feel the strength in your leg, then only try to walk."

Rajen

"How are you feeling now?"

Esben

"Now I don't feel any pain in my legs. I am much better now.

Rajen

"Unfortunately, the second medicine 'Arunim' has not been found so far, otherwise you would have become perfectly all right by now."

Lata

"God would not be unkind. Esben would soon be perfectly healthy. Esben, please try to walk."

Though Esben's legs are shaking he walks and comes up to Lata. Lata lifts him up to her lap and kisses him. She is very happy to find Esben walking on his legs.

Lata

"Bravo, my boy. You are brave. You should try and walk every day. You will soon be strong enough to run on your legs."

Rajen

"I am very happy. You would soon be running."

Esben

"I do not like the wheelchair."

Rajen

"Till the time you are strong enough, you have to be on the wheelchair."

Lata

"Soon you would be without the wheelchair."

Rajen puts his hand through Esben's hair. Esben is in Lata's lap. Everyone is happy.

Fade out:

Fade in:

<u>60:INT: BEDROOM OF SANGLA'S HOUSE: MIDNIGHT</u>

It is midnight. Flashes of lightening are coming into the house from the window intermittently and the cloud's thunder is also heard. It is heavily raining outside and the constant dripping sound is heard. Rajen, Lata and Esben are awake on their beds. There is a leakage from the roof of this house and the water is dripping from one point of the roof. So, a bucket is kept underneath to collect the rainwater.

<u>Rajen</u>
"Does it rain so heavily here?"

<u>Lata</u>
"Yes, it does."

<u>Rajen</u>
"The rainy season is the test for thatched and earthen tiled roof. This roof is also leaking."

<u>Lata</u>
"Few tiles may have broken. The roof would be perfect if we replace them tomorrow."

<u>Rajen</u>
"Where do we get these tiles?"

<u>Lata</u>
"People of this area build tiled roof only. Hence tiles are amply available. You have to climb on the roof to replace the broken tiles."

<u>Rajen</u>
"I think I might break my bones while climbing on the roof."

<u>Lata</u>
"Don't worry, if you fall ...I will hold."

<u>Esben</u>
"Dad, be courageous."

<u>Rajen</u>
"If this rain stops tomorrow, then there won't be any need to climb on the roof."

Lata

"This rainy season is not going to be over soon. So be ready to climb."

Everyone is desperately waiting for the rain to stop.

Cut to:

61: EXT: SANGLA'S HOUSE : DAY

Rajen has climbed on the roof to replace the earthen tiles. Lata is throwing tiles upward, which Rajen is carefully catching. After, he has collected enough tiles, he removes the broken tiles and replaces with the new tiles while sitting on the roof. Esben is watching his father working on the roof. Esben appears healthy.

Rajen

"I was under impression that climbing the roof is not very difficult. Though I have easily climbed on this roof, now I realise that coming down from the roof may not be easy."

Lata

"You will follow the same course for coming down that you followed for climbing up."

Rajen

"Now my work is over. How should I get down? The roof is slippery now due to rain. I may slip and fall."

Esben

"Dad, you have to try."

Rajen

"Okay my son. I cannot afford to sit here. I have to climb down."

Rajen carfully gets up and moves ahead to come to the edge from where he has to climb down. But he is imbalanced and he skids. He slides down from the roof, pushing many earthen tiles and comes on the ground. Lata rushes to him and helps him to get up. There are many thatches and earthen tiles scattered on the ground.

Rajen

"Thanks."

Lata

"Mention not."

Rajen

"How will I put these thatches and tiles back on the roof?"

Lata
"Londoners cannot do this. We have to find labourers for this work."

There is something wrapped in a plastic sheet and is visible within the scattered tiles on the ground. Esben notices that.

Esben
"Dad, something has fallen from the roof. There is something wrapped in the plastic sheet. Can you see that."

Rajen
" Yes, I can see that. What is this?"

Rajen picks up that plastic. It is tied with a thin thread. He opens it and finds the half portion of a notepad. He reads it and finds that the notepad has some details of medicine'Arunim'.

Rajen
"Oh God, thank you. This torn notepad has got the details of 'Arunim'."

Lata
" Read it. What does it contain?"

Rajen (He carefully flips through the notepad)
" This has got the total details of Arunim. It has got also the details of a King, his family and a infant prince. The fact of lost diamonds appear to be true. This says that a box full of diamonds has been kept hidden in a Lion's den."

Lata
"What? Please read it fully."

Rajen
"As you wish."

DISSOLVE TO:

62: EXT: ROAD CORSSING A DESOLATE JUNGLE :NIGHT

A chariot, pulled by a horse, is running fast on a deserted path of a dense forest. The charioteer is whipping the horse to speed the chariot. This chariot is uncovered. A lady from a royal family with a new-born baby is sitting on the chariot. The lady and charioteer is panicking.

Charioteer
"Her highness, the queen. Military commander's men are very far behind but they can find us. Our horse cannot run endlessly. The horse has also not eaten fodder today and is hungry. Now kindly tell me, What to do?"

<u>Queen</u>

"My dear charioteer, you are my saviour. Can you tell me if I can find a trustworthy citizen in my kingdom here? Please take me to him. I just want to secure my child's safety. Thereafter, I won't be afraid even if the traitors kill me the way they have killed my husband."

<u>Charioteer</u>

"Royal physician Chandrakant Sangla's house is nearby."

<u>Queen</u>

"Take me to him."

<u>Charioteer</u>

"As you wish."

The charioteer changes the course of the chariot and moves the horse towards the house of the Royal Physician.

Cut to:

<u>63: INT: SANGLA'S HOUSE : MIDNIGHT</u>

Royal physician Chandrakant Sangla is sleeping in his house and a lantern is mildly lit. The sound of forceful knocks on the entrance door of his house is heard. The physician wakes up and gets up from his bed.

<u>Chandrakant Sangla</u>

"Who is on the door at this midnight?"

<u>The sound of Charioteer</u>

"Please open the door, Royal physician. The Queen has come to see you. Please open the door."

Chabndrakant Sangla opens the door and the queen along with her infant son and charioteer enter into the house swiftly.

<u>Chandrakant Sangla</u>

"What happened to our infant prince? Is he sick? You could have called me."

<u>Queen</u>

"My dear Royal physician, we are in a dangerous situation. The military commander has done a military coup. He has killed your king...my husband. His militarymen are after my prince and me. I would like you to provide safety to my child. I have brought a boxful of diamond. Please accept this box and my child. Please ensure that my child is not found by the militarymen."

Chandrakant Sangla

"My dear queen. Do not worry. The tyrants will not be able to harm your child and our prince."

The queen hands over her child to the Royal physician along with a diamond box. The coversation between Chandrakant Sangla and the queen makes everyone of the family get up. They also come to see as to who is the visitor at this midnight.

Queen

"I shall immediately go otherwise the tyrants may guess about the Prince's whereabouts. If the tyrants come to know about my child, it will be equally dangerous for you and your family."

Chandrakant Sangla

"I shall soon make arrangements to send the Prince to a secured place."

Queen

"If I remain alive, I shall come to meet my child. I shall leave now."

Chandrakant Sangla

"My dear queen, I wish the tyrants to go down."

The queen and charioteer exit from the room. Chandrakant Sangla hands over the infant prince to his son. He opens the diamond box which is full of diamonds. There is a chain with a locket in the box. He opens the locket and find the photograph of the king and queen. A similar chain with a locket is also around the neck of the prince. He opens the locket of the other necklace and finds the same photographs of the king and queen.

Chandrakant

" Chwayan, my son. Make your horse ready and go to Itanagar with the Prince tonight. Go to the 'Sukant Orphanage' and meet the owner, Mr Sukant, who is very well known to me. Request him to kindly look after this child for at least two months. Thereafter, I shall collect the Prince from him. Please do not divulge the fact that he is a Prince."

Chwayan

"As you wish, dad."

Wife of Chandrkant Sangla

"Son, it is midnight. Remain alert and careful. There are military men on the road."

<u>Chwayan</u>
"I shall follow the path of the jungle. There may not be any military men there."

<u>Wife of Chandrkant Sangla</u>
"May god help you."

Chwayan touches the feet of his mother and father. He exits from the room along with the infant child. Chandrakant Sangla secures the diamond box.

Cut to:
<u>64: INT: SANGLA'S CLINIC : DAY</u>

Though the Royal physician, Chandrakant Sangla, is taking stock of the pulse of a patient to diagnose the ailment in his clinic in the basement of his house, he appears to be worried. His assistant is standing nearby to give medicine to the patient as per his prescription.

<u>Chandrakant Sangla</u>(to patient)
"You are suffering from cough. Just take in equal proportion of honey and juices of tulsi and ginger thrice a day and you will be fine. There is no need of medicine."

<u>Patient</u>
"Thank you very much."

The patient just walks away and exits from the clinic. Just then the footsteps of a horse is heard which becomes louder and louder. Thereafter, the sound of the footsteps stops. After few seconds, his son Chwayan enters into his clinic.

<u>Chandrakant Sangla</u>
"How are you my son? What is the news?"

<u>Chwayan</u>
"I have left the prince in the Sukant Orphanage. I requested Mr Sukant to look after him. I also told him that we will take him back after two months. He gladly agreed to keep the prince there as he admires you very much."

<u>Chandrakant Sangla</u>
"I am sure you have not divulged anything about the prince."

<u>Chwayan</u>
"Yes, of course. Though he wanted to know but I told him that I will let him know later, and askd him to take care of the infant child for

two months. Thereafter, I told him, you will come to collect him back. He didn't insist to know the detail."

Chandrakant Sangla

"You must be very tired and hungry. Eat something and then rest."

Cut to:

65:INT: SANGLA'S HOUSE : DAY

Chwayan is eating food while sitting on a spreadsheet. Chandrakant Sangla, his wife and other members of family are watching him eat. When he finished eating, he goes out of the room to wash his hand and mouth. Just then someone knocks at the entrance door. Chandrakant Sangla gets up to open the door. Chwayan has also returned in the room.

Chandrakant Sangla

"Who is there?"

Chandrakant Sangla opens the entrance door and finds that the charioteer, who had brought the queen to his house, is at the door in a panicking and breathless condition.

Chandrakant Sangla

"What is the matter? Why are you so worried?"

Charioteer

"Sir, one of the maids, whom the Queen trusted, has proved herself ungrateful. She has told everything about the Queen and the infant prince to the military commander in return for money and wealth. The military men found the queen and have killed her. The military men are coming to you. Somehow I managed to know all this and have come to warn you. Please leave this place immediately otherwise it would be fatal for you and your family."

Chandrakant Sangla

"Where are you going?"

Charioteer

"I am leaving this kingdom. I will cross the river Toonga and go to Myanmar. I am going now. Please run and save yourself and your family. The military men may reach at any moment. You have no time. Hurry...please."

The charioteer does not wait for his response and runs from there. Everybody gets panicky in Sangla's house.

<u>Chandrakant Sangla</u>

"We have to rush to Myanmar now, just collect the valuables and let us go."

<u>Chwayan</u>

"Just get ready within a minute before the military men arrive."

<u>Chandrakant Sangla</u>

"Chwayan, we have left our Prince with Sukant Orphanange. So, we should leave the diamond box here somewhere. In case the military men of this Kingdom or Myanmar catches us on our way out, they will take away the diamonds belonging to the Prince. We must secure his belongings here in this kingdom."

<u>Chwayan</u>

"Where should we hide it?"

<u>Chandrakant Sangla</u>

"This is day time. The lions are out of their den. You take a 'fire' with you and go to the Girnar forest. Leave this diamond box in one of the lion's den and come back to the riverbank of 'Toonga'. We shall wait for you there."

<u>Chwayan</u>

"The lion's den is a good place as no one would ever expect that the diamond box is hidden there. Okay Dad, I shall meet you at the riverbank."

Chandrakant Sangla gives the diamond box to Chwayan. Chwayan exits from the room. Chandrakant Sangla takes out a torn notepad and writes something on it. He wraps the notepad with a plastic sheet. He pulls a stool and stands on it. He pushes the plastic sheet in the thatches of roof in order to hide it.

<u>Wife of Chandrakant Sangla</u>

"What are you doing? Get ready quickly."

<u>Chandrakant Sangla</u>

"I have noted down the details of the Prince, his diamond box and the details of my medicine 'Arunim'. We are leaving our house in a dangerous situation. We do not know as to what is going to happen to us. So for any future use, these details are necessary to secure."

<u>Wife of Chandrakant Sangla</u>

"We are ready. Please get yourself ready. We must move out immediately otherwise we will be caught by the military men."

<u>Chandrakant Sangla</u>
"Have you taken the valuables and money with you?"

<u>Wife of Chandrakant Sangla</u>
"Yes".

<u>Chandrakant Sangla</u>
"I have nothing to prepare. Now let us get out of this place."

Everyone exits from the room in hurry. The entrance door remains open.

Dissolve to;

Fade In:
<u>66: EXT: SANGLA'S HOUSE : DAY</u>

Rajen has read the notepad. He is happy to know the details of 'Arunim'.

<u>Rajen</u>
"God is very kind that just after completion of three months, he has provided the details of the other medicine 'Arunim', I am sure my Esben will be perfectly all right now."

<u>Lata</u>
"I have also got the details of the diamond box. Girnar forest is nearby. Due to the deforestation, there are no lions or tigers now."

<u>Rajen</u>
"But it does not have the details of your family."

<u>Lata</u>
"The charioteer had crossed the Toonga River, whereas my family was in the middle of the river stream. Just then the military men chased and came to the riverbank. They could see my family members fleeing on a boat. They fired numerous poisondipped spears. In order to save themselves, everyone of my family jumped into the river. It was the time of hightide in the river, which took toll of my family. No one could save themselves. Everyone drowned. The charioteer was the witness of this horrible scene. He sent this message to my village. I was away with my maternal uncle. That is why I survived to bear the horror of the genocide of my family in the Toonga River."

<u>Rajen</u>
"What happened thereafter?"

<u>Lata</u>
"Soon thereafter India got its independence. The military commander

holding the kingdom was not recognised as a king of the area in the independent India. It was considered that the property of the kingdom or the palace belongs to the next of kin of the slain King or a blood relative of the slain king. Since everyone of the King's family was also killed and the whereabouts of the Prince could not be known, the properties and the palace was not handed over to anyone. The Government of India is the caretaker of this property and palace. The magistrate of Itanagar is the incharge of this majestic landscape."

<u>Rajen</u>

"The owner of the 'Sukant Orphanage' in Itanagar must be knowing about the prince's whereabouts."

<u>Lata</u>

"During the course of independence struggle, there was a lot of turbulance. He had handed over the prince, the infant child then, to someone for adoption, details of whom he does not know and does not remember. He does not know whether the prince is still alive."

<u>Rajen</u>

"Let us forget about the prince. Let us make the new medicine for my prince, Esben. Now it is the time to give him the new medicine 'Arunim'."

<u>Lata</u>

"Tomorrow we need to go to the Girnar forest to trace the diamond box in the lion's den. If we get the box then we will deposit it in the government treasury. Those diamonds belong to the lost prince."

<u>Rajen</u>

" Would you not like to keep those diamonds?"

<u>Lata</u>

"I am not greedy. I do not need those diamonds."

Both move towards house to enter into it.

Cut to:

<u>67: EXT: GIRNAR'S JUNGLE: DAY</u>

Rajen and Lata are alert and slowly moving within the Girnar forest. They appear to be tired. Rajen is holding a spade on his soulder.

<u>Rajen</u>

" We have walked around this jungle but we could not get a lion or his den."

Lata

" What would you do with a lion?"

Rajen

"At least I can ask the address of his den."

Lata

"This is a suicidal step."

Rajen

"After walking for such a long time, I am halfdead. I think we must return now."

Lata

"No return till we get the lion's den."

Rajen

"It is unbearable now."

Lata

"Are you afraid of this forest."

Rajen

"No, not at all. What about you?Are you afraid?"

Lata

"Yes, I am afraid, that is why I need you with me."

Rajen

"But I can see a lioness in you, who is fearless."

Lata

"Let us look for the lion's den."

They move ahead. After walking for a few yards, they find a dune with dry hedges and bushes on it. It appears that these hedges and bushes were green once upon a time, but are dry and dead now. Rajen burns the dry vegetation on the dune. When the bushes are burnt, they find an opening in the dune. Rajen gets upon the dune and peeps into the opening. Lata is watching him.

Rajen

"There is a bog room within this opening. Perhaps, this is the cave or the lion's den."

Lata

"Use the spade to widen the opening, so that we can enter into it."

Rajen is trying to widen the opening by using his spade. He is moving the soil from the opening.

Cut to:

68: INT: CAVE : DAY

Rajen and Lata are inside the cave. The cave is empty. In one corner of the cave, there appears to be something as the surface is uneven. Lata uses Rajen's spade to dig the soil. She finds a small box hidden under the soil. She becomes happy to see the box. She picks up the box and calls for Rajen's attention.

Lata
"Look, what I have got, a box...perhaps diamond box."

Rajen
"Is it the same box? Please open it."

Lata
"Lions do not keep small boxes to keep their jewellery. This is the same box."

Rajen
" Please open the box to check whether the lions have sold the diamonds and the box is empty."

Lata
"Rubbish."

She opens the box and the sparkling shine of diamonds spread within the cave. The box is full of diamonds. There is a locket as well as letter is in the box. Lata picks up the locket and checks it carefully.

Lata
"This locket is similar to the locket in your neck."

Rajen
"Read the paper."

Lata
"The diamond box belongs to the Prince. The infant Prince has been left in 'Sukant Orphanage' for proper care, away from the assailants. He can be recognised by a similar locket of his chain. This locket contains the photograph of his mother and father, I mean the King and the queen."

Rajen
"What?"

Lata
" Now you, please open the locket of your chain."

<u>Rajen</u>
"It does not open. I have never opened it."

<u>Lata</u>
"Try hard to open."

<u>Rajen</u>
"It may break."

<u>Lata</u>
"So be it. But open it."

<u>Rajen</u>
" Okay, I will open it, come what may."

Rajen applies force to open the locket and to his surprise it opened. Photographs of the king and queen similar to the locket found in the box are seen. Lata and Rajen are looking each other in utter disbelief.

Cut to:
<u>69: INT: SANGLA'S HOUSE:DAY</u>

Rajen, Esben and Lata are in the house. They are very silent. They are watching each other's faces.

<u>Lata</u>
" I do not understand as to how you got this locket. Either you are the Prince or a thief."

<u>Rajen</u>
" This has been with me since my childhood. I understand that my grandpa had given it to me."

<u>Lata</u>
" Then ask your grandpa as to how did he get this locket?"

<u>Rajen</u>
" How to find out? My cellphone is nonfunctional for three months now."

<u>Lata</u>
" Switch it on, may be it is working now."

Rajen opens the suitcase and takes out the cellphone and switches it on. Just then the cell phone rings.

<u>Rajen</u>
"Hurrah, the cell phone is working. My grandpa is calling."

Rajen picks up the phone and tries to here. Sound from the ear piece of mobile phone is quite loud and can be heard. The sound is identifiable. His grandpa is on the line.

Grandpa's sound from the ear piece of mobile phone: "Hello, my boy, where are you? I have been trying to contact you for the last many months. But you were not contactable. What happened?"

<u>Rajen</u>
"Grandpa, my cell phone was not functioning. Today, to my surprise, I found it to be working. I am still at the same place. Esben is still under treatment. He is much better than before. Now he walks by himself without the wheelchair. I am sure he would be recovering very soon."

Grandpa's sound from the ear piece of mobile phone: "That is a very satisfying news. I am very happy. When would you be able to come back?"

<u>Rajen</u>
"I think in a month or two."

Grandpa's sound from the ear piece of mobile phone: "Actually in your absence and with no contact at all, the business has been affected adversely. Keep in touch and please advice Rana suitably so that he could put everything in order."

<u>Rajen</u>
"Where is Rana? Can I talk?"

Grandpa's sound from the ear piece of mobile phone: "He is not here right now. I am calling from home."

<u>Rajen</u>
"Grandpa, I need to know about the locket in my chain. Where did you buy this locket and when?"

Grandpa's sound from the ear piece of mobile phone: " Why do you need to know this all of a sudden?"

<u>Rajen</u>
"Just for my knowledge. A similar locket belongs to a Prince of the erstwhile Kingdom of this area. The whereabouts of the Prince is not known."

Grandpa's sound from the ear piece of mobile phone: "What? What Prince..."

The cellphone is quiet.

Rajen

"Grandpa, are you there? Please answer my queries?"

Grandpa's sound from the ear piece of mobile phone: "Now I need to tell you some real facts which you are not aware of. I brought you from an orphanage named" Sukant Orphanage" in Itanagar and later you were adopted by my son as my grandson. The locket that you are referring to was already with you since then. I do not know as to how this locket was put in your neck."

Rajen

"Then this answers my queries. It means I need to find my root here in Itanagar. Thanks for this information."

Rajen switch off his cellphone. He is in a serious mood.

Lata

"Since the locket is in your neck since childhood, you may be the prince."

Rajen

"I do not know ...what destiny god has assigned to me. Today I find that the family which I adored since my childhood is not mine. Who is my kin?"

Lata

"You need to enquire from Itanagar, from Sukant Orphanage."

Rajen

"Yes, I will have to go to Itanagar."

Cut to:

70:INT: DOOR LEADING TO THE CABIN OF MAGISTRATE OF ITANAGAR:DAY

Rajen, Esben, Lata and a very old and fragile man are sitting on visitors'chairs outside an office room, the door of which bears the name-plate of the magistrate of Itanagar. There are many visitors in the visitor's room, waiting for his or her turn to meet the magistrate. A peon in his official uniform comes to Rajen.

Peon

"Now it is your turn to go inside the office room to meet the magistrate. You can go now."

The peon opens the door of the office room to allow Rajen, Esben (he can walk now), Lata and the old man to enter into the room of magistrate.

Cut to:

71: INT: MAGISTRATE'S OFFICE ROOM: DAY

The magistrate is sitting on his chair, whereas Rajen, Esben, Lata and the old man are sitting opposite him. Everyone greets him. The magistrate goes through a paper from his office tray.

Magistrate (To the old man)

"Dear Mr Sukant, I have read the affidavit that you have put up and I fully believe the affidavit to be true. As you are very old and fragile in health and you tend to forget also, I just wanted to meet you to reconfirm that you have made no mistake while making this affidavit and that you have carefully checked every details. I need to be careful before handing over the assets of the erstwhile King of this area to a person, whom I do not know."

Mr Sukant

"Sir, I am fully confident that Mr Rajen is the Prince. Since Doctor Chandrakant Sangla did not come to collect him after two months, I handed over the infant prince to a cook of the then English magistrate of this area. His name was 'Jai Kishan. He had left this area and I did not know his whereabouts. Now I have come to know that when the English left India, declaring it to be independent, Jai Kishan went to England with the English Magistrate to serve him. Now he is known as Jackson Cook in London. Had Rajen not come to this place to find a cure for his ailing son, we might not have come to know about this. The locket in his chain is the evidence that he is the prince. The locket is similar to the locket found in the diamond box and bears the photographs of Late King and queen. I am absolutely confident that he is the prince and he should inherit the assets of his deceased parents."

Magistrate

"You are the only living person, who knows this fact and can recognise the legal successor of the assets of the erstwhile Kingdom. Now I have spoken to you and as per your recommendations in the affidavit and as per the 'will' of the slain King, I am handing over the movable as well as immovable assets including the diamond box to Mr Rajen. I am authorising to make appropriate documents in favour of Mr Rajen."

Mr Sukant

"I am very sure that Mr Rajen is the Prince. There is no doubt whatsoever."

Magistrate (To Rajen)
"Mr Rajen, being the magistrate of this area, I was the caretaker of the movable and immovable properties of Late King Gaj Singh. Apart from the palace and the money in the bank, there are many rice mills, oil mills and other factories that I used to monitor, which are still functional and are earning good amount of money. The total assets would work out to be more than two thousand crores in Indian rupees. From today onwards, you would be the proud owner of this asset and I am sure you would keep the momentum of growth in the earning of these mills and factories which are the source of livelihood of thousands of people of this area."

Rajen
"I did not know about myself. Now that I know the truth, I feel very attached to the soil of this place. I assure you that the work that was started by my father would be continued."

Magistrate
"You may go to Minjong and I will meet you in the Palace. I will then hand over the documents as well as the keys to important assets under lock and key. I shall show you the assets for your familiarisation."

Just then a sub-ordinate officer of the magistrate enters into the room and hands over a bunch of documents to the magistrate and thereafter leaves the room.

Magistrate
"These are the property deeds that you should keep carefully as it authorises you to be the owner of the assets of the erstwhile kingdom."

Rajen
"In case I happen to lose or misplace it, I am sure, I can get another copy from your office."

Magistrate
"These are original copies and carry more weightage than the copies. You must keep it safely."

Rajen
"Don't worry, I shall take care of it. Now we will take your leave."

Magistrate
"I shall meet you in Minjong the day after tomorrow."

Rajen
"Thanks".

Rajen shakes his hand with the magistrate, whereas Mr Sukant, Esben and Lata greet him.

Cut to:
72: INT: SANGLA'S HOUSE : DAY

Rajen is packing his bags. Lata is sitting on the bed and watching him. Esben is on the door.

Esben
"Dad, the magistrate's car has arrived. He may come in."

Rajen
"Let us go and meet him."

Rajen and Esben exit from the room.

Cut to:
73: EXT : SANGLA'S HOUSE:DAY

Rajen goes near the magistrate's car. The magistrate is sitting on the back seat of his car and the wind-shield of the window is open.

Rajen
"Good morning, Sir. Please come in."

Magistrate
"Mr Rajen, I have to return to Itanager quickly. I am in a hurry. So please come with me quickly, so that I can finish my task."

Rajen
"Please give me minute and I will be with you."

Rajen and Esben return to the house.

Cut to:
74: INT: SANGLA'S HOUSE: DAY

Rajen and Esben enter into the room. Rajen closes his suitcase and puts on his shoes. Esben is ready but is not happy to leave Lata behind. He is sad to leave Lata.

Esben
"Aunty, you...please come with us."

Lata
"I came to search for a cure of your disease. Now you are fit and fine

and my work is over. Tomorrow I shall return to Itanagar for my job. You and your father are the prince of the erstwhile kingdom. Go with your father and be happy in the new palace. There you will find many new friends. You will have fun."

Esben

"I do not feel good without you. Aunty, please come with us. Dad, please request aunty to come with us."

Rajen

"If your aunty wishes to come with us, I welcome her."

Lata

"It would not be good for me to go with you now. Esben is all right now, my work is over. I shall return to Itanagar. You may go now, the magistrate is waiting. "

Rajen takes his suitcase and moves towards the door to exit. He finds that Esben is not moving.

Rajen

"Esben, now let us go. We do not have time. The magistrate is waiting."

Esben is very sad and looks towards Lata, requesting her silently to come with him. But Lata is firm. They both exit from the room, whereas Lata watches them leaving the place. She is also sad.

Cut to:

75: INT: PALACE OF MINJONG: DAY

This is an internal portion of the elegant Palace, the walls have many portraits of his ancestors, who were kings. The interiors of the palace are lustrous and elegant. Rajen and Esben are very happy to see the interiors of the palace. The magistrate, Rajen and Esben are standing in a big hall, which has a dome like high ceiling and many wide pillars. There are many servants of the palace who are also present there to hear from the magistrate.

Magistrate

"Mr Rajen, I have shown you almost everything that now belongs to you. They are your staff members and the servants of this palace. If you like them, you can keep them. If you do not like some of them, you can ask them to leave. But I am sure, you would need their services to manage and maintain this palace and properties."

Rajen

"Sir, I am grateful to you."

Magistrate (beckons a staff member)
"His name is Kipgen. He is the accountant of this palace. He is very loyal to this palace. You can trust him fully. (To Kipgen) You need to take care of the Prince and his son now."

Kipgen
"I am privileged to serve my Prince and his son. I can die for them. No danger can come until I am alive. Sir, you will never find me wanting, you will never get a complaint."

Magistrate
"Mr Rajen, now I shall take your leave as I need to return to Itanagar. You must be tired. Now you take rest in your own palace."

Rajen
"Sir, I am grateful for your time and efforts. Many thanks."

The magistrate shakes hand with him and then goes away. Kipgen comes to Rajen.

Kipgen
"Prince, you are tired now. Please come to your bedroom and relax. I shall make quick arrangements for your lunch."

Rajen
"Okay."

Kipgen takes the suitcase of Rajen and climbs the staircase to go to the bedroom on upper floor. Rajen and Esben follow him.

Cut to:
76: INT: BEDROOM OF PALACE:NIGHT

It is midnight. Rajen and Esben are lying on a bed in a bedroom of the palace. The room is mildly lit. Rajen is trying to sleep, whereas Esben is silently weeping. He is trying to stop his sobbing by putting his palm on his mouth and is feeling overwhelmingly sad about Lata and is emotionally disturbed. He is not able to control his sobbing. Rajen listens Esben's sobbing and gets up to see him. He finds Esben in tears. Esben is weeping.

Rajen
"What happened? Why are you weeping?"

Esben
"I miss Lata aunty."

<u>Rajen</u>
" Why ?"

<u>Esben</u>
"Aunty is very good. She is better than my mom. She left everything selflessly to find cure for my disease. Now I am fine. Why can't she live with us now? We have a big palace. She can live with me like my mom."

<u>Rajen</u>
" Why like mom?"

<u>Esben</u>
" Don't you like her?

Rajen is not able to answer Esben's sudden volley of the question. He is quiet.

<u>Esben</u>
"If not like mom, she can be a governess in our palace. There are a lot of other workers. She can be one of them. She can at least be with me always. Can you not bring her for me?"

Rajen has no answer. He is thoughtful and silent.

<u>Esben</u>
" Aunty has been with us selflessly but Dad we are selfish. When her work to help us is over, we have left her in lurch and have come to this palace of pleasure, treasure and wealth. We are selfish. She is great."

Rajen does not have anything to pacify Esben. He is still quiet and lost in his thought.

Dissolve to:

<u>77: EXT: SANGLA'S HOUSE: NIGHT</u>

Rajen walks towards the house, where Lata and Esben are sleeping. He knocks at the door and says 'Please open the door...please open the door.'

After a few knocks, the door is opened. Lata is on the door.

<u>Lata</u>
"What is it?"

<u>Rajen</u>
"It is very cold out here. I am shivering. Please allow me to sleep inside the house. It will be a great favour, otherwise I shall die in two days."

Lata

"How can you sleep inside the house?"

Rajen

"It is extremely cold outside. Please allow me, I shall die otherwise. Please believe me."

Lata

"People would talk rubbish, if they come to know that I am sleeping in the same room with a stranger."

Rajen

"People will never come to know. Please do not kill me in this cold."

Lata

"Okay. Come in and sleep on Esben's bed."

Rajen

"Thank you. I am grateful."

Rajen enters into the room and Lata closes the door.

Cut to:

78: INT: BED ROOM OF SANGLA'S HOUSE: MORNING

Rajen and Esben are sleeping on the same bed. The window of the room is open and sun-light is coming in the room. Lata makes tea and brings it in a tray towards Rajen and Esben. She tries to wake Rajen up.

Lata

"Mr Rich and Wealthy get up. Bed tea is ready."

Rajen gets up lazily and straightens his limbs.

Rajen

"Is it already morning, I still feel sleepy."

Lata

"You appear to be carefree, don't you remember your mission?"

Rajen

"I do remember. Thank you for reminding me and also for the bed tea."

Rajen takes a sip of the tea and finds it very tasty.

Rajen

"The tea is fantastic. Thank you."

<u>Lata</u>
"Please wake up Esben also."

<u>Rajen</u>
"Let him sleep for a while. Yesterday he got very tired. Now where is our toilet? I am now feeling the punch in my stomach."

<u>Lata</u>
"Do not expect a toilet here. Go to the bushes and relieve yourself. There is a pond nearby. That would help you to clean and bathe.

<u>Rajen</u>
"Oh God, this is a big problem."

<u>Lata</u>
"Mr Rich and Wealthy, today is just the first day. Many more problems are ahead but remember your mission."

<u>Rajen</u>
"Oh, I can not control myself. I have to rush."

Rajen takes a towel and runs away from there.

Cut to:
<u>79: INT: BED ROOM OF SANGLA'S HOUSE:NIGHT</u>

Rajen, Esben and Lata are sleeping in the bedroom. Rajen and Esben are sleeping on one bed whereas Lata is sleeping on the other bed. It is midnight but the bedroom is dimly lit because of the moon light coming in from windows. Esben is unable to sleep. While lying on bed he is trying to see out of the window. Lata also moves while sleeping and her sleep is disturbed. She wakes up and sees Esben awake. She is surprised to see him awake and calm.

<u>Lata</u>(slow voice)
"Esben, Are you awake?"

<u>Esben</u>
" Yes, aunty."

<u>Lata</u>
"How long have you been awake?"

<u>Esben</u>
"For quite some time. May be more than an hour."

<u>Lata</u>
"I will sing you a lullaby."

Lata starts singing.

<u>Esben</u>
"Aunty, you are singing."

<u>Lata</u>
"It has a story also. Please listen..."

Lata starts singing and Esben is quietly listening. Rajen's sleep is disturbed despite of Lata's soft and low voice. He does not move but quietly listens her song. He watches her glowing face in the dim moon light and finds it very innocent and lovable. After some time Esben feels sleepy and his eyes gradually droops. Esben falls sleep. When Lata finds him fast asleep, she stops singing. She takes a stock of the surrounding. Rajen closes his eyes as if he is fast asleep. Lata is assured. She also sleeps.

Cut to:
<u>80: EXT: SANGLA'S HOUSE: MORNING</u>

Esben sitting on his wheelchair watches Lata watering the kitchen garden. He appears to be healthier. Rajen is trying to massage the body of the cow. He is serving fodder, water and oil cakes to the cow as well as her calf.

<u>Esben</u>
"Aunty, I want to work in the kitchen garden with you. Can I join you?"

<u>Lata</u>
"My dear, you would be able to do everything. Just wait till the time you are fully recovered from the ailment. How are you feeling now after taking the medicine for two weeks?"

<u>Esben</u>
"I am much better now."

Rajen's cellphone rings. He picks it up.

<u>Rajen</u>
"Hello...Hello."

He cuts the call, as he ca not hear anything.

<u>Rajen</u>
"Bad connection..."

<u>Lata</u>
"Go and milk the cow. I have to give Esben his medicine."

Rajen takes a bucket with him to collect the milk. The calf is sucking milk from the udder of the cow. After some time he moves and tie calf away with a pole in front of the house. Thereafter, he starts milking the cow.

Esben

"Dad, you have learnt to milk a cow."

Rajen

"It is the necessity that makes you learn."

The cow is not feeling comfortable with the style of milking by Rajen. She moves ahead and kicks with her two hind legs. Thus Rajen is imbalanced and his cellphone in front pocket of his shirt falls in the bucket of milk. Rajen too falls on the ground but is able to save the milk from falling on the ground. Lata rushes to help him. She takes the milk-bucket from him and takes out the cellphone.

Lata

" What happened? Are you hurt? Why did cow kick her hind legs? Did you pinch her?"

Rajen

"I was gently milking her. I do not know as to why she kicked me? I have a mild sprain in my back."

Lata

"Go and take rest. The milk is saved but your cellphone may go out of order."

Rajen

" Oh God".

He takes the cellphone in his hand and tries to wipe out the milk. He dials a number but it does not function.

Rajen

" What to do? It is out of order. How will I contact London?"

Lata

"Don't you think, it is fine that no one will disturb you any more?"

Rajen walks back to the house limping. Lata also follows him with the bucket of milk.

Lata

"I will massage your back with hot oil. Do not worry, you will soon be all right."

Cut to:

81: INT: BED ROOM OF SANGLA'S HOUSE: DAY

Rajen is lying on the bed. Esben is sitting on his wheelchair. Lata is giving him medicine and a glass of milk.

Lata

"Esben, take this medicine."

Esben

"I really do not like this medicine. It is horribly bitter."

Lata

" But it will cure you. Gulp quickly and drink the milk. Do not keep it for long on your tongue."

Esben gulps the medicine and drinks the milk. Lata also gives a glass of milk to Rajen.

Lata

"After the hot oil massage, take this hot milk. You will be relieved of your backache."

Rajen

"I don't take milk."

Lata

"No, excuses now, just take the glass of milk and drink."

Rajen

"You just sound like my mom."

Lata

"Esben, then you drink this glass of milk."

Esben

"No aunty, not any more."

Lata

"You have eaten very little. Just take this glass of milk."

Esben

"No aunty, please. Not again."

Lata

"You must be obedient to your grandmother."

Esben

"Who is my grandmother here? You?"

Lata

"Yes, I sound like mom to your dad."

<u>Rajen</u>
"Sorry, I didn't mean it. Okay I will drink the milk."

<u>Esben</u>
"Aunty, you can surely set my dad right. He is not an innocent guy."

<u>Rajen</u>
"Esben, your dad is an innocent guy."

<u>Esben</u>
"No, not to my aunty."

<u>Lata</u>
"Esben is right. You need to be straightened."

She speaks in a humorous tone and everyone roars in laughter.

Dissolve to:

Fade in:
<u>82: INT: BEDROOM OF PALACE:NIGHT</u>

It is midnight. Esben is fast asleep, whereas Rajen is lying on his bed, lost in his thought. There is a pindrop silence. Esben's sound echoes in Rajen's ear.

<u>Esben</u> (O.S)
"Aunty is very good. She is better than my mom. She left everything selflessly to find cure for my disease. Now I am fine. Why can't she live with us now? We have a big palace. She can live with me like my mom."

Rajen is still thoughtful on Esben's words.

<u>Esben</u> (O.S)
"Aunty has been with us selflessly but Dad...we are selfish. When her work to help us is over, we have left her in lurch and have come to this palace of pleasure, treasure and wealth. We are selfish. She is great."

Rajen is pondering on Esben's words.

<u>Rajen</u> (V.O)
"Esben is right. She was treating him like her own child. She was a perfect mother, better than Lina, Esben's biological mother. Lina remained away from Esben and mostly busy in her parties when Esben wanted her the most. Lata came to Minjong to find cure for my son. Now he is fine due to her help, support, wishes and prayers. She has been totally selfless. She was not after the diamonds but

worried to safely pass on the diamond box to its real owner. Her grandpa has been the savior of my life. He was killed along with his family members to save my life. Why did I leave her in her grandpa's house? I owe my life to her. She is an innocent and beautiful girl. Her beauty has been fascinating me but I remained immersed in my selfish, arrogant mindset. She is a perfect mother of my child. She would make my life meaningful and happy. I am used to her now. I can not live without her. I am in love with her. "

Cut to:

83: EXT : ROAD : MORNING

It is morning and a gentle breeze is blowing. The sunlight is very mild. The weather is serene and soothing. A car is racing ahead on the road as if there is an emergency. The car is roofless and so the driver as well as the passenger of the car is visible from a distance. Rajen is driving the car and Esben is sitting on the front seat beside him.

Esben

"Dad, drive fast. Aunty is to leave for Itanagar by the morning bus."

Rajen

"At what time will the bus leave?"

Esben

"I have no idea. You should have asked aunty."

Rajen

"Son, I am very sorry for this lapse. If we do not find her, we will go to Itanagar."

The car is still racing fast on Minjong's road. After a while, Lata is seen standing on the bus stop beside the road leading to Itanagar. She is holding her purse and a rolling suitcase. Rajen stops his car near her. Both Rajen and Esben get out of the car and approach Lata. Esben runs towards her, calling her "aunty…aunty…please do not go…" Lata is happy to suddenly see Esben. She is emotionally charged to see Esben. She takes Esben in her arms and hugs him. She kisses him and her eyes are moist.

Lata

"I am happy to see you before boarding the bus."

Esben

"You will not go anywhere."

<u>Rajen</u>

"Are you going?"

<u>Lata</u>

"What do I do here? Esben is fine and my work is over."

<u>Rajen</u>

"You had a temporary job in Itanagar. I am sure they have hired someone else by now. What would you do there?"

<u>Lata</u>

"Yes, that may be true. But sitting idle will not help. I have to search a job now. I am sure I will be able to find a job for myself."

<u>Rajen</u>

"I have a full time job for you."

<u>Lata</u>

"Yes, now you are a prince, you can give me a job. What kind of a job you can offer?"

<u>Rajen</u>

"You can be a saviour."

<u>Lata</u>

" What ?"

<u>Rajen</u>

"You have saved Esben's life from a terminal condition. Now I am sick with a dangerous condition. I will not live long."

<u>Lata</u>

"What happened to you?"

<u>Rajen</u>

"I have realised last night that I am also in a terminal condition."

<u>Lata</u>

"Tell me, what happened to you?"

<u>Rajen</u>

"I will certainly die without you. I cannot live without you. Please save me from this terminal condition. Lata, I beg for your love. Please be my wife and mother of Esben."

<u>Esben</u>

"Aunty, I cannot live without you."

<u>Lata</u>

"I was also feeling disturbed without you."

Esben

"Aunty, can I call you my mom? My dearest mom..."

Lata

"Yes, my son."

Rajen

"And can I call you my darling."

Lata does not answer but smiles blissfully.

Esben

"Thank you, Dad."

Rajen

"For what?"

Esben

"For finding my mom. My dearest mom."

Rajen takes the rolling suitcase of Lata and keeps it in his car. Lata, Rajen and Esben sit in the car. Rajen is on the driving seat, whereas Lata is sitting on the front seat beside him. Esben is sitting in her lap. Rajen reverses his car and drives back towards the palace.

Esben

"Aunty...sorry... mom."

Lata

"I am still your aunty and will become your mom when your father marries me."

Rajen

"I hereby take all the bright stars, sun and moon, the cool breezes under the sky as a witness; I solemnly accept you as my wife and mother of my son, Esben."

Esben is ecstatic and joyful. He kisses Lata on her cheeks and repeats "Mom.......mom". Lata also kisses him and hugs him. Rajen is driving his car. He is also delighted to find a new love in his life. Suddenly, the surrounding appears to be melodious and marvellous.

Fade out

The End

3

A Bunch of Lies
(A Short Story)

It is 2020 AD. The Middle East nations are very rich and prosperous thanks to the oil reserves. The importance of oil is still at its peak. Rivalry between Iran and Iraq continues.

Mr Richard Blantyre is a TV-correspondent of ABC-TV in Washington and his wife, Mrs Lizzie Blantyre, is a cinematographer. They move to Baghdad from Washington to take up their new assignments. They find a new friend in Mr Sartaj Jamani, an Iranian journalist in Baghdad. The husband-wife team covers day-to-day developments and the dispute between Iraq and Iran. Relation between Iran and Iraq are strained following a dispute over territorial rights of both the countries over sea-reserve of oil and gas discovered by Iraqi explorers in Satt- al Arab strait. This dispute is settled through extensive mediation of the OPEC Secretary General. Iran and Iraq finally agree to exploit the Satt- al Arab reserve immediately for economic benefit and share the production at the ratio of seventy per cent for Iraq and thirty per cent for Iran as provided under applicable International law. Iran's demand is for a 50 percent share of the oil based on the fact that though the sea border between the two countries divides the natural reserve area in a 70:30 ratio, the onshore oil reserve on the Iranian side is much higher than the Iraqi side. Iran agrees to abide by the international law for the present and to continue talks with Iraq to create a congenial atmosphere for its request of a 50:50 per cent share.

After one year, Iraqi President Asfaq Hussain takes an urgent secret meeting of his cabinet colleagues. In this meeting a minister announces that an Iraqi technologist has made a prototype of an almost perpetual motion machine with the help of magnets, round springs, fission of silicon and a device able to convert gravitational energy to linear energy whereas an Iraqi Chemical Engineer has created a new gas, which has marvellous property of instant expansion and instant contraction in its volume due to change in temperature. Another Iraqi technologist took note of this marvellous property and has made a marvellous machine, which has propelling function like a steam engine. Actually cyclic rotation of this gas within solar electricity fuelled hot and cold chambers creates effect of sudden burst and contraction in the volume of this gas, resulting into a propelling action that gives various speed to a wheel or a fly wheel, based on the temperature level in hot & cold chambers. These two inventions can effectively replace fossil fuel driven engines. The Iraqi cabinet decides to make all the arrangements for large-scale manufacturing of these engines and automobiles as well as its storage for sale at a later date. It also decides to keep this invention secret till such time that all its oil and gas reserves are sold out, since the invention renders oil and gas redundant. In fact, the President make these instructions to accelerate Iraqi sale by lowering the price below the level fixed by the OPEC and to route the sale through an agent in London to facilitate cover up in case of discovery by the OPEC. With this move, Iraqi sale of oil multiplies manifold and comes under scrutiny of OPEC, which finds that Iraqi sale is at a price below the prescribed level. OPEC convenes a meeting in Cairo to discuss the situation. In the meeting the Iraqi representative defends that its agent in London is responsible for the sale of its oil. OPEC, therefore, decides that from now on sales shall not be routed through agents, brokers or intermediaries but shall be direct to the buyer countries.

After a month, Mr Blantyre finds that the Iraqi sale has not come down despite Iraqi pledge to sell oil at OPEC prices. He becomes suspicious about the actual mode of Iraqi oil business and ultimately finds from the bills of oil exports and imports that the benefit is concealed in the form of an adjustment item towards import, which never occurs. Since he finds that USA is also a beneficiary, he believes that his report would not find favour and would not be telecasted in TV. Hence he gives his report to Mr Sartaj Jamani, a Iranian journalist, for publication in an Iranian newspaper on the presumption that the report in the Iranian newspaper would look like a result of Iranian espionage.

The revelation of this fact in the Iranian newspaper makes all OPEC countries, particularly Iran, furious about Iraq's blatant breach of International agreement. OPEC convenes an urgent meeting in Cairo, where the Iraqi representative remains defiant and accuses Iran of fabricating false allegation and propaganda against it. OPEC, however, sees some truth in the Iranian allegations because Iraqi-sales are booming. This meeting reaches nowhere due to Iraq's defiant posture. Mr and Mrs Blantyre are not able to understand why Iraq is selling its oil at a price below OPEC level. Mr Blantyre and Mr Sartaj Jamani try to intrude into an out-of-bounds area of Iraqi Scientific Research Centre to find a clue to this mystery. But they were not successful.

In the city of Baghdad there is an old Mullah. He runs a small grocery shop in a congested lane of downtown. He sits in this shop with his deaf and dumb grandson Ahmed. His grandson helps him. The Mullah lost almost everyone except his grandson during the war of 2003 when Americans and their allies attacked Iraq. He is very poor and has a small piece of land in downtown Baghdad on which his provision shop is built. They live happily. Ahmed loves his grandfather very much as he communicates with him very well despite his being deaf and dumb.

One Mr Anwar Aziz, a shrewd real estate dealer, intends to buy the land owned by the old Mullah in downtown as it is in the prime area of business. Anwar Aziz wants to build a big business centre on this piece of land. Mullah turns down all offers for the sale of his land. The old Mullah makes it clear that he has no intentions to sell his ancestral property at all. At last, Aziz decides to grab this land by hook or crook. One night, he along with three muscle men and a pre-dated sale deed goes to the shop of the old Mullah just before the time of the closure of the shop. The downtown is deserted. Anwar Aziz demands Mullah to sign the sale deed and threatens to kill Ahmed on refusal. The old Mullah is frightened and therefore signs the sale deed under pressure. After the sale deed is signed, one muscle man takes out his pistol and shoots the old Mullah in the head. He dies instantly. On seeing his grandfather dead, Ahmed becomes frantic and takes out a sharp knife from a cupboard. He attacks the three muscle men and after a tough struggle manages to kill them. In the mean time, Anwar Aziz runs away from the scene and informs the police. At the sight of police approaching, Ahmed flees. He manages to escape from the police in the complex lanes of downtown Baghdad and gets onto a running goods train heading for Iran.

It is a small town within the territory of Iran bordering Iraq. There is a small house in the ruins of this town just near the only mosque. One crippled old man along with his old wife and their granddaughter live in this house. The old lady earns livelihood by working in the neighbourhood houses. This Iranian couple has lost their son's family in the Iran-Iraq war except their granddaughter,Laila, who happens to be deaf and dumb. She is young and very pretty.

Imam, the religious man at the Mosque, is publicly known to be a celibate but he lusts after young women and secretly leads a life of pleasure. He desires Laila secretly, as he feels she cannot disclose his wrong doings and make him infamous among the people of this small town. With the help of his three henchmen he attempts to catch hold of Laila but she manages to escape her pursuers. Her grandfather and grandmother come to know about this but are not able to resist the Imam because of the fact that Laila can not speak and substantiate any allegation against him. Secondly, the Imam is a highly influential person. Since the Imam is not able to do anything to Laila in the presence of her grandfather, he decides to eliminate the hurdle in his way. Under his influence and conspiracy, the local police trump up false theft charges against the old man and woman. The police arrest the grandmother and grandfather and imprison them. Now a few hired thugs of the Imam are after Laila to bring her to Imam. But Laila casts about for help. Ahmed, who happens to reach this small town of Iran by the goods train, notices her. He helps her in hiding from the muscle men who are after her. When both come to know that they both are deaf and dumb, they are happy as they can communicate easily in sign language. Both of them are young and their knowledge of their plight brings them closer. Fed by their need for company, their love blossoms. They hug each other to signal that they would live together forever. They leave this town again in a goods train leading to a certain destination and get down after some time from the train when it slows down while crossing an old bridge above a river. This place is actually a no man's land between the border of Iran and Iraq and is very beautiful. This is a green valley with many flowering plants and lots of palm, coconut, almond and other fruitbearing trees. There is a river passing through this valley, where a rich variety of birds make nests. This place is uninhabitated. They are very happy to see the green area and river with no human habitation. They realise that they are away from the society of human and are alone. A deserted and partially destroyed old security post becomes their shelter, a very sweet home for them where they live and sleep at night after passing their day-to-day playful and happy life. It was heaven-like for them.

After sometime Laila gives birth to a beautiful baby. Their happiness knows no bounds. The valley seems to have come alive again and become joyful.

Two years on, nothing appears to be abnormal in the relation between Iran and Iraq until Iraqi intelligence finds that Iran had secretly put additional pipelines to its oil drilling station in Sat Al Arab strait. Iraq learns that Iran took away more than 30 per cent of its share because it wanted to make up for its losses by stealing oil from the sea reserve. Iraqi President goes to the UN with the documentary proof to put up a demand for compensation from Iran. The UN Security Council appeals to Iran by its resolution to pay up the compensation to Iraq. But Iranian President refuses to pay the compensation, terming UN's appeal as an appeal from the beneficiary countries to benefit its benefactor, who sells oil at a price below the OPEC level.

Following Iranian refusal, Iraqi President orders his military to be on alert, though he clarifies that this is a routine military exercise. Many believe that this is an Iraqi ploy to pressurise Iran to come to a compromise on the presumption that Iran may not like to enter into a war that would prove costlier than paying compensation because it has been isolated in the international community. Iran on the contrary, moves its military forward and orders its air force to strike Iraq to pre-empt any possible Iraqi strikes against it to prevent any damage. Continuous air strikes for two days on the civilian population in Baghdad cause a large number of casualties. Iranian air strikes stop only when the UN threatens to impose all round economic sanctions against Iran. Iraq, however, demands that UN impose economic sanctions against Iran for targeting civilian population in Baghdad and for violating human rights. The UN agrees to examine the cases of human rights violation by Iran and if found guilty, to impose economic sanctions against it.

Iraqi President, however, vows to get even with Iran and orders Iraqi air force to mildly punish Iran by air-attacks on Iranian cities for a day. "No human casualty" was their brief, to showcase Iraq's commitment to human rights. After the token airstrikes for a day, Iraqi spokesman says that Iraq's human rights records have become more vibrant by ensuring no human casualties in its successful token air attacks on Iran.

He says that Iraq has always been advocating compliance of human rights on every one including its neighbour. He alleges that Iran's record in this field has always been the worst. Once again, Iraq demands all-round economic sanctions against Iran for killing civilian population in Baghdad.

Mr and Mrs Blantyre do not believe Iraq's claim that it was able to ensure hundred per cent safety of human lives in the war. They along with their friend Mr Zamani go to the Iranian side and visit the sites, which were targeted by Iraqi bombers to find out if there is any death. After extensive search they discover three dead bodies. The green valley, the paradisal abode of Ahmed and Laila, has been completely devastated. All fruitbearing trees, vegetation and the only shelter for Ahmed, Laila and their baby have fallen due to continuous, merciless bombing. The dead bodies of Ahmed, Laila and their infant son are laying on the ground within a roofless security post, a sweet home for the three of them. Laila and Ahmed are seen holding their infant son while holding each other before their death. It appears as if they were braving the gruesome act of bombing before their death. The scene is extremely pathetic, which make Mr and Mrs Blantyre emotional.

Mr Blantyre in his TV report says, " Iraq's claim of sparing human lives in a token war is totally wrong. You can see on your TV screen three dead bodies found in the area of this no man's land bordering Iraq. The dead bodies have been identified. One was that of Ahmed of Iraq and the others were that of Laila of Iran. They were deaf and dumb and the parent of the dead infant. Iraq may now defend that the Iranians killed Ahmed and therefore it had targeted Laila, the Iranian woman. But what about the infant child who was born in no-man's land and had parents from Iran and Iraq? Why should he bear the brunt of the hostility between the two countries to which he does not belong? History is witness to the fact that innocent people have always suffered the consequences of hostile circumstances created by the Governments to meet selfish ends. Why to go to a war? When it would kill human beings. Pushing the circumstances towards war is also an abuse of human rights, which is what both Iraq and Iran did."

For filing this report on ABC TV, Mr Richard Blantyre earns the wrath of Iraqi Government, because this report can weaken Iraq's request in UN to impose economic sanctions against Iran on the basis of human rights violation. Iraq declares him persona non-grata for his report on ABC-TV news, saying that his report was a bunch of lies and a fabricated video recording against Iraq. Mr and Mrs Blantyre return to America with the feeling that they did their job well by telling the truth known to them.

XXXXXXXXXX

A Bunch of Lies
[Screenplay]

FADE IN

1:EXT : OFFICE BUILDING OF ABC -TV NEWS IN WASHINGTON : DAY

2020 AD–Washington (On screen caption)

A heavy traffic is moving in the by-lanes of a building carrying a neon-sign "ABC -TV" on the roof. Mr Richard Blantyre of ABC-TV manages to navigate his car up to the open parking enclosure at the front of the building. His wife is also beside him in the car. After parking the car, they come out of the car. After that they move towards the building.

Cut to:

2:INT ; PROJECTOR ROOM

The room is dark. A slide projector shows a photograph of a man on the screen.

(Loud voice in the projector room)

"He is Mr Asfaque Hussain, the President of Iraq. He was a military ruler till last year. We, the Westerners, now consider him liberal, progressive and staunch supporter of human rights and support him in his pursuit to establish democracy in Iraq. Poll processes were held peacefully and impartially as per our standards. He is a very sensitive man and is known to uphold human rights issues."

The photograph changes on the screen and is replaced by the photo of a bearded man.

"He is Mr Rege Altani, the President of Iran. He is the new successor in the line of fundamentalist rulers in Iran. He is known to adopt brutal attitude in implementing Islamic laws and has no regard for human rights. He is very difficult to deal with."

The photograph on the screen changes again. This is a photograph of a panoramic view of sea.

"This is the sea of Sat-Al-Arab, the scene of current dispute between Iran and Iraq. Beneath the sea, there are large reserves of oil and gas. As both the countries claim it their territorial rights, exploitation is difficult until they resolve their differences. With their present level of relationship, it is going to be difficult. We will watch the events as it unfolds.

The projector is switched off and a man named Garry switches on the light.

Mr Richard Blantyre and Mrs Blantyre are in their respective seats.

Garry
"This is a most important issue for both of you. You need to focus a lot while in the Middle East."

Mr Richard Blantyre and his wife get up from their chair. Mr Blantyre shakes hand with Garry.

Mr Richard Blantyre
"Thank you Garry! It was excellent."

Garry
"When are you both leaving for Baghdad?".

Mr Richard Blantyre
"Next Saturday."

Mr and Mrs Richard Blantyre exit from the room waving their hands.

Cut to:
3 : EXT ; BAGHDAD AIRPORT ; DAY

2020 : BAGHDAD (On screen caption)

An American Delta Airlines flight lands and rolls to a halt. The airport servicemen attaches a staircase to the craft. The passengers are coming out and among them are Mr and Mrs Richard Blantyre.

Cut to:
4:INT ; IMMIGRATION AREA OF AIRPORT ; DAY

An immigration officer looks at the passports of Mr and Mrs Richard Blantyre and clears them. Later, they both come out of the area.

Cut to:
5: EXT ; OUTSIDE AIRPORT ;DAY

Mr and Mrs Richard Blantyre leave the airport along with their luggage and get into a taxi. They head towards a Hotel.

Cut to:
6:INT ; RECEPTION AREA OF HOTEL ; DAY

Mr and Mrs Blantyre reach the reception desk of the hotel. The receptionist welcomes them with a smile.

<u>Mr Richard Blantyre</u>
"I have done a booking in this hotel. My name is Richard Blantyre and she is my wife, Lizzy Blantyre."

<u>Receptionist</u>
"Welcome to Baghdad. It is indeed a great pleasure for us to have you and your wife as our guest."

<u>Mr Richard Blantyre</u>
"Thank you."

<u>Receptionist</u>
"This is the key of your room on the 3rd floor. The bellboy would bring your luggage. This is the other key of your office room on the 4th floor. Please also take the key of your car Mercedes Benz."

<u>Mr Richard Blantyre</u>
"You are a great help."

Mr and Mrs Blantyre head towards the elevator.

Cut to:
<u>7:INT ; INSIDE ELEVATOR</u>

Mr Richard Blantyre hugs and kisses his wife.

<u>Mr Richard Blantyre</u>
"What a hectic flight."

<u>Mrs Blantyre</u>
"I am tired. I will take a shower and sleep."

<u>Mr Blantyre</u>
"So will I."

Cut to:
<u>8: EXT ; OVERVIEW OF DOWN-TOWN OF BAGHDAD ; DAY</u>

This is the overview of busy lanes in downtown Baghdad.

Cut to:
<u>9:EXT ; A PROVISION SHOP ; DAY</u>

A bearded young businessman comes out of a Mercedes Benz and walks into a provision shop.

Cut to:
<u>10:INT ; PROVISION SHOP ; DAY</u>

The provision shop is full of grocery items. One old Mullah with long beard is sitting with an eighteen-year-old boy. The young boy is deaf and dumb. His name is Ahmed. He is playing with the old man and talking in sign language. The old man in reply is saying, " Yes, Yes my boy. I love you very much. You are my darling."

A young bearded man, whose name is Anwar Aziz, walks into the shop and goes straight to the Mullah.

Mullah

"What?"

Anwar Aziz

"My name is Anwar Aziz. I would like to talk to you."

The Mullah spreads a small carpet. They both sit on it. Ahmed is on the cash desk.

Anwar Aziz

"Who is this boy?"

Mullah

"He is my grandson, Ahmed."

Anwar Aziz

"Tell me something about you. Where is your son?"

Mullah

"Why don't you tell me about yourself? "

Anwar Aziz

"I deal in real estate . What about you and your family?"

Mullah

"He is my grandson and the only survivor in my family to have escaped the American military attack in 2003. He is my only kinsman."

Anwar Aziz

"Mullah, I am concerned about you. You should now concentrate on a spiritual life and go for Haj piligrimage."

Mullah

"Thank you for the advice, but Ahmed is not selfsufficient. He is deaf and dumb."

Anwar Aziz

"Oh God, this is terrible. (Pause) Anyway, Ahmed is a young man and should be able to take care of himself. You can sell your shop. It would fetch you good money, which would be sufficient for Ahmed."

Mullah
"What do you mean?"

Anwar Aziz
"I am a real estate dealer and always on the lookout for viable land. Your land can be used for lucrative commercial purposes. Would you sell this plot? I will give a very good price."

Mullah

"So this is your motive...!"

Anwar Azi

"Yes"

Mullah (Angrily)
"You get out of my shop immediately. I do not want to sell my ancestral property."

Anwar Aziz

"Please take your time to think. It will be beneficial for you. I will come again."

Mr Anwar Aziz gets up and walks out of the shop.

Cut to:
11:EXT ; DOWN TOWN LANE OF BAGHDAD ; DAY

Mr and Mrs Richard Blantyre come out from their car and walk along the pathway of a lane. Mrs Blantyre is holding a video camera. Suddenly a jeep carrying affluent and drunken boys approaches them at a high speed. Mr and Mrs Blantyre are frightened to see that and run away from the speeding jeep to save themselves. A man on the path far behind them opens a door and pulls both of them into the doorway for safety. The boys on the jeep laugh and shout, 'Long live democracy'.

Cut to:
12: INT ; INSIDE DOORWAY ; DAY

Mr and Mrs Richard Blantyre find themselves safe inside.

Mr & Mrs Blantyre
"Thank you very much. You saved us."

Man
"Do not mention it".

Mr Richard Blantyre

"My name is Richard Blantyre and she is my wife. I am an American journalist for ABC TV. She is my cinematographer. We are grateful to you."

Man

"I am Sartaj Zamani. I am an Iranian newspaper journalist based here. This is a strange meeting."

Mr Blantyre

"Nice to meet you Mr Zamani."

Zamani

"These democratic Iraqis have no respect for the law of the land. They think democracy is a freedom to flout norms. You do not find these kind of hooligans in Iran. If found, they would be shot dead."

Mr Blantyre

"We are staying in hotel Holiday Inn."

Zamani

"I am also staying in this hotel."

Mr Blantyre

"That is great. We can meet easily now."

Zamani

"Of course, we can mee.,"

Everyone exit from that place.

Cut to:

13:INT ; ROOM OF ANWAR AZIZ ; NIGHT

There are two people sitting on a sofa. Mr Anwar Aziz serves them beer from his drawing room' bar-cabinet.

Anwar Aziz

"Sagir, that plot is extremely valuable. I have a plan of making a multi-storey building and selling to a multinational organization for a good profit. It is in the middle a busy market place."

Sagir

"Yes, you are dead right."

Anwar Aziz

"I would like you to convince the Mullah to sell this to me."

Sagir

"I will try. Though he is tough at times."

Anwar Aziz

"You are his neighbour. You should be able to do it. If I am able to get that plot then, you will also benefit."

Cut to:

14:EXT; CITY ROAD ; MORNING

The Mullah and Ahmed are seen in a pony carriage going towards the market place. They are in a playful mood and are laughing among themselves.

Cut to:

15:INT ; CONFERENCE ROOM ; DAY

A meeting is being held between Iranian and Iraqi diplomatic officials. Table flags of both the countries are visible on the conference table.

Cut to:

16:EXT ; MINISTRY OF FOREIGN AFFAIRS BUILDING ; DAY

Many cameramen and journalists are waiting outside the building to note down the outcome of the meeting given by the spokesperson of Iraq. Many TV journalists are covering the event live. Mrs Blantyre is holding her camera and Mr Blantyre is reporting live into the camera.

Mr Richard Blantyre

"Eight rounds of talks between the Iranian and Iraqi diplomats have failed to produce an agreement on sharing the oil and gas reserves found in Sat-al Arab strait. Finally an agreement has been reached. This is not an agreement to share the oil reserves, but to accept mediation by OPEC Secretary General in this matter to reach a mutually acceptable solution. The OPEC Secretary General has agreed to mediate. He is expected to begin his shuttle diplomacy between Baghdad and Tehran very soon."

"This is Richard Blantyre reporting from Baghdad."

Fade out:

FADE IN
17:EXT ; SMALL TOWN OF IRAN BORDERING IRAQ : MORNING

Small town of Iran - 2020 (on screen caption)

Overview of a town. Several small houses surrounding a mosque with many by-lanes are seen. Early morning 'Azan' is heard from a loudspeaker," Allah Akbar Allah, o Akbar."

Cut to:
18:INT ;A SMALL DILAPIDATED HOUSE ;AWAY FROM MOSQUE ;DAY

This house has three people. One old disabled man on bed, an old woman and a very beautiful girl. They all are having their food. As soon as they finish eating, the old lady takes away the utensils and then comes back.

Old lady
"Omar, I am going to the factory now. Take your medicine in time."

Old man
"Don't worry."

The beautiful girl is deaf and dumb. She is trying to tell something to the old lady in sign language but the old lady is puzzled.

Old man
"Laila wants to go out and play."

Old lady (Loudly)
"Okay, Okay, do not wander too far, and come back quickly to your grandpa."

The girl nods in agreement. She appears happy as she gets the permission to go out.

Cut to:
19:EXT; MOSQUE GATE ; DAY

A crowd is waiting in front of the door of the Mosque. A vacant four-seater horse carriage waits outside the Mosque. After some time a long-bearded and strong middle aged man in white robe comes out of the mosque. His supporters shout slogan raising their arms "Long live Imam." The Imam gets into the horse carriage and three of his close associates sit beside him. The horse carriage moves in the by-lane.

Cut to:

20:EXT ; IMAM'S HORSE CARRIAGE ON ROAD ;DAY

The Imam's carriage passes through the by-lanes of the small town and people on the roadside pay respect to him by bowing their heads. The carriage moves ahead and reaches a lonely area of the town with old houses and walls in ruin. At one point, Laila, sitting on a broken wall, is trying to tuck a flower in her hair by squinting into a broken piece of mirror. The Imam and others see her and are mesmerized by the charming adolescent beauty. The Imam stares at her in lecherous way.

Imam

"Who is this girl? Is she new here?"

One man

"No Sir, she is the granddaughter of Omar, the famous boxer of his time. Now disabled and helpless after a road accident."

Imam

"What about her father?"

Another Man

"You forgot? His son and daughter-in-law died in the bombing...war with Iraq."

Imam

"She is very beautiful. How could I not see her earlier?"

One man

"She is deaf and dumb. She stays at home most of the time."

Imam

"She is a perfect beauty with no tongue."

Another man

"Yes, the tongue makes things difficult."

Imam

"Try and bring her to me."

One man

"As you wish, Sir."

Cut to:

21:EXT ; A OPEN FARM LAND ; DAY

Mustard farm spread over many hectares is seen. Laila is running to catch a butterfly. Two close associates of Imam approach and call her loudly.

<u>One man</u>
"Laila! Take this money."

Laila cannot hear him but from the corner of her eye she catches the glimpse of someone holding out money to her. Laila is little surprised to see their kind gesture. She, however, accepts the money happily.

<u>Another man</u>
"You have to do something for us."

Laila looks questioningly.

<u>One man</u>
"Come to the Mosque. The Imam would specially bless you."

Laila agrees and follows them.

Cut to:
<u>22:INT ; ROOM OF A MOSQUE</u>

The interior decoration of the room is luxurious. The Imam is sitting on a very expensive carpet. A ray from another room cuts through the dim light of the room. Laila walks into the room and the door is closed from behind. Startled, Laila turns towards the door. The Imam gets up.

<u>Imam</u>
"Come here, don't worry."

Laila is not feeling comfortable. The Imam gets closer to her and instead of blessing her, embraces her tightly. He eyes her with lust. This angers Laila and she kicks him hard. The Imam yells in agony. The moment his associates hear the Imam cry out, they open the door and rush into the room to help. Seeing the door open Laila runs out from the room.

Cut to:
<u>23:EXT; COURTYARD OF THE MOSQUE ; DAY</u>

A large crowd has gathered and is offering the Friday prayer 'Namaj' on the ground. The Imam is facing the crowd and leading the prayer. The prayer ends and everybody sits on the ground. The Imam is on the stage and his helpers fixes the microphone of a PA system before his mouth.

A Koranic verse is read on the loudspeaker.

Imam

"God wishes us to follow a simple, honest and nonviolent life. To honour each other and not to hurt each other...."

Three of his associates comes to the stage and speak to Imam in a very low voice.

One man

"Sir, we have offered her more money but she is not ready at all."

Imam

"Then use force but try to avoid attention of anyone."

He nods and his associates leave the place.

Cut to:

24:INT ; BEDROOM OF OMAR ; NIGHT

Omar and his wife are upset by the incident narrated by Laila in sign language.

Omar's wife

"The way the rascal eyes any young woman, it was not affection but lust."

Omar

"I will expose this bastard."

Omar's wife

"You are not a boxer anymore. The Imam is very influential and we are helpless. Laila must not go outside alone. She will not be able to substantiate any proof against the Imam."

Fade out;

FADE IN

25:EXT ; MINISTRY OF FOREIGN AFFAIRS BUILDING ; DAY

Baghdad: After three months (On screen caption)

Many journalists and cameramen are waiting outside the building for a update by the Iraqi spokesperson about the meeting between Iranian and Iraqi officials under the auspices of OPEC Secretary General. Mrs Richard Blantyre is handling the camera and Mr Richard Blantyre is reporting live into the camera.

Mr Richard Blantyre

"After an extensive mediation of OPEC Secretary General, Iraq and Iran have agreed to exploit the Sat-Al Arab reserve for economic benefit and share production at the ratio of seventy per cent for Iraq and thirty per cent for Iran as per thė applicable International law. Iran was pushing its demand for fifty per cent of the production though the sea border between the two countries divided the natural reserve area in the ratio of 70: 30. The onshore reserve on the Iranian side is much higher than on the Iraqi side, thus containing almost the same volume of reserves. Iraq was insistent on 70 per cent share as the oil field had cost Iraq a considerable sum in the exploration and equipment. Iran has, however, agreed to follow the international law for the present and continue talks with Iraq to create a congenial atmosphere for its request of 50:50 per cent share. Iraq gave the contract for exploitation to an American oil company whereas Iran has given this contract to a Russian company 'Gas Prom'. The oil export is expected to start from this reserve within the next three months."

"This is Richard Blantyre reporting from Baghdad".

Cut to:
<u>26:INT ; PROVISION SHOP OF MULLAH ; DAY</u>

Mullah, Ahmed and Anwar Aziz are agitated and talking loudly.

<u>Mullah</u>
"I will not sell my ancestral property, no matter what."

<u>Anwar Aziz</u>
"You must sell this plot to me. This will benefit you and everyone else."

<u>Mullah</u>
"My answer is no. Get out from my shop. Do not come here again. I do not want to see you."

<u>Anwar Aziz</u>
" I will come again."

<u>Mullah</u>
"Get out !"

Mr Anwar Aziz walks out of the shop in a huff.

Cut to:
<u>27:INT ; ROOM ; NIGHT</u>

It is a room with opulent decoration. Anwar Aziz is sitting on a sofa and three muscle men are on the other sofa. Anwar Aziz is talking on the phone.

Anwar Aziz

"Advocate Rahman, this is Anwar. Please prepare a pre-dated sale deed confirming the sale of Mullah's plot to me. I would like to have this by tomorrow evening."

His conversation on the phone is over and Anwar Aziz addresses the three muscle men.

Anwar Aziz

"I need help from all of you. I need the signature of Mullah on the sale deed by any means, fair or foul. Tomorrow night we will go to him when the market place is deserted."

The three men nod in agreement.

Cut to:

28: INT; MULLAH'S SHOP; NIGHT

Mullah and Ahmed are preparing to close the shop. Mullah is counting the money and Ahmed is closing the cupboards. Just then Mr Anwar Aziz and three muscle men walk into the shop. Mullah and Ahmed look up in surprise.

Mullah (Loudly)

"You are here again?"

Anwar Aziz

"You will sign on these papers."

Mullah

" What is this?"

Anwar Aziz

"You are selling this plot to me."

Mullah

"No! I am not. You have brought these goons to threaten me?"

Anwar Aziz

"This is for real. If you do not sign the papers, Ahmed will die".

The two muscle men cover Ahmed and point the pistols at him. The Mullah is frightened now.

Mullah

"Do not do this. He is my only family."

Anwar Aziz

"I told you. I need this plot. Sign the sale deed and take the money. Then both of you can live happily."

Mullah

"Okay, I will sign but do not hurt my Ahmed."

The Mullah then signs the sale deed. One of the muscle man holding a pistol shoots Mullah in the head. The Mullah dies instantly. On seeing his grandfather dead, rage overcomes Ahmed and he quickly takes out a sharp knife from a cupboard. He attacks the three musclemen. In first attempt he cuts the throat of the muscle man holding pistol towards him and cuts the palm of another man who shot dead the Mullah and then kills him with his knife. The third muscle man did not expect the sudden change of situation and after realizing it he tries to overpower Ahmed but he is not able to. They both fight each other. Seeing the situation out of control, Mr Anwar Aziz walks out of the shop.

Cut to:

29: EXT; A ROADSIDE TELEPHONE BOOTH; NIGHT

Mr Anwar Aziz inserts a coin in the telephone machine to make a call.

Anwar Aziz

"Hello! Police! Three murders have taken place in Mullah's grocery shop in the downtown lane. Come quickly."

Cut to:

30:EXT; DOWNTOWN LANE OF BAGHDAD; NIGHT

Two police patrol cars are approaching the shop of Mullah. The police siren is heard.

Cut to:

31: INT; MULLAH'S SHOP; NIGHT

Ahmed and the last muscle man are grappling with each other. Suddenly Ahmed finds a knife and pushes it into the stomach of the muscle man, who dies instantly. Ahmed sees the headlight of police patrol car from inside the glass door of the shop. He realises the situation and quietly walks out of the shop. Four corpses are lying in the shop.

Cut to:

32:EXT; DOWN TOWN LANE AGAINST MULLAH'S SHOP; NIGHT

Two police patrol cars stop near the shop. Ahmed walks out of the shop and runs away from the police cars. One police car remains on the site and four policemen walk into the shop. The other car chases Ahmed in order to arrest him.

"Catch him" (O.S)

The police car follows Ahmed. One policeman inside the car fires on him. Ahmed ducks the gunshot and scrambles, swiftly turning and running to dodge the police. In a chase through the narrow lanes of Baghdad, the cars are not the best way of pursuit. While the police turn and reverse the car, Ahmed gets time to run away but the speeding car can be seen following him. After a few minutes of the cat and mouse run, Ahmed reaches the dead end of a lane. There is a rail track at the end of the lane on which a goods train is seen approaching. This is good opportunity for Ahmen so he runs along the moving goods train and climbs onto it. The police car comes to the end of the lane. Seeing the goods train leave with Ahmed, the police are disappointed and drive off towards the scene of crime.

Fade out;

FADE IN

33: INT; OMAR'S HOUSE; DAY

Omar, Omar's wife and Laila are inside the room. They are surprised to see four policemen forcefully enter into the room. The policemen are searching the room thoroughly and find a bag from the corner of the room.

Policeman

"Mr Omar and Mrs Omar, You both are under arrest for stealing Mosque's property."

Omar

"This is a fabrication against us."

Policeman

"You can defend yourself in the court of law now."

Omar

"I know the crafty man who has done this to us. Anyway, kindly take my granddaughter along. She is helpless as she is deaf and dumb girl."

Policeman

"She is an innocent girl. She cannot be taken to the prison."

Omar

" But how would she survive?"

Policeman

"God is great. Now come on."

The policemen forcefully take them away. Laila cries and falls at the feet of a police. The policeman mercilessly pulls his leg away and gets out of the room. Laila cries and follows them.

Cut to:

34: EXT; LANE IN FRONT OF OMAR'S HOUSE; DAY

The policemen forcefully make Mr Omar and his wife sit in the police jeep. The police jeep speeds up. Laila is crying and running behind the jeep. Mr and Mrs Omar are also weeping. Laila is not able to match the speed of the jeep and falls on the road. She can see the police jeep vanishing. She lies on the road and weeps bitterly.

Cut to:

35: EXT; DESERTED LANE; MID NIGHT

It is a full moon night. Four muscle men are running after Laila through the complex lanes of the small town to catch her and take her to the Imam. Laila runs to save herself. As she turns to the right from one lane to another, one powerful hand grasps her arm and pulls her into the dark. The palm then presses against her lips to smother her shrieks. She could not have shouted even if she wanted to. Four muscle men are puzzled as they were not able to trace Laila from the scene. After prowling around in the branching streets, they give up the chase and return.

The hand which grasps Laila's arms to save her happens to be of Ahmed's. With the muscle men gone, Ahmed removes his hand from Laila's mouth. They both come out from the dark and sit on a broken wall. Ahmed tries to ask about her in his sign language. Laila is happy to find someone just like her. Before long, the two are animatedly sharing their inner feelings. Ahmed tells about himself and Laila about herself. They hold each others hand compassionately. They feel that they are made for each other. They hug each other to signal that they would never leave the other.

Cut to:

36: EXT; A SMALL RAILWAY STATION AND A STATIONARY GOODS TRAIN; NIGHT

Ahmed and Laila are on a railway station holding each other's hand. They intend to climb on the goods train, which is about to leave the station. They climb and walk into an empty wagon.

Cut to:

37: INT; WAGON ; NIGHT

As the wagon door is open, moonlight comes in. There is straw lying on the floor of the wagon. Ahmed and Laila lie down on the floor and speak in sign language. Ahmed holds her hand and gazes into her eye with love.

Cut to:

38:EXT; RAILWAY STATION AND GOODS TRAIN; NIGHT

The goods train begin to move away from the railway station.

Cut to:

39: EXT; A GREEN VALLEY; MORNING

A very beautiful green valley where flowers have grown and a lot of wild palm, coconut palm, almond and other fruit-bearing trees are visible. A river meanders through the valley. The valley is not spoilt by inhabitation. There is a rail track on an old bridge over the river. A goods train is seen approaching the river bridge. The train slows down gradually as it is nearing the bridge. The train passes over the bridge in slow motion. One wagon doors open and Ahmed and Laila look out to see the area outside. A steel board alongside the bridge bears the sign 'NO MANS LAND BETWEEN IRAN & IRAQ BORDER'. Ahmed and Laila jump out of the wagon and the goods train leave them behind in the valley. Both are very happy to see the greenery with no human habitation but many birds flying within the valley. Many ducks are floating in the river. Ahmed and Laila are laughing as if they have found a heaven. They are running from one fruit-bearing tree to another to pluck the fruits and eat. They are showing different types of fruit to each other. When they have eaten enough, Ahmed plucks a flower and puts it in Laila's hair and gives a bunch of flower to her as a present. Laila is moved by Ahmed's sentiments and gets lost in his eyes. She sees love in his eyes and is overwhelmed and her eyes are full of tears. Ahmed hugs her. After a minute they are roaming around the area holding each other's hand. They reach a spot where trees bowing from the high winds of storm have formed a canopy of leaves. They go closer to the thicket and find a hut covered by bush. The hut is surrounded by a broken wall. The outside wall has a small plate bearing the sign: 'Security Post'. Ahmed and Laila go inside the broken walls and find that the door of the hut is locked from outside. Ahmed picks up a stone and hits on the lock of the door. The locks gives way. Ahmed and Laila walk into the room. The hut has three rooms. One of the room is damaged but the other two are liveable.

Cut to:

40: INT; BEDROOM; DAY

Ahmed and Laila are in the bedroom. Ahmed opens the windows. Now there is ample light in the room. The room has all the required furniture for two people: one sofa, two armchairs, four chairs, one double bed with mattress, bed sheet, towel and pillows. They find a cupboard full of clothes for man and woman. There is another door which leads to another room. Ahmed opens the door and walks into the room. Laila follows him.

Cut to:

41:INT ; KITCHEN ROOM ; DAY

This is actually a kitchen. Ahmed and Laila open the windows of the kitchen. They start dusting the room. After cleaning it, they return to the bedroom.

Cut to:

42:INT; BEDROOM; DAY

Ahmed and Laila dust the room. They are very happy to find a shelter in this lonely place. They hug each other. They choose suitable clothes and towels for themselves from the cupboard and walk out of the room.

Cut to:

43: EXT; RIVER BANK; DAY

Ahmed and Laila are on the riverbank. They are preparing to take bath in the river. They are standing a little away from each other. They take off their clothes and go into the river to take a dip. Laila is feeling shy. Ahmed is looking the other side to make Laila comfortable. After swimming for a few minutes, they come out of the river and dry themselves with their towel. After wearing their clothes, they come closer and look into each other's eye for a few minutes and then embrace each other.

It seems as if they have got their ultimate desires fulfilled. The valley appears to be happy and very beautiful among the two lovers who are innocent and in love with each other.

Fade out;

FADE IN

<u>44:INT; A CONFERENCE HALL; NIGHT</u>

After one year (on screen caption)

President Ashfaq Hussain of Iraq calls an urgent meeting of his cabinet colleagues in his conference room. The Iraqi flag is seen on the two sides of the chair of the President. This is a secret meeting.

<u>President</u>

"There is a sudden development which you all should know."

He beckons one of his Ministers to elaborate.

<u>Minister</u>

"One of our technologists has made a prototype of almost perpetual motion machine with the help of magnets, round springs, fission of silicon and a device able to convert gravitational energy into linear energy. Secondly while doing continuous research in chemistry, one of our Chemical Engineers has created a new gas, which has marvellous property of sudden expansion and contraction in its volume due to the change in temperature. Whereas another technologist has taken note of this marvellous property and has made a sophisticated machine, which has propelling function like a steam engine. Actually the cyclic rotation of this gas within the solar electricity fuelled hot and cold chambers, creates effect of sudden burst and contraction in the volume of this gas, resulting into a propelling action that gives various speeds to a wheel or a fly wheel, based on the temperature level in the hot and cold chambers. These two inventions can effectively replace fossil fuel driven engines. We need to start large-scale productions of these engines for sale around the world. This would make oil and gas redundant. The President needs to formulate our policy now."

Everybody looks at the President.

<u>President</u>

"We should start a large scale production of the machine and keep them in our store houses till the time our oil and gas stock are exhausted. We need to accelerate our sale. Now how can we increase our oil sale?"

<u>Minister</u>

" We can lower our prices."

<u>President</u>

" This is sure to invite OPEC's criticism."

<u>Minister</u>

" We would stop direct sale but route through an agent in London so that we could shift our blames to the agent."

<u>President</u>

"The contract with the agent should be such that the agent may not be able to expose us."

<u>Minister</u>

"I will take care of that."

<u>President</u>

" This whole operation will be treated as top secret. I expect all of you to keep it a secret including your family members."

Everybody nods in affirmation.

<u>President</u>

"Now we can dismiss the meeting."

The President gets up and so does his entire cabinet colleague.

Fade out;

FADE IN

<u>45:INT; MERIDIEN HOTEL'S LOBBY, CAIRO; DAY</u>

There are many journalists and cameramen in the lobby of this hotel. A big board indicates that a meeting of OPEC members is going on in this hotel. Mrs Richard Blantyre handles the camera and Mr Richard Blantyre speaks into the camera. On a TV screen Mr Blantyre is seen reporting live.

<u>Mr Richard Blantyre</u>

"The OPEC met today in Cairo to review the situation arising from Iraq's export of oil and gas. They have increased the quantity of export. Iraq is selling its oil and gas at a price lower than that fixed by OPEC. Iraq responded that its agent in London is responsible for the sale. In today's meeting it has been decided that, henceforth, sales will not be routed through agents, brokers or intermediaries anymore. The OPEC sale will be direct to the buyer countries. Iraq has also agreed to this proposal. But the question, why did Iraq sell its oil at a lower price, remains unanswered?"

"This is Richard Blantyre reporting live from Cairo."

Fade out;

FADE IN

<u>46: INT; HOTEL BAR; NIGHT</u>

<u>After one month (on screen caption)</u>

Mr and Mrs Richard Blantyre are in a relaxed mood and accepting two mugs of beer from a bartender, they go to a table and sit.

<u>Mr Richard Blantyre</u>

"Darling, why has Iraq's oil sale not reduced? It still is higher than fixed by OPEC."

<u>Mrs Blantyre</u>

"There must be some mechanism or some trick to achieve that, I suppose."

<u>Mr Blantyre</u>

"There may be some concealed benefit of some form and that is why the Iraqi oil sale would not come down."

<u>Mrs Blantyre</u>

"But why are they doing this?"

<u>Mr Blantyre</u>

"I wish I knew! But we can figure out their mode of operation if we can get the copies of bills of oil export and import."

<u>Mrs Blantyre</u>

" Mr Tariq Hussain, the old drunkard, you met in Aziz's party can help. He is the head clerk in Oil export billing department."

<u>Mr Blantyre</u>

" What about import?"

Mr Sartaj Zamani, the Iranian journalist, is seen taking a mug of beer from a mini bar. Mr Blantyre beckons Mr Zamani to come to their table. Mr Zamani joins them.

<u>Zamani</u>

"A nice way to spend the evening!"

<u>Mr Blantyre</u>

" Do you know someone in the import depot, who can provide the copies of bills of recent imports".

<u>Zamani</u>

" Why do you need them?"

<u>Mr Blantyre</u>

"This will be helpful in my research. I will give you a copy of my research papers later."

Zamani

"Yes, I know one person but I doubt his resourcefulness."

Mr Blantyre

"I can suitably reward this man."

Zamani

" Well, then there should be absolutely no problem."

Mr Blantyre

"Can you get this information as soon as possible."

Zamani

"Okay".

They enjoy their beer and the calm evening.

Cut to:

47: INT ; HOTEL ROOM; NIGHT

Mr and Mrs Blantyre are sitting on chairs and studying some papers.

Mrs Blantyre

" Your doubt was well placed."

Mr Blantyre

"You can see that the oil export bill has an adjustment item towards the cost of import, which never occurred. You can see the import bills."

Mrs Blantyre

" Why are they clearing their stock by selling cheap?"

Mr Blantyre

" Now, that is a million dollar question".

Mrs Blantyre

"This report cannot go through the telecast because USA is also a beneficiary. What if we give this to Zamani for publication in his paper."

Mr Blantyre

"That is a great idea. It would look like a result of Iranian espionage."

They look at each other smilingly.

FADE OUT ;

FADE IN

48:INT; THE MERIDIAN HOTEL'S LOBBY, CAIRO;DAY

There are many journalists and cameramen in the lobby of the hotel. A big board indicates that an emergency meeting of the OPEC nations is going on in this hotel. Mrs Richard Blantyre handles the camera and Mr Richard Blantyre is in front of the camera. He is seen reporting live.

<u>Mr Richard Blantyre</u>

"After Iran discovered the fact that Iraq was deceitful in exporting its oil at prices below OPEC level, an emergency meeting of OPEC has been convened today in Cairo to consider the whole issue. All OPEC countries, particularly Iran, are furious about Iraq's blatant breach of International agreement. Though Iraq's representative repeatedly accused Iran of making false allegations and propaganda against it, OPEC, however, finds some truth in Iran's accusations because the evidence show that Iraq's sale is booming. This meeting has reached nowhere due to Iraq's defiant posture."

"This is Richard Blantyre reporting from Cairo."

FADE OUT;

FADE IN

<u>49:EXT; GREEN VALLEY; DAY</u>

The green valley is breathtakingly beautiful with a verdant view of flowers. Ahmed and Laila are extremely happy. Ahmed is holding Laila in his arms and running around the surrounding area of flowers. He looks up at the sky to thank God. After a few moments, he puts Laila down on a thick grass bed. Ahmed also lies down and fondles Laila. He brings his head towards the swollen belly of Laila and tries to feel the pulse. He is gently tickling on her swollen belly. Laila is pregnant and both are very happy. Ahmed takes out a fruit from one of his pocket and put it in Laila's mouth and then tries to bite the half of the fruit with his teeth. Both eat each half of the fruit.

FADE OUT;

FADE IN

<u>50:EXT; HIGH SEA OF SAT AL ARAB; NIGHT</u>

Overview of high sea area. Oil drilling station with Iranian flag is seen. There are many oil tanker-ships within and around the drilling station. The Iranian guards in their trawlers are actively policing the area using binoculars to see any intruder. Activity in the area appears unusual.

Cut to:
<u>51: EXT; UNDERWATER; NIGHT</u>

There are many divers with oxygen cylinders on their back and carrying a huge pipe trying to connect to a storage tank underneath the sea. They are putting caps to seal this pipe under water against any leakage.

Cut to:
<u>52: EXT; HIGH SEA AREA OF SAT AL ARAB; NIGHT</u>

Divers are on the surface of the sea and are happily shaking hands with one another. One diver amongst them waves a torch to signal the completion of task assigned to them. One man standing on top of the oil drilling station after seeing the signal turns around and makes his thumbs up with a smile to let his senior officers know about the completion of the task, who are looking at him from a office window far behind in the drilling station.

FADE OUT;

FADE IN
<u>53:EXT; OUT OF BOUND AREA, BAGHDAD; MIDNIGHT</u>

Mr Richard Blantyre and Mr Sartaj Zamani are parking their car far away from the Iraqi Scientific Research Centre in Baghdad, an off-limit area for foreigners. They are carefully approaching the boundary of the Centre from behind and cross the boundary with the help of one bamboo. They reach the main area of the Centre. They are looking at any possible entrance point to enter into the Centre but are not able to find one. They hide themselves from a night patrol police car running around the Centre. Mr Sartaj Zamani is frightened.

<u>Sartaz Zamani</u> (low voice)
"If we are caught, you would go scot-free because you are American but I would be tortured to death on charges of espionage."

<u>Mr Richard Blantyre</u> (low voice)
"Do not worry."

<u>Sartaj Zamani</u>
"I am a journalist and not a spy. I should not have come here."

<u>Mr Richard Blantyre</u>
"Okay, we would go back."

Sartaj Zamani

"Unsuccessfully."

Both stealthily return to the boundary wall and again jump with the help of the bamboo to cross the high security wall. They come back to their car unhappy over the failure of their mission.

FADE OUT;

FADE IN

54: INT; ROOM; DAY

Laila is suffering with labour pains. Ahmed is trying to console her.

Cut to:

55: EXT: GREEN VALLEY: DAY

There is pin-drop silence outside the shelter of Laila and Ahmed as if nature is holding her breath to hear the sound of the arrival of new born baby.

Cut to:

56: INT:ROOM: Day

Laila and Ahmed are seen in the room. Laila feels relieved after delivering her child. A child is born. Ahmed happily holds the child in his hand, while Laila looks on. Ahmed keeps the child beside Laila. Laila is feeding her child happily.

FADE OUT;

FADE IN

57: INT; A BAR IN BAGHDAD; NIGHT

After two years (on screen caption)

Mr and Mrs Richard Blantyre are sitting on a table with their mug of beer. Mr Sartaj Zamani joins them.

Mrs Richard Blantyre

" Your Government has done the same. It is like tit for tat."

Zamani

"Iraqis are painting themselves as saints and us as sinners. Ashfaq Hussain has gone to the UN for justice in the matter with all his documentary proof and is demanding a huge compensation, which Altani has bluntly refused today."

<u>Mr Richard Blantyre</u>
"Iranians are equally good."

<u>Mrs Blantyre</u>
"Good or bad ?"

<u>Mr Richard Blantyre</u>
"Equally good in deceitful affairs."

<u>Zamani</u>

"Of course, they earned a lot and we stole a lot."

He laughs and so too Mr and Mrs Blantyre.

<u>Mr Richard Blantyre</u>
"Anyway Iraq's intelligence has done a good job by catching your people redhanded."

<u>Zamani</u>
"They cannot do anything to us."

They sip their beer.

FADE OUT;

FADE IN
<u>58:EXT; GREEN VALLEY; DAY</u>

Laila and Ahmed are running after their two-year-old child. They are playing hide and seek with their child. They are happy and laughing. Their surroundings appear lively due to the greener pasture including the variety of flowers and fruitbearing trees. It appears heavenly.

FADE OUT;

FADE IN
<u>59: EXT; IRAQI AIR-FIELD; DAY</u>

<u>Iraqi Air-field (on screen caption)</u>

Overview of Iraqi airfield, where heavy missile and ammunition movements are seen. It seems as if war has started. Fighter planes are taking off the ground. Air force personnel are extremely busy in their activities.

Cut to:
<u>60: EXT; OPEN FIELD NEAR BORDER; DAY</u>

Army personnel's activities are seen in the Iraqi area bordering Iran. Tank and heavy artillery's forward movement is seen. It gives a feel of war-like activity.

Cut to:

61: INT; UN SECURITY COUNCIL CHAMBER

This is an overview of a meeting of UN Security Council, where placards give the introduction of different countries. The Chairman appears to have passed an UN resolution in favour of Iraq as Iraqi representative looks happy. He shakes his hand with the Jordanian Ambassador. Whereas the Iranian representative is unhappy, tense and sitting alone.

Cut to:

62: INT; HOTEL ROOM; MORNING

This is the hotel room of Mr and Mrs Richard Blantyre. Morning sunlight is coming in from windows. Mr Blantyre is making tea. Mrs Blantyre is awake and is in bed in her nightgown. She puts on a small radio on the sideboard near the bed.

(Loud Voice from radio)

"This is the BBC World Service. Todays' top story is the dispute between Iraq and Iran, which is hotting up. Our Middle East specialist Mr Tim Baker is in the studio to analyse the situation for our listeners."

"Good Morning Mr Baker, tell us about the situation in the Middle east."

"Good morning, Nick. Actually the situation in Middle East is now explosive after Iran's refusal to honour the UN resolution. Iran has rejected the appeal of International community to honour the UN resolution, terming it as an appeal from the beneficiary countries to benefit its benefactor. Keeping in view Iran's defiant posture, Iraq has ordered its military to be in a state of high alert. Though it has clarified that this is a routine military exercise but many believe that this is a signal to Iran to come to a compromise. Perhaps Iraq's line of thinking was that Iran may not like to enter into a war that would prove costlier than paying compensation because it has been isolated in the International community."

[Pause]

"But contrary to this thinking, it is learnt that Iran has moved its military forward and is ready to pre-empt possible Iraqi strikes. This situation is extremely explosive. Both countries should refrain from a full-scale war, which would be devastating. Iran's thinking appears to be that despite the sympathy of the International community towards Iraq, no country would aid Iraq with military hardware. There may be a lip service but not actual material support. Hence to put Iraq on defensive, Iran has prepared itself for military showdown. This is a matter of prestige for both and hence a limited or a full-scale war is imminent in the present circumstances, which must be avoided. International community must help prevent a war in this region."

"Thanks Mr Baker."

Mr and Mrs Blantyre are sipping their morning tea.

Cut to:

<u>63:EXT; IRANIAN AIRFIELD; NIGHT</u>

<u>Iranian airfield (on screen caption)</u>

Overview of Iranian airfield where fighter planes are taking off one after another and missile launchers are firing continuously.

Cut to:

<u>64: EXT; BAGHDAD CITY; NIGHT</u>

<u>Baghdad city (on screen caption)</u>

This is an overview of Baghdad city in the night. Military siren is heard. Missiles are exploding after hitting the targets. Iranian fighter planes are flying above the city sky and bombing. Noises, cries, and wails fill the air.

Cut to:

<u>65: EXT; BAGHDAD CITY; MORNING</u>

Overview of Baghdad city appears to be reeling under the effect of devastating Iranian air attack. Smoke, fire, devastation and damaged buildings are visible. Movements of fire fighter vans are visible.

Cut to:

<u>66: EXT; BAGHDAD CITY, A DAMAGED BUILDING; MORNING</u>

Mr and Mrs Richard Blantyre are in front of a damaged building. Mrs Blantyre is filming the situation and her husband is reporting news live.

<u>Mr Richard Blantyre</u>

"Continuous Iranian air attack over last two days has inflicted large scale human casualties and damage to the property in Iraq. Last night's UN resolution and threat to put all around economic sanction against Iran has stopped the insane attacks today. Iraq has requested the UN to impose economic sanctions against Iran as it has violated human rights by targeting civilian population. More than five thousand people have died. Iraq exercised restraint and did not attack. The UN Security Council members have agreed to examine the details of human rights violation by Iran next week and discuss possible economic sanctions as per Iraq's request. President Ashfaq Hussain of Iraq has said that Iraq would not be sitting back and watching it like a coward but would settle the score. It would carry out a token air-attack on Iran for a day and would ensure that there is no human casualty."

"This is Richard Blantyre reporting from Baghdad."

Cut to:

67: INT; MINISTRY OF FOREIGN AFFAIRS,BAGHDAD

Iraqi spokesman is briefing the newsmen about the Iraqi token attack.

Spokesman

"Our human rights record has become more vibrant by ensuring that there was no loss of human lives in our successful token air attacks on Iran yesterday. Iraq has always upheld human right and desired similar actions by its neighbour. Unfortunately, the Iranian record in this matter has always been worse and we demand an all-round economic sanction against it for killing civilian population in Baghdad."

Cut to:

68: INT; HOTEL ROOM; DAY

Mr and Mrs Richard Blantyre are relaxing in their hotel room.

Mr Blantyre

"I cannot believe their claim that in a war they have been able to ensure hundred per cent safety of human lives."

Mrs Blantyre

"I am as sceptical as you are. Perhaps we can check on it."

Mr Blantyre

"Yes, we will. Perhaps Zamani can help us."

Cut to:

<u>69: EXT; HYATT REGENCY HOTEL, TEHRAN; DAY</u>

Tehran - Iran (on screen caption)

Mr and Mrs Blantyre and Mr Zamani come in a car, which stops in the compound of the hotel. Mr and Mrs Blantyre get down from the car and Mr Zamani drives the car away. Mrs Blantyre sits on a bench in the compound along with her camera and equipment. Both are very tired.

<u>Mrs Blantyre</u>
"I am extremely tired."

<u>Mr Blantyre</u> (sits near her on the bench)
"Yes, it was too hectic."

<u>Mrs Blantyre</u>
"Should we back off? So far we have found nothing."

<u>Mr Blantyre</u>
"They have bombed only the military buildings or open fields away from population."

<u>Mrs Blantyre</u>
"Yes."

<u>Mr Blantyre</u>
"Let us try once more tomorrow and then back off."

Cut to:

<u>70: EXT; GREEN VALLEY; DAY</u>

Green valley, the paradisal abode of Ahmed and Laila has been completely devastated. It is in ruins. All the fruitbearing trees and vegetation have ruined due to continuous and merciless bombing. Mr and Mrs Blantyre and Mr Sartaz Zamani are carefully approaching the shelter of Ahmed and Laila. The hut is completely destroyed. The dead bodies of Ahmed, Laila and their infant son are lying on the ground within the roofless hut. Laila and Ahmed were clutching their infant son and holding each other by arms before their death. It appears that they were braving deranged, gruesome acts of bombing before their certain death. The scene is extremely tragic, which brings tears in the eyes of Mr and Mrs Blantyre. Mrs Blantyre is filming whereas Mr Blantyre is looking at the dead bodies in utter shock. Mr Zamani is trying to console Mr Blantyre.

Cut to:

71: INT; HOTEL ROOM;

Mr and Mrs Blantyre are watching the TV report filmed by them.

(Mr Richard Blantyre on TV screen) (V. O)

"Iraq's claim of sparing human lives in a token war is totally wrong. You can see on your screen three dead bodies found in the area of no man's land bordering Iraq. The bodies have been identified: one as Ahmed of Iraq and the other Laila of Iran. They were deaf and dumb, and parents of a dead infant. Iraq may now defend that Iranians have killed Ahmed, and therefore it had targeted Laila, the Iranian woman. But what about the infant child who was born in no mans land and had parents from Iran and Iraq? Why should he bear the brunt of the hostility between the two countries when he does not belong to either country? History is witness that innocent people have always suffered the consequences of hostile circumstances created by the Governments to meet their selfish ends. Why go to a war when it would kill human being? Pushing the circumstances towards war is also an abuse of human rights, and both Iraq and Iran are guilty on this count."

Cut to:

72: INT; NEWS CONFERENCE ROOM, MINSTRY OF FOREIGN AFFAIRS, BAGHDAD

Many journalists are assembled in this room. The spokesman of Iraq is standing on the podium to answer questions of journalists.

One Journalist

"Do you think that the discovery of three dead people in token war contrary to your claim is a matter of concern and that it would weaken your request in UN to impose economic sanctions against Iran."

Spokesman

" No, first of all, there was no death. The story on ABC TV by Richard Blantyre is a bunch of lies and a fabricated video recording directed against Iraq. Richard Blantyre is an undesirable man and our Government has asked him to leave Iraq within twentyfour hours."

Cut to:

73: EXT; BAGHDAD AIRPORT; DAY

Mr and Mrs Richard Blantyre are going along with their cabin bags towards airplane of Delta Airlines parked at a distance. Mr Blantyre's mood appears to be gloomy.

Mrs Blantyre

"Honey, you look thoroughly dejected. Why should you brood over the events when you know that we did our job well by telling the truth?"

They are climbing the staircase to get into the plane.

FADE OUT

The End

4

A Molten Motive
(Short Story)

Mr John Fein, his wife Mrs John Fein and daughter Ms Lisa lived in a small town, 100 km north of Belfast. Mr John Fein was an ideal Irish Republican Army activist and had disagreements of ethos with his fellow colleagues, who were threatened by his ethics and decided to eliminate him. So they murdered Mr John Fein.

After her husband's murder by his IRA colleagues due to his dissent, Mrs John Fein found her life miserable at her native place in Ireland and decided to move to London along with her nine- year-old daughter Lisa with an objective to settle down there.

She got a job in a Girl's school in London and her daughter was also admitted in the same school. They both finally settled in London. Lisa was an intelligent girl and as she grew up she opted for physics as her subject. She was very impressed by initial wireless device, i.e Morse's key device. She innovated and improvised two micro devises – one of them was a ring with a micro tip placed on the knob of the ring to work like a key to send radio messages and another a micro digital receiver, which used to receive the messages and decode it. The message could be seen on the digital panel of the receiver and could be heard from the inbuilt microphone. The receiver operated on battery whereas micro keyring used to send messages due to energy from body warmth and earth contact. Though this device was not commercially viable due to tremendous advancement in communication technology, she used this device to communicate with her mother when she was out from her home. The micro receiver was placed in the drawing room of their flat.

Lisa finished her college education and got a job of research scholar. Later she married Mr Geoffrey Hunt, a police officer from bomb disposal unit of London. She gave birth to a boy. He was named Sharn. Lisa in order to complete her research work, needed to go to Wisconsin University in USA for six months. She required visas for herself, her son and her mother. So she went to the Embassy of USA in London along with her son, Sharn. She waited in the consular hall to receive the visas, which was said to be ready in two hours.

During this hour, thirty heavily armed terrorists stormed the Embassy building and took position on the vital points. They cut all the connections of telephone, telex, fax, wireless and also seized all the cellular, satellite and wireless phones. All the officers of the Embassy along with the Ambassador were locked in the Ambassador's room. All the visa and passport applicants were taken hostage in the consular hall where four armed men kept watch on them. The armed men installed sophisticated bombs on the walls of the Embassy. All the hostages in consular hall were stunned wi h the sudden incident. None was sure as to what actually happened. After a while a CNN live coverage on the TV in the consular hall disclosed the sudden incident.

CNN flashed a live news coverage sayin: "This is total surprise for all of us that a moderate member of the house of Lords of UK, Mr John Goldsmith, has now resorted to extortion in order to teach America a lesson for its favour to the settlement of the Irish problem. A wireless message received by the London Police Headquarter confirms that Mr Goldsmith and his armed ultranationalist comrades have stormed the USA Embassy building in London and has held all the officials including the Ambassador hostage. They have also taken hostage the visitors and visa applicants in the consular hall. They have severed all the connections of communication. They can contact the outside but not vise versa. He has demanded that the visiting delegation of IRA in Washington may be arrested, and for favouring IRA, the USA must pay his new found organization, 'Group of Ultra Nationalists of UK' a sum of US$ 1 Bn,10 percent each in pound sterling, US$, Euro and Yen, and the rest in god and diamond to meet its expenses to fight the forces meant for disintegration of UK. The amount must be paid within 24 hours, failing which will lead systematic slaughter of hostage. They also request for four helicopters so that they can easily flee from there. Authority in

Washington is worried about the safety of the diplomats. Police and military forces have cordoned off the area and a stand off is expected till a solution is found to this problem."

Everybody in consular hall became frightened to learn that after 24 hours, killing would start if demands were not met. A few old and weak ladies were having nervous breakdown and were yelling. A few were hurt in initial scuffle with armed man. A few were oozing blood from their wound or nose. They needed immediate help of a doctor but were denied by the armed men.

Sharn gets up after his two-hour sleep and starts crying. As he was hungry, he became restless and was crying. Four armed men asked Lisa to stop the boy from crying. She told that he was hungry and needed milk, as he was not breastfed. Despite her efforts to comfort Sharn, he was crying non-stop, which made all the armed men uneasy. At last, they allowed Lisa to go to the kitchen of the Embassy on the first floor to prepare milk for the child. She fed Sharn. While returning she was surprised to notice the familiar faces of three armed men in position. She tried to recollect as to where she had seen these three faces. At last she remembered them as the three assassins out of six who came to slay her father. She concluded that Mr Goldsmith may be doing all this under pressure from these IRA men. These IRA man cannot be part and parcel of 'The group of ultra-nationalist of UK'. These IRA extortionists may be using him to give the scene a different colour and are working in disguise to get the ransom. But what could be the reason of pressure to Mr Goldsmith?

When night set in, Lisa sent a message to her mother through her micro-key of her ring. She advised her mom to keep her presence in USA Embassy secret as she can now provide information about inside scenario. She says that Goldsmith is working under pressure of IRA as she has recognized three armed IRA men as murderers of her father and that local authority must find out the reasons of Mr Goldsmith's pressure. On receipt of this information a few expert detectives worked hard and found the reason of pressure. They found that his daughter, supposed to be holidaying in Spain is missing. Spanish Police got a confidential red alert about the kidnapping of Nina, Goldsmith's daughter. The quick combing operations during whole night by Spanish police in and around the area of sea-beach hotel resort brought a good result. She was rescued by the police from a basement of a dilapidated house in a village after encounter of four suspected person heavily armed with ammunitions. The police managed to kill them and save Nina. She was brought to the London Police Headquarters. Next day in the morning, when Mr Goldsmith contacted officials in London Police Headquarters with his demand, he was surprised to hear the voice of his daughter, who informed him that the Police had rescued her after killing all her captors. She was now free and he need not work under pressure.

After knowing this Mr Goldsmith became vocal and non-cooperative. Realizing the truth and seeing non-cooperation from Mr Goldsmith, the actual man behind the scene Mr Rudar Fienman exposed himself as the key-man. He said that Mr Goldsmith was a scapegoat and that he belonged to a group of actual IRA. He threatened to kill all the hostages if the ransom was not paid before deadline.

CNN flashed this new development in its headline news, which Lisa came to know from the TV in consular hall. On the second day every body in the consular hall were very tired including Lisa as they had not been able to sleep properly on their chairs. Lisa saw that the bombs planted were very powerful and even if the ransom was paid, these IRA extortionists would keep the bombs live before they leave the Embassy to reach their safe hideouts. She sent a message for his husband to disguise himself as a doctor and come inside the Embassy for treating ailing patients.

Sharn again started crying for food in the morning, she was again allowed to go to kitchen on the first floor to prepare milk. While returning from the kitchen, she became instrumental for an accident, making it seem natural. Sharn fell down from the stairs and started bleeding from nose. Lisa started crying asking for medical help for her child. She argued either she may be allowed to go out or a doctor may be allowed to come in to treat her son. She said that her husband was a doctor and that he should be allowed to come in. The IRA men granted permission and allowed her husband to come inside the Embassy to treat her child. Mr Geoffrey Hunt came in along with a medical kit and treated his son and other yelling old men and women. Sharn was happy to find his father. Mr Hunt sat in the consular hall till the final stage of incident.

Before deadline, the local authority in London provided the IRA terrorists the ransom and four helicopters. All the armed men before climbing onto helicopter switched on the bomb devices. Mr Rudar

Fienman took Mr Goldsmith along with him at gun point to use him as a bargain chip to ensure the safe return to his hideout in the jungle of Northern Ireland. He warned the inmates of the Embassy and the local authority to refrain from entering or leaving or even touch the building of the Embassy as the whole premise had been effected with a laser beam and any major disturbances in the wave length of laser rays emitted by the bomb device planted in the Embassy would explode killing all the inmates. If any attempt were made to harm them enroute to their hideout in the helicopter, they would explode these bombs by remote control device in their hand.

Mr Rudar Fienman along with his associates and Mr Goldsmith flew from the roof of the Embassy building and were heading towards the jungle of Northern Ireland. As Mr Goldsmith is also with them, the local authority had to save him from the clutches of IRA terrorists as it was suspected that they would kill Mr Goldsmith to avenge his being an anti-IRA force.

Hence local authority made arrangement to rescue him. Sixteen military helicopter followed the four IRA terrorists carrier helicopter. Mr Fienman repeatedly warned the military helicopter of the consequences if an attempt was made to harm them. Military captain leading the helicopter squadron promised and assured not to harm them at all but pleaded for the release of Mr Goldsmith. Mr Fienman threatened to kill Mr Goldsmith if any attempt to rescue him was made or to obstruct them before reaching their hideout. All sixteen helicopters were flying over the sea of England and the military captain was talking to Mr Fienman for releasing Mr Goldsmith.

When Mr Rudar Fienman left the Embassy along with his associates and took away all the communication equipment, Mr Hunt started diffusing the bombs. He was impressed to see the masterly crafting of bomb devices. He was puzzled to think as to how he should defuse these bombs. The local authorities were in touch with him only through one-way communication device at the residence of Lisa. Authorities were not able to order the military captain on the helicopter to take any action until they got a confirmation from Mr Hunt that he had defused all the bombs. The military captain had an action plan provided he got a confirmation from the authorities on successful diffusion of bombs before IRA terrorists crossed the sea of England. Local authorities at Lisa's residence were awaiting Hunt's confirmation about the bomb disposal.

After a long drawn effort Mr Hunt was able to defuse few bombs and clear a passage. He asked for help from bomb disposal squad. The bomb squad could enter into the building and defuse all the bombs. The military captain was eagerly waiting for the confirmation of everyone rescued from the Embassy.

Just before the completion of journey above the sea of England, Mr Hunt confirmed the completion of task and on instruction of the military captain all sixteen helicopters shot an arrow, tail of which was tied with strong nylon rope and in control at their end. Arrow was pointed towards the bottom hold of enemy helicopter and therefore a group of four helicopters were in control of one enemy helicopter due to the rope tied with it. Suddenly military helicopters dived towards sea surface very fast making each enemy helicopter imbalance, and making them fall into the sea. In this course of action all sixteen helicopters were flying just above the sea surface, whereas enemy helicopters were drowned in the sea with every body on board. Drowning into the sea did not allow the enemy helicopters to burst in flame. Armed military divers jumped from their helicopter into the sea to save Mr Goldsmith and the box containing ransom amount. As divers were more in number, they killed Mr Rudar Fienman and all his associates. Thus the entire IRA terrorists found their sea grave. Military personnel came back to their bases safely along with Mr Goldsmith and the box containing ransom amount.

All the hostages in the Embassy of USA were free. They were very happy with tears in their eyes as they found a new lease of life. Ms Nina was happy to get his father Mr Goldsmith back. Lisa's mother was happy to get back Lisa, Hunt and Sharn safe and sound. Everybody was very proud of Lisa's radio communication device, actually a micro Morse device improvised by her.

XXXXXXXXXX

A Molten Motive
[Screenplay]

Fade In:
1 -INT: Flat , Drawing Room: Day

Mr John Fein, father of an eight-year-old daughter named Lisa, is sitting on a chair. Lisa is also sitting on another chair. They are in a relax mood.

Mr John Fein
"Initially solid such as metal, earth, etc, was considered to be the medium of communication."

Lisa
"But now wireless technology is the in thing."

Mr John Fein
"But in olden days when the communication system was not yet developed, earth or metal was considered a medium for it."

Lisa
" How?"

Mr John Fein
"If you put your ear on a Railway track, you will be able to hear the sound of a train that is running on the track in the close vicinity even though you may not able to see the train due to distance."

Lisa
" Which was the first communication device?"

Mr John Fein
"In fact, I do not know but I think it was Morse's device."

Lisa
"What does it contain Papa?"

Mr John Fein
"Morse had developed a sound code. The sender could send messages by ticking the device at one place and the recipient could hear these ticks of a particular pattern prescribed by Morse at the other place and then decode."

Lisa
"Do we use it now?"

Mr John Fein
"No, this is an obsolete device now. The wireless technology has taken over."

Mrs John Fein steps into the drawing room from the exit door with two cups of tea and gives one cup to Mr John. Lisa is busy reading a book.

Mrs John Fein
"Honey, where are you going? What is that action plan?"

Mr John Fein
"Darling, I do not know anything."

Mr John Fein
"Our IRA bosses keep their action plan secret till the last minute. Anyway I do not bother as long as it helps liberate our mother land from the English rule."

Mrs John Fein
"How long would it take? When will you be back home? Is there any danger? This is your first adventure. I am afraid, please be careful."

Mr John Fein
"I am a freedom fighter and so I have to accept dangerous situations. Anyway, I shall be extremely cautious. I will be back by tomorrow morning."

Mrs John Fein
"May God help us."

Cut to:
2- EXT: IN FRONT OF A MANSION, ROAD: MIDNIGHT

The night is dark and the atmosphere weird. It rains from time to time. Between the thunderclaps and the flashes of lightning, fearsome faces of masked men are seen.

Masked men are seen spread over in this area equipped with AK-47 rifles. They all are very alert. After a few second, the mansion's door is opened and one elderly man in his night gown is forcibly brought by a group of masked man. He is made to sit in a van parked on the side of road. All the masked men get into the van and it moves fast on the road.

There are three people including a driver in the frontal section of the van. They are uneasy. They have unmasked themselves. Mr John Fein is one of them.

Mr John Fein
"Jack, is this your action plan to kidnap our own man, an Irish businessman? What has he done wrong?"

<u>Jack</u>

"He plays an anti IRA role. He is pro-English."

<u>Mr John Fein</u>

"As far as I know he plays no role. He is a simple man and extends his help towards charity for Irish social welfare."

<u>Jack</u>

"No, you do not know anything."

<u>Mr John Fein</u>

"I know it. You want to take ransom from his family and enrich yourself. This will not help our freedom movement. If this is the fight for freedom, then I am not in."

<u>Jack</u>

"You are making a mountain out of the mole. For our action plans we need money and no one can give away what we need. I do not want to sustain on doles."

<u>Mr John Fein</u>

"A freedom fighter does not lead a luxurious life. This action plan is just to enrich the luxury for you and your goons. I am out of this freedom movement. "

<u>Jack</u>

" It is not a wise decision on your part. We do not allow dissent."

<u>Mr John Fein</u>

" You cannot stop me from quitting. Please stop the van, I will get down."

Jack murmurs something which Mr John Fein does not hear. The driver soon stops the van and Mr John gets down. The van moves fast again on the road.

<u>Jack</u>

"We do not allow any body to quit."

Mr John Fein is seen standing on the road.

Cut to:

<u>3- INT: FLAT, DRAWING ROOM : NIGHT</u>

Mrs John Fein opens the door and Mr John Fein steps in. He looks gloomy and is totally drenched in rain. Mrs John Fein gives him a large towel to dry himself. He takes off his shirt and trousers. He is drying himself.

Mrs John Fein

"What happened? You are back early?"

Mr John Fein

"I was in a wrong place with wrong people."

Mrs John Fein

"What?"

Mr John Fein

"They have a molten motive. They are not true freedom fighters. Actually they are criminals in the garb of freedom fighter. They kidnap our own people for ransom and luxury. They have kidnapped Mr David Cooper for extortion, the famous noble Irish business tycoon."

Mrs John Fein

"Is that so?"

Mr John Fein

"Yes, I have left them and I am out."

As they were conversing, Lisa, their eight-year-old daughter, wakes up and comes into the drawing room from her bedroom.

Lisa

"Mom, what is wrong?"

Mrs John Fein

"Nothing, my dear. Go to bed and sleep. I am coming."

Lisa goes to bedroom. Immediately the doorbell is heard. Mr John Fein opens the door. Six IRA personnel get into the room forcibly.

Mr John Fein

"What is this?"

One man

"Why dare you quit our organization? You are a freedom fighter."

Mr John Fein

"Yes I am a freedom fighter but you all are a group of criminals, extortionists and murderers".

Other man

"It is absolutely necessary to murder the foreign rulers. "

Mr John Fein

"It is right but not our own people like Mr David Cooper."

One man

"We need to do some kind of politics and for that sacrifices are required."

<u>Mr John Fein</u>

"Sacrifice of own people, murder of own people."

<u>Other man</u>

"You must understand our compulsions."

<u>Mr John Fein</u>

"I have understood and I have decided to quit."

Cut to:

<u>4-INT: LISA'S BED ROOM: NIGHT</u>

The bedroom was dark. Lisa could not sleep and is watching her father talk to six strangers in the drawing room from behind the curtains of her bedroom. Though she is able to see the faces of all the strangers she is not able to hear their conversation properly due to the thunderclaps and sound of gust which is shaking the windows. She is, however, able to sense the unpleasant argument.

Cut to:

<u>5- INT: DRAWING ROOM: NIGHT</u>

Mr John Fein is talking to six strangers. Mrs John Fein is looking at them.

<u>One man</u>

" You have finally decided to quit."

<u>Mr John Fein</u>

" Yes, I am not in your group now."

<u>Other man</u>

"So be it. We do not allow any dissenter to live. You need to die."

He takes out his pistol to shoot Mr John Fein, but Mrs Fein is alert and she pushes this man and thus his pistol slips out of his hand and falls out of the window, a portion of which is open for ventilation. She then starts shouting:" Help, Help, Help." But her voice is not heard by anyone due to heavy rain and thunderclaps.

The strangers bring out hockey sticks from behind their back and attack Mrs John Fein and Mr John Fein. Due to a hard hit on her shoulder, Mrs John Fein faints and falls down on the floor. She looks almost dead. All six people surround Mr John Fein and stab him in his stomach many times. He dies instantly.

Cut to:
<u>6-INT: BEDROOM: NIGHT</u>

It is dark in the bedroom. Lisa has not slept yet and is frightened to see six strangers beating her mother and father with hockey sticks. She hides herself behind the long curtains, hanging from the pelmet of the bedroom. She is sobbing and is full of tear. Her sob could not be heard due to heavy rain, frequent thunderclaps and sound of gust.

Cut to:
<u>7-INT: DRAWING ROOM: NIGHT</u>

After finishing their assignment of killing Mr and Mrs John Fein, the six IRA terrorists are preparing to leave the house.

<u>One man</u>
" Check all the rooms if anybody else is there."

Five of his accomplice go to the bedroom and come back.

<u>Other man</u>
" There is no one in this house."

<u>One man</u>
" He had a daughter."

<u>Other man</u>
" No, there is no one. She must have gone on vacation to her relative."

<u>One man</u>
" Then let us go."

They exit from the door.

Cut to:
<u>8- INT: DRAWING ROOM: NIGHT</u>

Lisa weeping uncontrollably comes into the drawing room from bedroom. She is splashing water on the face of her mother and father to wake them up. After a while Mrs John Fein wakes up and realizes the situation. She finds her husband dead. Mrs John Fein and Lisa are bitterly crying but their sound is not heard in the roaring thunderclaps.

Cut to:
<u>9- INT: DRAWING ROOM: MORNING</u>

Policemen are seen taking fingerprints and photographs of the dead body of Mr John Fein. Two journalists with their cameras and notebooks have also reached there to find about the incident.

<u>One Journalist</u>
"Chief Detective, Mr Fouler, could you please tell us about the motive for this gruesome murder?"

<u>Second Journalist</u>
"Have you found anything regarding this incident?"

<u>Chief Detective</u>
"Yes, We have questioned Mrs John Fein. This is a consequence of gang-war and nothing else. We have nothing to do in this case. Mr John Fein was an IRA terrorist and has been killed by his ganf members due to dissent and personal enmity."

<u>One Journalist</u>
"What action do you contemplate to take against the murderer?"

<u>Chief Detective</u>
" This was a personal revenge. We are doing our routine duty. The case is closed here and now."

Cut to:
<u>10- EXT: CORRIDOR OF A GIRL'S SCHOOL: MORNING</u>

Mrs John Fein is passing through the corridor. The students' great Mrs John Fein saying "Good Morning madam" but each of them stops for a while to see at her going towards the office of Principal. Mrs John Fein also greats them "Good Morning".

Cut to:
<u>11- INT : PRINCIPAL'S OFFICE ROOM ; MORNING</u>

Mrs John Fein enters into the room. The lady Principal is sitting on her chair and is going through some papers.

<u>Mrs John Fein</u>
"Good morning, Maam,"

<u>Principal</u>
"Good morning, Mrs Fein. Where were you these days? You took leave without any intimation to the school."

<u>Mrs John Fein</u>
"I guess you know maam. My husband was murdered and I was busy with all the formalities."

<u>Principal</u>
" You never told us that he was an IRA terrorist? "

Mrs John Fein keeps quiet.

<u>Principal</u>
" You should be knowing better as you are working in a British Government School. You must be truthful towards your school, colleagues and students."

<u>Mrs John Fein</u>
"It was his conviction and...."

<u>Principal</u>
" But you knew and abetted him. Mrs Fein, you cannot work in this school under these circumstances until we have your proven credentials."

<u>Mrs John Fein</u>
" Maam, I am helpless...."

<u>Principal</u>
"Then I cannot help you in these circumstances. Instead I dismiss you from this job, it would be better if you resign."

<u>Mrs John Fein</u>
" When you have already decided, then I have no choice."

<u>Principal</u>
"These are the instructions from my bosses."

<u>Mrs John Fein</u>
"Thank you. I will leave my resignation letter with your secretary."

She gets up from the chair and goes out of the room.

Cut to :
<u>12- INT ; BED ROOM OF MRS JOHN FEIN : NIGHT</u>

Lisa is in her bed. She is weeping. Mrs John Fein is lying beside Lisa and trying to console her.

<u>Mrs John Fein</u>
" Why do you weep? Tell me, what happened?"

<u>Ms Lisa</u>
"My friends in school are not talking to mel. They told me that they will not talk."

Mrs John Fein

"Do not worry. I will talk to your class teacher or alternatively you can go to some other school."

Lisa is pacified and tries to sleep in her mother's lap.

Cut to:
13 : EXT : TELEPHONE BOOTH ; DAY

One man after carefully watching the nearby area enters into telephone booth. He puts a coin into the telephone equipment and dials a number. After a pause he speaks: " Am I speaking to Mrs John Fein?"

Man (after a pause)
"Mrs Fein, my name is David and I liked your husband very much. He was truly a brave man. You must leave this place immediately because the IRA members thought that they had left you dead at your home. They fear that John might have told you many things, including their hideouts which you may divulge to the British police for revenge. They have ordered for your elimination along with your child. Now under these circumstances you must immediately leave the town and go to a safer place. This is my earnest advice to you being a friend of your husband."

After a while he hangs up the handset and goes away from the telephone booth.

Cut to:
14: EXT ; MOVING TRAIN ON ITS TRACK ; DAY

A British train is seen running fast on a railway track.

Cut to:
14 : INT ; TRAIN COMPARTMENT ; DAY

Mrs John Fein and Lisa are seen inside a compartment of the British train. There are many passengers . Everyone is talking in a low voice.

Lisa
"Where are we going, mom? "

Mrs John Fein
" We are going to London."

<u>Ms Lisa</u>
"But, why...?"

<u>Mrs John Fein</u>
"Our lives are in danger here. These gang members want to kill you and me just like your father."

<u>Lisa</u>
"Where will we live in London? We do not have anyone there."

<u>Mrs John Fein</u>
"You need not worry, my darling. I will take care of you. We can do something over there. Do not worry."

<u>Lisa</u>
"What about my school and my friends?"

<u>Mrs John Fein</u>
"You will go to a new school and find many new friends."

Lisa looks satisfied with her mother's reply.

Cut to:
<u>15 : INT ; A FURNISHED FLAT ; DRAWING ROOM ; DAY</u>

Mrs John Fein, Lisa and a lease broker are in a drawing room. Two suitcases of Mrs John Fein and Lisa are seen on the floor.

<u>Lease Broker</u>
"I think you like this flat. Don't you?"

<u>Mrs John Fein</u>
"Yes, I like the flat but the rental is very high in this suburb of London."

<u>Lease Broker</u>
"I must say that two hundred pounds sterling a month, all inclusive is really a reasonable rental. You do not have to worry about the payment of electricity, water or any thing else."

<u>Mrs John Fein (after a pause)</u>
"That is true. Okay, done."

<u>Lease Broker (handing over a key ring to Mrs John Fein)</u>
"This is the key of this flat. You can straight away make this flat your home. I will bring the document and deed tomorrow for your signature."

<u>Mrs John Fein (accepts the key)</u>

"Thank you, Mr David for your immediate help."

<u>Lease Broker</u>
" It is my pleasure to help you. Now I will leave so that you can relax."

Mr David exits from the door.

Cut to:
<u>16 ; INT ; LADY PRINCIPAL'S ROOM ; DAY</u>

Mrs John Fein and Lisa are sitting on chairs opposite the table of the Principal of a Girl's school. The Principal is looking at some papers.

<u>Principal</u>
"Mrs John Fein, I find your qualifications commendable and therefore offer you the job of a language teacher. I hope our girls would be benefited from your knowledge and experience."

<u>Mrs John Fein</u>
"I am extremely grateful to you for offering me this job. I was in dire need of this job."

<u>Lady Principal</u>
"You can join your duty as a teacher from tomorrow and Lisa can also attend her classes from tomorrow."

<u>Mrs John Fein</u>
"I am very thankful to you for giving me the job and also admitting my daughter in your school."

The lady Principal smiles.

Fade out:

Fade in
<u>17 ; INT ; A BIG HALL OF THE SCHOOL ; DAY</u>

After Ten Years (On screen caption)

This is a very big and spacious hall with many tables around. A big banner specifying the occasion as "LANCASTIOR GIRLS SCHOOL, SCIENCE EXHIBITION FROM SCHOOL CHILDREN, DISCOVERY/INVENTION/INNOVATION BY STUDENTS" is seen hanging. Students and teachers are very busy. Members of the public are looking at the exhibits placed on different tables/stalls. Each and every stall/table has a placard showing the name of the student, her class and the brief details of exhibit. Students including Lisa are seen standing opposite their exhibits. Their name and other details like 'Ms Lisa Fein, student–A level and Exhibits-Innovation of Morse's wireless technology to a micro technology' is seen on the placard. Every body appears to be excited. A podium is placed at the centre of the hall and a compere holding a wireless microphone is talking to some one. After a while, compere announces: " Ladies and Gentleman, attention please. Our today's guest of honour Mr Abraham Joy smith, the Director General of Education in City Council has arrived . He would inaugurate the exhibition and would then look at the exhibits. Kindly give a big hand while welcoming him."

The guest of honour, Mr Joy Smith, receives a thunderous applause on his arrival from everyone present in the hall. He is an elderly man and is escorted by the school teachers to the podium. He cuts a ribbon tied at the two poles to inaugurate.After that he is given the wireless microphone to make his speech. He said, "It is a great honour to inaugurate the science exhibition from school children today, who are going to be our next generation scientist and would do wonders.Thanks to everybody present here to boost the morale of these school children."

He then moves to see the science exhibits. Lisa's stall is the closest and hence Mr Joy Smith goes to her stall.

Mr Joy smith

"Hello, young lady! tell me something about your project."

Lisa

"Sir, my name is Lisa Fein and I have innovated the old and obsolete Morse's wireless device into a micro device which is very handy and does not cost a penny to send messages."

Mr Joy smith

"That is great. Tell me more about it."

Lisa (Shows a ring and receiver device)

"Sir, this ring has a micro tip which is used as a button for sending messages. While touching the earth by feet and the tip by finger many times as prescribed in Morse's code, this receiver device can receive these ticks and read the pattern and decode the message, which you can read or hear after a loud ring. In case of the need of recording the messages, a message recorder is available with answering machines which is added for benefits of those who mostly remains out of their houses."

Mr Joy smith

"How does this function? I mean the source of energy."

Lisa

"The ring can be put in the finger and hence it gets the warmth of the body for its energy, whereas the receiver needs AA size pencil battery."

Mr Joy smith

"Though it is cost effective, the set of device can be used for one-way communication only I suppose."

Lisa

"Yes, that is the minus point, Sir. For two-way communication, two sets of device are needed. I use this to communicate with my mom, when I am out of home. This is my innovation to make Morse's device somewhat useful now, when it has gone obsolete in surge of cellular and other fast communication technology."

Mr Joy smith

"Do not bother. You have done great. It is a great innovation. Though it may not be commercially viable now but many 'have-nots' can use it for their benefit in the developing countries. I appreciate your ability and innovation. You are a smart lady. Keep it up."

Lisa

"Thank you, Sir."

Mr Joy smith moves from her table to the next exhibit and so also the group of people escorting him.

Fade out:

Fade In

17- INT ; DRAWING ROOM OF MRS JOHN FEIN'S FLAT; DAY

After five years (On screen caption)

Mrs John Fein looks elderly now and Lisa a smart young beautiful girl. They are sitting on a couch in the drawing room of their flat. Mrs John Fein is sipping tea and Lisa is opening a postal envelope. After reading the content of the letter, she is excited and very happy. She kisses her mother and says: "Mom, great news. I have been appointed as Research scholar as well as Professor in the London Institute of Communication Technology. I would be paid two thousand pounds sterling per month as research stipend."

Mrs John Fein has no word to express as she is extremely happy. She hugs Lisa. Both look jubilant.

Fade out:

Fade In

18 – INT: LOWER HOUSE OF BRITISH PARLIAMENT ; DAY

The Lower House of British Parliament is in session and the members of Parliament are seen involved in important discussions.

One MP raises his arm up to seek permission from the Chairperson/speaker of the house to put up his viewpoint.

Speaker of the House

"Yes, Mr Jerald Goldsmith, you can speak."

Mr Jerald Goldsmith gets up from his seat and speaks in a wireless microphone.

Mr Jerald Goldsmith

"If our Government is seen sympathetic towards the cause of IRA and its terrorist outfit, then we would appear to be prostrating ourselves before IRA's treacheries and readying to accept IRA demands. We must not give such an impression at all and should be dealing with them with iron fist whatever the cost may be. I would like to know our Government's position."

Mr Jerald Goldsmith sits down.

Speaker of the House

"If the ruling Government has anything to comment then Secretary of Internal Affairs may speak before the house."

The Secretary of Internal Affairs then gets up to speak before the full house.

Secretary of Internal Affairs

"The impression gathered is not correct. The IRA terrorist outfit has been hitting soft targets. Innocent people are dying on the road. The Government has opened a series of dialogue to convince them that bloodshed is not the answer to their cause. They can benefit by mutual understanding and good work for their people under the framework of British Constitution. We would never prostrate to IRA treacheries and would be dealing IRA hardliners with iron fist. I would like to ensure every body on this account."

Fade Out;

Fade In

19: EXT : OXFORD STREET, LONDON; DAY

A young and handsome cop is seen guarding and keeping watch on the pedestrians at a cross-point of the Oxford Street. He hears a

SOS call on his walkie-talkie which says: " Mr Geoffrey Hunt, Mr Dan Burg or any other Sergeant policing Oxford Street must clear the public presence near a suspected blue Beetle car, actually a car-bomb meant to explode at any time. Please hurry."

After hearing this, the young cop runs along the street to see if a blue Beetle is parked in the street.

Lisa is in the Oxford Street carrying new purchases in a polythene bag. She is walking along the street.

The young cop spots a blue Beetle parked between two cars in front of an office building. This being not a shopping complex, the public presence is nil which makes him relieved. He hurriedly puts on two red stop signs covering the blue Beetle to stop thoroughfare on this street. He puts his walkie-talkie on and speaks.

Mr Geoffrey Hunt

"I am Geoffrey Hunt speaking. Blue Beetle has been spotted. No public presence at all. It may, however, damage adjacent buildings and people living in there since it is parked between two cars and can be catalytic for extensive explosion. Rush disposal help."

As soon as he finishes his message on walkie-talkie, he sees that Lisa is approaching towards the site of the blue Beetle car in order to cross the road. He runs towards her. He pulls her and runs away from the site to save her from the explosion.The Beetle explodes and so do the adjacent cars. Fire and flame of explosion is so strong that though Mr Geoffrey Hunt is able to save Lisa from explosion by covering her from above on the floor of the street-road, he is hurt at his back. His shirt burns in flame, which he puts off by rolling himself on ground. He takes out his shirt by tearing it from his body. Police cars reach the spot and one cop helps Mr Geoffrey Hunt to sit in the car and rushes him to hospital. Lisa is shocked and is not able to understand any thing. She is stunned and sees a Police jeep taking away her saviour Mr Geoffrey Hunt.

Cut to:

20: INT : HOSPITAL , RECEPTION AREA : DAY

Lisa along with her mother is standing before the Reception Desk of the hospital. The receptionist gets up to help them.

Receptionist

" May I help you, please?"

<u>Lisa</u>

"Yes, I am looking for Detective Sergeant Mr Geoffrey Hunt. I suppose he is admitted here after yesterday's bomb explosion in Oxford Street."

<u>Receptionist</u>

" Why do you want to see him? Are you a relative of his?"

<u>Lisa</u>

"No, he got hurt while saving me from the explosion. I would like to thank him."

<u>Receptionist (showing direction)</u>

"That is great, you are alive and so is he . He is in ward number –10, bed 2."

<u>Lisa</u>

"Thank you, thanks a lot."

Lisa Fein and her mother move towards the direction shown by the receptionist to reach the ward no 10, bed 2.

Cut to:

<u>21: INT ; HOSPITAL WARD NO-10 ; DAY</u>

Lisa and her mother enter into the ward no 10, a rest room for two patients separated by a hanging curtain. Lisa is able to recognise Mr Geoffrey Hunt who is lying in the bed.

Mrs John Fein, mother of Lisa, feels affectionate towards this young and handsome youth, saviour of her only daughter. She goes closer to him and kisses on his forehead with affection. Mr Geoffrey Hunt wakes up and opens his eye. He is surprised to see an elderly woman kissing his forehead. Later, he realises after seeing Lisa standing behind her mother that both have come to pay a visit to him. He tries to get up but Mrs John Fein advices him to remain lying.

<u>Mrs John Fein</u>

"My Dear son, do not worry about us. Take rest. You have been the saviour of my only family, my daughter Lisa. May god bless you with a very long and happy life."

<u>Mr Geoffrey Hunt</u>

"Do not mention. It was my duty. I am glad that I am able to see her safe and sound. It was a very swift incident and I was rushed away from the site for medical help so I could not know anything about her."

Lisa

"You appeared as an angel for me to push away from the explosion. I am extremely grateful to you."

Lisa holds his hand and kisses. Mr Geoffrey Hunt feels delighted and attracted towards her. Her beauty, loving touch and closeness trembles his heart suddenly.

Mrs John Fein

"I would like to see once the mother of the brave policeman."

Mr Geoffrey Hunt

"I was an orphan but looked after by Annie, Mother of the Anglican Church. Unfortunately, she also died last year. So, I am still an orphan."

Mrs John Fein (becomes emotional)

"You are no more an orphan. You are my brave child. You are my family. I am proud of you."

Mr Geoffrey Hunt (also gets emotional)

"I am glad to find my mom. God, you are great!"

A nurse enters the room and says: " You should allow him to rest. This is the time for medicine." She gives him a tablet and a glass of water. The nurse goes away.

Mrs John Fein

"Okay, my boy, take rest and get well soon. We will now be meeting often."

Mrs John Fein shakes his hand and bids him goodbye.

Lisa

"I will come again. Get well soon."

She also shakes his hand but Mr Geoffrey Hunt keeps holding her hand for a while as if he does not want to let her go from there.

Mr Geoffrey Hunt (low voice)

" I will miss you. I would like to meet you again soon."

Lisa smiles. She also feels the same. She exits along with her mother.

Fade out;

Fade In

22 : INT ; DRAWING ROOM OF MRS FEIN'S FLAT ; DAY

After six months (On screen caption)

Mrs John Fein and Lisa are sitting on a couch and going through a photo album of Mr Geoffrey Hunt. Both are laughing at a naked photograph of Geoffrey in his childhood.

Mrs John Fein

"Annie had been like a real mother of Geoffrey. She took a good care of him."

Lisa (laughing)

"Geoffrey says, he used to be naked while taking bath till the age of 12. This photograph is a proof."

Mrs John Fein (laughs)

"Do not worry baby. After marriage, you would see him that way very often."

Lisa (feeling shy)

"Mom! You are naughty."

Mrs John Fein

"You are going to marry him next month, baby! Why should you shy now? You are young and would soon be a wife and then a mother! I shall be privileged to become a Granny of your child. I am awaiting for that wonderful day, my baby. Geoffrey would be a wonderful husband for you and a great child for me. We would all live together."

Lisa (smiles)

"Yes mom, you are right. We would live together."

Fade Out;

Fade In

23 : INT ; MATERNITY WARD OF A HOSPITAL ; DAY

After two years (On screen caption)

Lisa is lying on a stretcher bed and a small newborn baby is seen beside her. She is breastfeeding her newborn child. Just then Mrs John Fein and Mr Geoffrey Hunt enter into the room with a flower bouquet. Lisa stops breastfeeding her child and gets up.

Mr Geoffrey Hunt

"Honey, keep feeding my boy. How are you? How is my Sharn?"

Mrs John Fein

"Sharn must be like his brave father, doing well."

Lisa

"He is very quiet except when he is hungry."

Mrs John Fein

"That is like a brave child."

Mr Geoffrey Hunt
"Sharn will soon be with us at home. The doctor says that you will be discharged tomorrow morning."

Mr Geoffrey Hunt holds the newborn baby in his hand and kisses his forehead. He looks jubilant and happy and so is Mrs John Fein.

Lisa
"That is great. I get bored here."

Mrs John Fein
"It is now a matter of a night in here, darling."

Mrs John Fein and Mr Geoffrey Hunt exit the ward.

Fade out;

Fade In
24 : INT ; DINING ROOM OF MR JERALD GOLDSMITH ; DAY

Mr Jerald Goldsmith, MP in British Parliament, is having breakfast in the dining room. The telephone bell rings and a houseboy brings the wireless receiver to him.

Mr Jerald Goldsmith
" Hello."

Mr Jerald Goldsmith (After hearing for a while)
"My child, wherever you go, be careful. Where are you going this time?"

Mr Jerald Goldsmith (After hearing for a while)
"Spain is a good country for holidaying. So you would be out for two weeks in Spain. Keep in touch and let me know your address as and when you reach your holiday resort."

Mr Jerald Goldsmith (After hearing for a while)
"Nina, take good care of yourself. You are my only family. Good wishes for your happy journey, my child."

He puts off the telephone and gives it back to the houseboy.

Cut to:
25 ; INT ; LOWER HOUSE OF BRITISH PARLIAMENT ; DAY

The Lower House of British Parliament is in session and members of Parliament are seen taking part in important discussions.

Mr Jerald Goldsmith raises his arm up to seek permission from the Chairperson/speaker of the house to put up his question.

Speaker of the House

"Yes, Mr Jerald Goldsmith, you can speak."

Mr Jerald Goldsmith gets up from his seat and speaks in a wireless microphone.

Mr Jerald Goldsmith

"To my mind the agreement reached between the British Government and the IRA leader Jerry Adams under the Political gimmickry of USA is wrong. We are eating our own words. Why should there be difference in words and deeds of our Government, I would like to oppose the agreement and like to know the compulsions under which this has been accepted?"

Speaker of the House

"As the Secretary of Internal Affairs and the Prime Minister are not available, the question of honourable Member of Parliament may be noted for answer in the next session."

Mr Jerald Goldsmith sits down.

Cut to:

26 : DRAWING ROOM OF MRS JOHN FEIN'S FLAT ; DAY

Mrs John Fein, Lisa and Mr Geoffrey Hunt are sitting on a couche. The infant, Sharn, is crawling on the ground and is happy to play with a doll. Mrs John Fein and Mr Geoffrey Hunt are looking serious whereas Lisa is trying to make her point with them.

Lisa

"Mom, this is a great chance for me to accept this scholarship in USA. I shall be able to complete my research work commendably in Wisconsin University. As you know this University has the best facility for this kind of research work and I am in the last phase of research work and would finish in next six months. This is a matter of six months only, mom."

Mrs John Fein

" But how will you manage on your own?"

Lisa

"No, mom. I am not going alone. You have to come with me otherwise it would be impossible for me with Sharn."

Mrs John Fein

"But how would Geoffrey be here all alone for six months?"

Mr Geoffrey Hunt

" I was worried about you and Sharn. If mom is going with you then I will have little relief. You need not worry, mom. For Lisa's carrier I shall be able to manage for six months."

Mrs John Fein

"I am not feeling good to leave you here, Geoffrey."

Mrs John Fein

"I am a cop, mom! I am a cop from the bomb disposal unit and I can defuse any type of bomb. I should be able to defuse this problem also. It is matter of six months only. In any way, I will be visiting you many times. You need not worry about me."

Mrs John Fein looks relieved and so too Lisa.

Lisa

"Tomorrow I shall be going to USA Embassy to obtain our visas."

Mrs John Fein

"Tomorrow I have to visit one of my friend, who is ailing."

Cut to:

27: EXT ; FRONTAL SIDE OF CONSULAR WING OF THE USA EMBASSY BUILDING, LONDON :DAY

Frontal view of the Consular Wing of the USA Embassy in London. A taxi stops in front of the gate of the Embassy building and Lisa along with her son get down. She opens her purse and takes out the money. She sees the taximetre and pays the taxi driver the required fare and moves towards the gate of the building, which is heavily guarded by securitymen.

Cut to:

28 ; INT ; CONSULAR HALL OF THE USA EMBASSY IN LONDON ; DAY

Many visa seekers are sitting on the chairs laid in the Consular hall of the Embassy. Some visa applicants are seen filling the visa forms while others are talking to the officers on the consularcounter. Lisa enters in the hall and reaches a consular counter.

Visa Officer on Consular Counter

"May I help you, please?"

<u>Lisa</u>

"I have been granted a research scholarship for six months in Wisconsin University and I need required visa for myself, my child and my mom. I have already filled the visa forms." (She gives the visa forms to the officer).

<u>Visa Officer</u>

"Let me check the forms."

<u>Ms Lisa Fein</u>

"All other required documents are attached with the visa application form. When should I come to collect my visa?"

<u>Visa Officer</u>

"The visa will be ready in two hours. If you like, you can wait in the hall or you can come some other time as per your convenience."

<u>Lisa</u>

" Then I would like to wait here. Thanks."

She holds Sharn in her arms and settles in a chair.

Cut to:

<u>29: EXT: ON RODA WITHIN LONDON MUNICIPAL AREA:DAY</u>

There are many cars moving on a one-way road. Mr Jerald Goldsmith is driving his car on the road. A van, which looks like a policevan, follows his car about which Mr Goldsmith is unaware.

Cut to:

<u>30 ; EXT ; ON A ROAD WITHIN LONDON MUNICIPAL AREA ; DAY</u>

There are many cars moving on a one-way road. Mr Jerald Goldsmith is driving his car on the road. A van, which looks like a policevan, follows his car about which Mr Goldsmith is unaware.

After a while his car reaches a red light crossing and he stops his car to await the signal to be green. The van also stops behind his car and three people get down from the van and come forward towards Mr Goldsmith's car. They forcibly enter into the car and point a pistol at the ribs of Mr Goldsmith.

<u>One Person</u>

" Do as we tell you otherwise your daughter will die in Spain."

Due to this sudden happening Mr Goldsmith is stunned and frightened.

Mr Goldsmith

"Who are you?"

Another man pushes him back and takes the driving seat. Crossing signal turns green and he drives the car on the road. He makes a turn and drive on a road other than the usual course.

Mr Goldsmith

" Where are you taking me?"

Another man sitting on the rear seat puts his cellular phone on his ear and says: " Now you talk to your daughter."

Mr Goldsmith can hear the voice and weeping of his daughter.

Ms Nina (In Phone)

" Dad, they are ruthless criminals. They would kill me."

Mr Goldsmith

"What happened?"

Ms Nina (In Phone)

" They have kidnapped me from the sea-beach hotel and I do not know where I am kept. I do not wish to be here. Dad, please save me. Please do something."

Mr Goldsmith

"Honey, do not lose heart. I will do..."

Before he could finish his sentence, the cell phone was taken away and switched off.

Man (Holding the pistol at his ribs)

"Now Mr Goldsmith, kindly speak to this number in the Embassy of USA. This is the number of the Counsellor there. Tell him that you are coming to the Embassy now to write in the condolence book. You must be knowing that a great humanist of USA , Mr Richard Charlton, has died and the Embassy has kept a condolence book open for visitors like you. And do not forget to tell Counsellor that you want to meet him."

The man dials a number on the cell phone and gives the cell phone to him. The cell phone's sound is quite high and hence ring tone is heard. After a few rings, someone on the other side picks up the phone and says: "Hello!"

Mr Goldsmith

" Hello, am I speaking to Mr Godson, the Counsellor of the US Embassy? I am Goldsmith speaking."

Mr Godson (Loud Voice from mobile phone)
" Yes, Mr Goldsmith. How are you? "

Mr Goldsmith
" Mr Godson, good morning. I am on my way to your Embassy to write in the condolence book and would also like to meet you. If you can leave a message at the reception for a quick meeting."

Mr Godson (Loud Voice from mobile phone)
"You are most welcome. I will arrange for your arrival.."

Mr Godson ends his conversation and then Mr Goldsmith ends his call and looks at the person holding the pistol for further instructions.

Man (holding pistol)
" That is like a gentleman's performance."

His car is driven by one of his kidnappers. The driver moves towards the road leading to USA Embassy in London.

Cut to:
31 : Ext : Overview of Road :Day.

Mr Goldsmith's car can be seen on the road along with other cars.

Cut to:
32: Int : A Big hall : Day

It is a very big hall, which is dimly lit. A big van is parked inside the hall. The van resembles a police van. A group of thirty people in police uniform are preparing themselves with weapons and explosives in their person. When they are fully equipped with these weapons and explosives in their person, they hold automatic weapons and sit in the van. The driver is alert and awaiting the signal on walkie-talkie before he could proceed. Everybody is patient and alert.

Cut to:
33: Ext; On Road: Day

Mr Goldsmith's car driven by his kidnappers enters into a narrow and almost deserted lane. A man is seen standing in front of a big shutter and holding a walkie-talkie.

Man (with the walkie-talkie)
"Mr Goldsmith's car driven by our man is here.. You people in the van may now move and follow the car."

The man puts off his walkie-talkie and opens the shutter hurriedly. As soon as the shutter opens, the van comes out from the hall onto the road to follow Mr Goldsmith's car.

Cut to:
34 : Ext : Overview of Road :Day.

Mr Goldsmith's car can be seen moving, followed by the van along with other cars on the road.

Cut to:
35 : Ext : USA Embassy : Day

Mr Goldsmith's car stops just near the main gate of USA Embassy, whereas the van stops a little behind. A sentry on the main gate comes up to Mr Goldsmith's car.

Sentry (looks at the people inside the car)
"Why are you here? "

A Captor (on the driving seat)
"Mr Goldsmith would like to write on the condolence book and meet Mr Godson."

Mr Goldsmith smiles and waves his hand.

Sentry (signals his fellow colleagues to open the gate)
"Open the gate. Mr Goldsmith is here."

The main gate opens and Mr Goldsmith's car moves inside. After Mr Goldsmith's car moves inside, a sentry closes the main gate of the Embassy. At this moment, the police van parked outside the main gate moves with a high speed and forcefully crashes into the main gate and reaches inside the Embassy premises. The sentries at the gate are stunned and are gearing to face the situation with their automatic weapons. But before they could do anything, thirty well-equipped men come out of the van and within seconds spray bullets at the sentries on the gate.

A group of twenty captors move inside the Embassy building along with Mr Goldsmith whereas ten captors carry sophisticated wallmountable bombs from the Van. They move outside of the building premises and mount the bombs on the wall. When all the Bombs are mounted, they activate the bombs. The rays of the activated bombs could be seen merging.

<u>One Captor</u>
"If anybody tries to defuse these bombs and obstruct the bomb-rays, these bombs will explode at once."

<u>Other Captor</u>
"If somebody tries to defuse it, while we are inside, it can be dangerous for us also."

<u>First Captor</u>
"No, the bomb will not be dangerous for us as these are remote controlled bombs. I will deactivate the bombs now and will activate when we move out. These bombs can be blasted with this remote control."

He shows the remote control and deactivates the bomb with the help of his remote control. All the ten captors then move inside the building premises.

Cut to:
<u>36: INT: CENTRAL HALL OF THE EMBASSY BUILDING: DAY</u>

A man surrounded by his six armed associates is seen inside the building. One of the associates carrying a walkie-talkie instructs the other associates on different floors of the Embassy building.

<u>Man (on walkie-talkie)</u>
"Jack..."

<u>Loud Voice (from walkie-talkie)</u>
" Yes, Chief. Instruction please."

<u>Chief (on walkie-talkie)</u>
"Gather all the Embassy officials including the Ambassador in a room and make them pass through metal detector to ensure that they do not have any communication device with them. Please take away their wristwatches as those might have a mobile communication device and keep them locked in the room with a security camera to monitor them from outside"

<u>Loud Voice (from walkie-talkie)</u>
" Yes, Chief. Sure."

<u>Chief (on walkie-talkie)</u>
"Gordon..."

<u>Loud Voice (from walkie-talkie)</u>
"Yes, Boss."

<u>Chief(On walkie-talkie)</u>
"I hope by now all communication devices, telephone, fax, telex, wireless systems are dead and all mobile sets seized. Confirm."

<u>Loud Voice (from walkie-talkie)</u>
"Positive, Sir."

<u>Chief (On walkie-talkie)</u>
" Thanks. Confirm your position."

<u>Loud Voice (From walkie-talkie)</u>
"I am in consular hall. It is quite big and there are a number of visitors for consular services."

<u>Chief (On walkie-talkie)</u>
"Send five armed men to keep a watch and do not allow these visitors to move. Also if you find anyone with muscle power and extraordinarily masculine, inject anaesthesia to make him senseless. Make sure that all of them pass through metal detector to ensure no entry of communication devices. Check their belongings thoroughly and keep their wristwatchesf.

<u>Loud Voice (on walkie-talkie)</u>
"Yes, Sir."

<u>Chief (on walkie-talkie)</u>
"I am positioning myself in Ambassador's room with Mr Goldsmith. You along with other keep your walkie-talkies on so that I can communicate and instruct you on further development. Confirm all sectors, positive"

<u>Loud Voice (from walkie-talkie)</u>
" All positive, Sir."

The Chief then moves along with his six armed associates towards a staircase to go to the first floor of the building.

Cut to:
<u>37: INT: PASSAGE AREA : DAY</u>

All the Embassy officials including the Ambassador are being pushed by ten armed men towards a big room on the first floor of the building.

<u>One Armed man</u>
"Quickly move into that room. Move, move."

One Embassy Official (Angrily)
" Yes, I am moving."

Another Armed Man
" Sorry, Ambassador, for this inconvenience. Bear with us."

All the Embassy officials including the Ambassador are forced into a big room by the armed men.

Cut to:
38: INT: A BIG ROOM WITH ALL THE EMBASSY OFFICIALS: DAY

All the Embassy officials including the Ambassador are helplessly looking at the armed men for further instructions.

Ambassador
"I am the Ambassador of USA and would like to know as to who you are and what are your motives?"

One Armed Man
"Do not worry Mr Ambassador, you would know everything from our Chief. Just wait a little and cooperate with us. We will not harm you."

Ambassador
"You all will be sorry for doing this to us."

One Armed man (angrily points his gun towards him)
"You need to shut your mouth and cooperate. Otherwise it would be your turn to pay."

A lady employee rushes forward and pleads before the armed man.

Lady Employee
"No. Please, do not do this. He is our Ambassador. Take my life but do not harm him."

One Armed man
"That will not be necessary if you people cooperate with us."

Then two armed men bring a metal detector into the room and plug it into a power point.

One Armed man
"Now all of you remove and put your wristwatches in this bag and move through the metal detector one by one. I must warn you that none of you should possesss any communication device, which would otherwise prove suicidal."

Another armed man

"Now, hurry up. Give your wristwatches and cross through the metal detector."

All the Embassy officials including the Ambassador put their wristwatches in the bag and then cross through the metal detector. As and when the metal detector signals an alarm, the armed guards check the belongings of the person and mostly find either key rings or coins in their pockets, which are taken away in another bag. After the metal belongings are taken away, the people are again instructed to cross the metal detector to double check.

Two armed men are mounting a security camera on the wall of the room near the door to cover the total eye view of the room.

Cut to:

39: INT ; PASSAGE AREA OUTSIDE THE BIG ROOM WHERE EMBSSSY OFFICIALS ARE LOCKED; DAY

Armed men come out of the room and lock it from outside. They mount a security TV on the wall and then drag a table and three chairs.

One Armed Man (points out to three armed person)

"You three would sit here and keep a watch on the security TV so that you all can keep eye on the inmates of this room."

Three armed men

"Yes boss."

Cut to:

40 : INT ; CONSULAR HALL ; DAY

All consular applicants are sitting on their chairs, whereas five armed men are keeping watch on them. A man with a walkie-talkie enters the consular hall along with five armed men, two of them bring a metal detectors.

Man (with a walkie-talkie points his finger towards the applicants sitting on chairs)

" Men and women separate yourselves in two groups. Hurry. Quick."

They quickly stand in their respective lines.

Man (with a walkie-talkie)

" Now all the men will take their clothes off and pass through the metal detector while holding their clothes. You will also remove your wristwatches and keep them in the bag provided. Quick. Move."

A visa applicant standing before an armed man hesitates; the very moment the armed man hits & abuses him-"You son of a bitch, follow the instructions fast, otherwise you would die. Do it fast."

The armed men point their gun towards the male applicants and they out of fear remove their clothes and pass through the metal detector. In case, metal detector detects any metallic item, quizzical glance of the armed men prompts applicants to take out the item which are inside their pockets. After that they drop their wristwatches in the bag. The armed men notice twelve male applicants extremely muscular and well built. The armed men instructs by pointing gun towards them to stand away from the rest.

Man (with a walkie-talkie)
" Now twelve of you will be injected intravenously."

One male
"But why injected?"

Man (with a walkie-talkie)
"You have no choice. Do you?

One male (nervous and puzzled)
"But..."

Man (with a walkie-talkie)
"You all are masculine and well-built. This injection will not harm you except make you feel relaxed and calm."

One armed man injects anaesthesia to all the twelve people chosen. After being injected, all the twelve men fall a sleep on their chairs. When the male applicants finish their turn of passing through the metal detector, the armed man holding the walkie-talkie instructs female applicants to follow the same course.

Man (with a walkie-talkie)
" Now all the females are requested to remove their clothes and do the same."

One female applicant
"Why should we be nude before you? We can simply pass through the metal detector with our clothes on for your purpose."

Man (with a walkie-talkie)
" No, you will will have to bare yourselves. We would like to see your muscles. I will not hesitate to kill any of you in case of resistance. So do as I say. Move. Fast."

This threat scares the women and they undress themselves and put their wristwatches in the bag. Lisa is among the group of female and does the same. She has removed her clothes and wristwatch and passes through the metal detector. A armed man searches her purse. After that she puts on her clothes.

<u>Lisa(holds Sharn in her arm)</u>
" Should I remove my son's clothes?"

<u>Man (with a walkie-talkie)</u>

"No. That will not be necessary. Thank you."

After all the females undergo thorough search done by their captors, they are allowed to sit on chairs.

<u>Man (with a walkie-talkie)</u>
" Now, listen carefully. You people are held hostages here."

<u>One male</u>
"Why? I would like to know your identity?"

<u>Man (with a walkie-talkie)</u>
"You are required to remain silent and not utter a single word. You would remain on your chairs without moving. If someone shows any kind of smartness, our armed associates are authorised to shoot anyone any time without any delay. Understood."

<u>Man (with a walkie-talkie turn to his five armed associates)</u>

" All of you keep a proper watch on these people. If you find anyone behaving funny, do not wait but shoot. I am going to the chief."

Five of his armed associates pull the chairs and sit down. The man with the walkie talkie exits from the place along with remaining five armed associates. There is a TV in this Consular Hall, which is generally used for entertaining the visitors. A film is shown on the TV.

Cut to:
<u>41 : INT: AMBASSADOR'S ROOM: DAY</u>

Mr Jerald Goldsmith, Mr Rudar Feinman (the conman of the operation) and his five associates holding automatic guns are in the Ambassador's room. Mr Rudar Feinman is sitting on the Ambassador's chair.

<u>Mr Rudar Feinman</u>
" It feels good to sit on the chair of the Ambassador of USA. Bring

him here. We need to talk to him. Mr Goldie (to Mr Goldsmith) , you be ready to talk to him as per my instruction."

As per his instruction three of his associates go out of the room to bring the Ambassador.

<u>Mr Goldsmith</u>
" What you are doing is very inappropriate."

<u>Mr Rudar Feinman</u>
" Politicians do appropriate things but patriots like us do everything keeping in mind about our goal. Now do follow my instructions, otherwise you would find your daughter's head severed."

<u>Mr Goldsmith</u>
" Please do not hurt my daughter. I am at your beck and call."

<u>Mr Rudar Feinman</u>
"That is like a good politician and a good father. I would give you few written papers with instructions in it, which you would follow."

Three of his associates come back into the room with the Ambassador.

<u>Mr Rudar Feinman</u>
" Hello Mr Ambassador. Sorry for the inconvenience. Could you kindly help us? Please intimate the local government that you have been held hostage in your Embassy itself. (He dials a number on his Cellular phone and gives it to the Ambassador) Kindly talk to the headquarter of London police."

<u>Ambassador (holds the cellular phone)</u>
"Hello, I am Terry Grant, the Ambassador of the United States of America, speaking."

<u>(Loud Voice from the Cellular phone)</u>
"Yes, Ambassador. I am David Lean speaking. How are you? It is quite a long time that we did not meet. Tell me if I can do something for you."

<u>Ambassador</u>
"I need your help. My embassy, embassy personnel including me have been held hostage."

<u>(Loud Voice from the Cellular phone)</u>
" What? Who are they? What do they want?"

Mr Rudar Feinman takes away the cellular phone from the Ambassador and gives it to MrGoldsmith so that he can proceed with the demands written on the papers.

<u>Mr Goldsmith (sees the instructions in the paper)</u>

"Hello, Mr David Lean. I am Jerald Goldsmith, the Member of Parliament of UK, the House of Lords and now an ultranationalist. You have already been informed by the Ambassador of USA that the embassy has been taken as hostage. It is required to teach America a lesson for supporting the cause of an independent Ireland. We, the comrades of the Ultranationalist Group of UK, cannot allow degeneration of our motherland and would fight for the national cause. We demand that the visiting delegation of IRA group in Washington may be arrested and for favouring the IRA, USA must pay our new found organization, 'Group of Ultranationalists of UK', a sum of US$ 1 Bn, 10 per cent each in Pound sterling, US$, Euro and Yen and the rest 60 percent in gold and diamond to help us meet the expenses to fight the forces which are disintegrating UK. We also need four big size military helicopters to leave the Embassy scratch free. The cash and helicopter must be arranged within 24 hours otherwise the hostages will be killed one by one in every hour till our demands are met. We have distinguished Diplomats and some visa seekers in consular hall to put on altar to sacrifice for the cause of integrated UK. I warn you against any possible adventurous action by your department. All the walls of the Embassy have been mounted with a powerful remote controlled bomb and all the comrades associated in this mission are equipped with remote controls to explode these bombs in a second at the slightest provocation from your side. We are ready to die in explosion along with the hostages in fight against the forces who want to disintegrate United Kingdom. I hope everything is very clear to you."

<u>(Loud Voice from the Cellular phone)</u>

" Mr Goldsmith. I would need some time to talk to the authority and arrange your demands."

<u>Mr Goldsmith</u>

"It is good that you have understood the gravity of the situation. Do not try to forcefully enter into the Embassy building. It would be fatal for everyone including me. Talk to anyone you like but fulfil the demand. I will call you tomorrow in the morning around 8 O'clock to check whether you have arranged all the demands or should we start killing exactly after 24 hours. You can not call me as I am in command of all the communication systems. I can call the shots but you can not. So we will talk exactly at 8 O'clock tomorrow. Till then goodbye."

Mr Goldsmith puts off the cell phone and gives it back to Mr Rudar Feinman.

Mr Rudar Feinman

" That is marvellous Mr Goldsmith. Thank you. You were great. (to his associates) Take the Ambassador away. We do not need him any more."

His three associates take the Ambassador away at the gunpoint in another room.

Cut to:

42: EXT: EMBASSY OF UNITED STATES OF AMERICA, LONDON: DAY

The London police cordons off the Embassy building by surrounding it with metal barricade on the road. Many police car and military van of rapid action force arrive at the site. Policemen and personnel of rapid action force have taken positions with telescopic automatic guns in their hands. By and by press and media personnel are arriving at the site. The place is noisy and busy due to the siren of police car and conversations of police and military personnel on their walkie-talkies. Media personnel from BBC, CNN, ABC, Sky TV, etc are filming the situation live. One BBC cameraman is filming the situation and the correspondent is reporting live into the camera.

BBC Correspondent

"You can see the Embassy of USA in London at the background which appears calm as activities are not visible at all. But London Police headquarter confirms that the Embassy has been seized by a group of Ultranationalists of UK, who are opposed to the formation of an independent Ireland and did not like USA's approval to IRA cause. Hence they intend to teach America a lesson by holding its diplomats hostage. They demand the arrest of visiting IRA delegation in USA and a ransom of US$ 1 Bn, 10% each in US$, Pound sterling, Euro, Yen and the rest sixty percent in gold and diamond. They have also demanded four helicopters to leave for their safe haven. If demands are not met within 24 hours, hostages would be killed. The Embassy is fully fitted with remote controlled explosives and any rescue attempt by any one would be fatal for hostages as well as captors."

Cut to:

43: ENT : CONSULAR HALL, EMBASSY OF USA,LONDON : DAY

Gunmen on their chairs are keeping eye on the consular applicants.They are alert with their weapons, whereas consular applicants including Lisa are watching the wall mounted TV, which is showing showbiz programme in CNN. This programme is abruptly stopped and 'headline news' is being telecasted. CNN's live news telecast is shown on the TV in which the CNN correspondent is narrating the top story of the hours, 'This is shocking news for all of us that a moderate member of the House of Lords of UK, Mr Jerald Goldsmith has now resorted to extortion in order to teach America a lesson for its favour to the settlement of the Irish problem. A message on the cellular phone received by the London Police Headquarter confirms that Mr Goldsmith and his armed ultranationalist comrades have stormed the USA Embassy building in London today and held all the officials including the Ambassador hostage. They have also held men and women as hostage who visited the Embassy for consular services. They have severed all the connections of communication. They can contact the police but police can not. They demanded that the visiting delegation of IRA in Washington may be arrested and for favouring the IRA, USA must pay their new found organisation ' Group of Ultranationalists of UK' a sum of US$ 1 Bn, 10 percent each of which may be paid in US$, Pound sterling, Euro and Yen and rest 60 percent in gold and diamonds to meet the expenses of the organisation to fight the forces which are responsible for disintegrating the United Kingdom. They have also demanded four helicopters to fly away to their safe haven. The amount must be paid within 24 hours and four helicopters provided, failing of which will result in killing of the hostages. Authorities in Washington are worried about the safety of their diplomats. The President of USA has spoken to the Prime Minister of UK, who assured the President that all steps would be taken to ensure safety of the Diplomats including the payment of ransom. Police and military forces have cordoned off the area and a stand off is expected till a solution is found to this problem as each wall of the Embassy has been mounted with a remote controlled explosive. The entire explosive can be exploded at once by using the remote control, which is stated to be in possession of each comrade. They have threatened of fatal consequences if any rescue attempt or attempt to storm the building is made. I am Richard Cook reporting live from the Embassy site in London.'

After hearing this news from the TV, all the consular applicants including Lisa look worried but Lisa's infant son Sharn is unaware of the impending problems and is happy playing with his mother.

Cut to:

<u>44: EXT: EMBASSY OF UNITED STATES OF AMERICA, LONDON: DAY</u>

Overview of the Embassy of USA building and stand off situation is seen on the road adjacent to the building, where gunmen from Police force and rapid action force are still in their respective positions. Police cars and military vans are seen parked in the area.

Cut to:

<u>45: INT : DRAWING ROOM OF MRS JOHN FEIN IN LONDON : DAY</u>

Mrs John Fein is strolling in the drawing room and looks worried. She picks up the phone and dials a number.

<u>Mrs John Fein</u>

"Hello, Geoffrey. Lisa has gone to the USA Embassy and has not returned yet. I do not know whether she is also caught in the middle. Sharn is also with her."

<u>Loud Voice (from telephone)</u>

"Do not worry mom. Has she not called you on her micro device to you."

<u>Mrs John Fein</u>

"No not yet. I do not know why? Perhaps she is not there otherwise she would have informed me."

The micro receiver on top of the TV set in the drawing room beeps thrice.

<u>Mrs John Fein</u>

"Geoffrey. Her message has just come. Please hold on. I will let you know."

The message is heard from the micro receiver after decoding it in a mechanized manner.

Loud Voice (from micro receiver)

"Mom, I am being held hostage in the USA Embassy. Sharn and I are otherwise well. There are many gunmen keeping watch on us. Do not worry. I will contact you again."

Mrs John Fein

"Oh my god! Geoffrey, She and Sharn are held as hostages in the Embassy."

Loud Voice (from telephone)

"Do not worry mom, the Government will perhaps provide the ransom amount for the safety of the Diplomats and common people. So do not worry, she will be back by tomorrow morning."

Mrs John Fein

"Okay son, if you get any news from your police department, let me know immediately."

Loud Voice from telephone

"Okay mom, I will let you know."

Mrs John Fein keeps down the telephone handset on the instrument.

Cut to:

46 : INT : CONSULAR HALL OF USA EMBASSY, LONDON

After five hours (on screen caption)

All the visa applicants are tired of sitting on their chairs. Sharn is also not feeling comfortable. Lisa is trying to play with him but he starts crying. She is trying to comfort him but he is unstoppable. She gets up from the chair and moves around in the hall to comfort him but it does not yield any result. He is still crying.

One gunman

"What is the problem with him?"

Lisa

"He is hungry now."

Gunman

"Then breastfeed him."

Lisa

"I do not have milk in my breast. He takes powder milk, which I prepare every time to feed him."

<u>Gunman</u>
" Where will you get that?"

<u>One visa applicant</u>
"Allow her to go home to feed this little boy. Otherwise how will he survive without milk?"

<u>Gunman</u>
"It is not possible to let her go."

<u>Lisa</u>
"There must be a kitchen in the Embassy. Will you allow me to go to the kitchen to search for milk."

<u>Gunman</u>
"I need to ask my boss. Wait."

<u>Gunman (on walkie-talkie)</u>
"Boss, there is a small infant child in the consular hall, who is crying a lot as he is hungry. Can his mother be allowed to go to the kitchen to make milk for the child."

<u>Loud Voice (from walkie-talkie)</u>
" That may not be a problem, but keep a watch on his mother."

<u>Gunman (he puts off the walkie-talkie)</u>
"Okay, Boss."

<u>Gunman (to Lisa)</u>
" Now you can go to the kitchen on the first floor.(to another gunman) Ronny, you would escort her ."

Lisa takes Sharn will and follows Ronny, the gunman, to go to the kitchen at the first floor of the Embassy. They exit the Consular Hall.

Cut to:
<u>47: INT : KITCHEN OF THE EMBASSY OF FIRST FLOOR</u>

Lisa enters into the kitchen along with Sharn and Ronny, the gunman. Ronny opens the refrigerator of the kitchen and takes out a beercan and starts drinking. He stands at the kitchen door. Lisa opens the wallmounted cupboards to find if milk powder is available. She finds the can of "Nido" milk and takes out of the cupboard. She puts water in the kettle and few spoon of powder milk in it. She plugs in the kettle for warming. Exactly after a minute she puts off the electricity and pours the milk in a bowl. She sits on a kitchen stool and feeds Sharn with a tablespoon. He is happy to have his milk. When Lisa finishes feeding her child, she keeps the utensils back in the cupboard as before.

She exits from the kitchen with Sharn followed by Ronny, the gunman.

Cut to:

<u>48: INT: CORRIDOR OF THE FIRST FLOOR ADJACENT TO THE KITCHEN</u>

Lisa is walking through the corridor of the first floor of the Embassy along with Sharn. Sharn is now happy after having his food and prefers to walk holding the fingers of his mother. Lisa is happy to see Sharn walking and so is Ronny, the gunman.

Three gunmen on the first floor come to Ronny. They were about 50 to 60 years.

<u>One man</u>
"Hi Ronny, who is this lady? Why are you here?"

<u>Ronny (pointing his finger towards Sharn while Lisa is looking at the three faces which appears familiar)</u>
"This little man was very hungry and was shouting a lot. The boss allowed him to have his milk from the Embassy kitchen."

<u>Another man</u> <u>(smiling at Sharn)</u>
" Very lucky guy indeed. I am feeling jealous of him."

<u>Ronny</u> <u>(laughs)</u>
"Boss would happily allow you to eat if you crawl like the little guy who is fully unaware of the situation around him."

<u>Man</u>
"Nonchalant little guy."

<u>Ronny</u>
"Okay, guys. I will catch up later."

Ronny, Lisa and Sharn climb down from the staircase leading to the ground floor. Lisa is trying to recollect the three familiar faces, which she has seen just at the first floor talking to Ronny. Lisa looks very serious after seeing them.

Cut to:

49: INT : CONSULAR HALL OF THE EMBASSY OF USA

Lisa, Sharn and Ronny come back into the Consular Hall. Lisa sits on her seat and hold Sharn in her lap. Ronny also sits on his chair with his gun to watch the visa applicants in the hall.

Lisa is very serious and is trying to recollect the incident where she has seen the three familiar faces. After a while, she remembers the incident, which took place during her childhood.

Fade out:

Fade in

50 : INT: BEDROOM: NIGHT

It is dark in the bedroom. Lisa has not slept and is frightened to see six strangers in the drawing room beating her mother and father mercilessly with hockey sticks. She hides herself behind the long curtains hanging from the pellets of the window of the bedroom. She is sobbing and in tears. Her voice cannot be heard due to heavy rain, frequent thunderclaps and gust of wind shaking the windows.

Fade out:

Fade in

51: INT: CONSULAR HALL OF EMBASSY FO USA

Lisa is able to recognise the three familiar faces out of the six IRA activists who had come to kill her father in her native town in Northern Ireland.

She is surprised to see the three IRA activists in a hostage-taking mission and being a part of the Ultranationalist of U.K. She concludes her view and starts sending messages on her micro-tip Morse ring device in her finger. She is touching her micro-tip many times to send messages, which the gunmen are not able to see. Her feet are in contact of surface to pass the messages.

Cut to:

52 :INT : DRAWING ROOM OF MRS JOHN FEIN :DAY

Mrs John Fein and her son-in-law, Geoffrey Hunt, are worried about the well being of Lisa . They are silent but tense. They have kept the TV on which is telecasting the top story of the hour. The correspondent on TV screen says, 'There is no headway in this stand off as no one can talk to the terrorist till tomorrow 8 O'clock and then only any negotiation is possible. Mr Jerald Goldsmith's plan appears to be extremely full proof, giving nobody a chance to play psychologically. We will be giving minute-to-minute reports to our viewers. Thanks."

Mrs John Fein (angrily)

"This bastard Goldsmith should be hanged. I do not know what is happening to my child."

Mr Geoffrey Hunt

"Do not worry mom. Everything would be allright. The Government would pay the ransom and get everybody out of there."

Micro-receiver's beep is heard thrice and catches the attention of Mrs John Fein and Mr Geoffrey Hunt. They switch off the TV and approach near it to hear the messages.

Loud Voice (from receiver, which sounds mechanised)

"Mom, I am allright and so is Sharn. I have seen and recognised three IRA activists amongst the gunmen of Mr Goldsmith. They are the ones who came to slay my father. I suspect if Mr Goldsmith is doing this on his own. The IRA activists and UK's ultranationalists can not share one platform. You said that Dad got wrongly entangled with a criminal organisation who were publicising themselves as the messiahs fighting for the independent Northern Ireland. It may be a possibility that Mr Goldsmith is working under pressure for these IRA criminals and these criminals are using Mr Goldsmith as their shield to give the whole scenario a different colour before escaping from the scene with the ransom. Tell Geoffrey to inform this fact to his department and find out the cause of pressure on Mr Goldsmith. Also kindly do not make this information or my presence public otherwise my life would be endangered. Thanks."

Mr Geoffrey Hunt

" Mom. I am going to David Lean at the London Headquarters. Only he can find the cause of pressure on Mr Goldsmith."

Mrs John Fein

"Tell him to keep this secret."

Mr Geoffrey Hunt

" Yes mom. I will..."

After wearing his leather jacket and cap he leaves the room.

Cut to:

53: INT: OFFICE OF Mr DAVID LEAN, THE CHIEF OF LONDON POLICE

Mr Geoffrey Hunt and Mr David Lean are talking in the office room. Mr David Lean is on his chair whereas Mr Hunt is standing on the otherside of the table.

Mr Geoffrey Hunt

"Sir, you need to believe me. Though they have cut all the communication but my wife is in consular hall of the Embassy and has a micro communication device as a ring in her finger that she innovated during her school days, which is unfortunately a one-way communication device. Due to this limitation, it could not get a commercial viability but is used by my wife and her mother to let the other their well being if one of them is out and another is at home."

Mr David Lean

"The situation is such that I have to believe you in a hope to find some clue of the real criminals. Let it be true."

Mr Geoffrey Hunt

"Thank you, Sir. We must find the reason as to why Mr Goldsmith is doing this."

Mr David Lean dials a number on his telephone and speaks....

Mr David Lean

"Hello, Mr Roland. Please find out about the family details of Mr Goldsmith and also see whether all of them are available at their respective places safe and sound. Kindly let me know this information as early as possible.Send your detectives right away to check on their well-being. Maintain secrecy at all point in this matter."

Mr David Lean disconnects the call.

Mr David Lean

"I think one can only follow someone's instruction because of threat to his own life or the near and dear. I cannot imagine anything else now."

Mr Geoffrey Hunt

"I am grateful, Sir. You believed me and I am sure some clue would be found in this matter. Sir, I will be back in an hour."

Mr David Lean

"Okay, see you soon."

Mr Geoffrey Hunt exits from the room.

Cut to:

<u>54: INT: MR JERALD GOLDSMITH'S HOUSE,DRAWING ROOM: DAY</u>

One Police detective is questioning the servant of Mr Jerald Goldsmith.

<u>Police Detective</u>
"Do you know today's incident?"

<u>Servant</u>
"Yes, I know."

<u>Police Detective</u>
"Could you kindly tell me the family details of Mr Goldsmith?"

<u>Servant</u>
"He is a widower and has a daughter."

<u>Police Detective</u>
"Where does she live? Where is she now?"

<u>Servant</u>
"She lives in Yorkshire. She is a Bank executive and holidaying in Spain these days at Valencia."

<u>Police Detective</u>
"Do you know if anyone else is a regular visitor to him?"

<u>Servant</u>
"He seldom meets anyone at home. He prefers meeting in his Parliament office or in lobby."

<u>Police Detective</u>
"Do you know someone who is very intimate to him."

<u>Servant</u>
"No, not to my knowledge."

<u>Police Detective</u>
"Thanks, thanks for cooperation."

<u>Servant</u>
"It's my privilege."

<u>Police Detective</u>
"Okay for now. I may come to you again."

Servant

"It's allright."

The Police detective walks away from the drawing room.

Cut to:

55: INT: LONDON POLICE HEADQUARTER:DAY

There are activities going on by police personnel inside the London Police Headquarter. The Police Detective who was questioning Mr Goldsmith's servant is dialing a telephone number.

Police Detective

" Hello, is it Spania Novotel Hotel in Valencia."

After hearing for a second, he again responds.

Police Detective

"Hello, I am calling from London. I am a friend of Nina Goldsmith who is staying in your hotel. I would like to talk to her please."

After hearing for a while, he again responds.

Police Detective

"How long she has been out of the hotel?"

After hearing he again responds and puts off his handset.

Police Detective

"Okay, I will call again."

He thinks for a while and again dials a number.

Police Detective

" I am sergeant Rudyard speaking. Could you put me through to Mr David Lean I need to talk to him.

He waits for a while before talking.

Police Detective

" Sir, I am Sergeant Rudyard speaking. Mr Goldsmith has a daughter named Nina Goldsmith who is presently holidaying at Valencia in Spain. I called at the Spania Novotel Hotel, where she is supposed to be staying. The receptionist of the hotel tells me that she has not collected her room key since the day before yesterday and has not checked out yesterday as scheduled, but her luggage is still in her room. I suspect some foul play with her by someone."

After hearing for a while, he responds.

Police Detective
"Okay. Thank you, Sir."

He leaves the handset down.

Cut to:
56: INT: LONDON POLICE HEADQUARTER, MR DAVID LEAN'S OFFICE ROOM:DAY

Mr David Lean and Mr Geoffrey Hunt are facing each other.

Mr David Lean
"Mr Hunt. Your information may be true. I am told that his daughter is missing from her hotel room, where she is supposed to be holidaying. She has not collected her room key since the day before yesterday and has not checked out from the hotel yesterday as scheduled. Her luggage is still in the hotel room. There may be a foul play by these IRA men."

Mr Geoffrey Hunt
"In that case, what action do you suggest for investigation?"

Mr David Lean
"As Spain is out of my jurisdiction, I need to talk to the Prime Minister to talk to his Spanish counterpart for possible help in finding her whereabout."

Mr Geoffrey Hunt
"But we do not have much time as they have threatened to kill the hostage by tomorrow morning."

Mr David Lean
"I am aware of that. I will suggest a combing operation around her holiday resort during the night so that we have results by tomorrow morning. If someone has kidnapped her, I sincerely hope that she may not have been taken out of the holiday resort."

Mr Geoffrey Hunt
"Let us hope, Sir."

Mr David Lean (asks his secretary on intercom)
"Miss Jenny, could you put me through the Prime Minister. I need to talk to him urgently."

Mr Geoffrey Hunt
"I will take your leave,Sir."

Mr David Lean

"Okay, Sergeant. I will come to your residence to see the information device. In case you get some more information from you wife, kindly let me know immediately."

Mr Geoffrey Hunt

"Yes Sir, certainly."

Loud Voice (from intercom)

"Sir, You can pick the receiver now. The Prime Minister would be talking to you, Sir."

Mr Geoffrey Hunt leaves the room.

Cut to :

57: EXT: OPEN GRAZING FIELD, A BEAUTIFUL LANDSCAPE IN SPAIN: DAWN

Four Spanish shepherd with a large contingent of sheep are riding on their horses slowly in the grazing ground. Their four watchdogs are keeping the sheeps in one flock. They are moving towards a desolate place which is an old, dilapidated and deserted farmhouse. These four shepherds on their horses are actually cops, who are on a combing operation to look for IRA kidnappers of Ms Nina Goldsmith. These shepherds are wearing cowboy hats that has a sealed walkie-talkie. When they are required to talk, they bring their hats near their month.

One Shepherd

"Everything appears to be normal."

Second Shepherd

"We will check the deserted farmhouse."

They reach near the dilapidated farmhouse and get down from their horses. They move towards an old hand pump for water. Suddenly two people in red robe and beard appear from the dilapidated building.

One bearded person

"What are you guys doing here? You cannot trespass to another's property."

One shepherd

"Sorry Sir, we are shepherds and feeling thirsty. We have come here looking for water or a can of beer, Sir."

Another bearded person

"That is not available here. Sorry."

<u>Second Shepherd</u>

"Thank you Sir. (to other shepherds) Guys let us go."

They go away from that place. Both the bearded men disappear from there.

Cut to:

<u>58: EXT: OPEN GRAZING FIELD, A BEAUTIFUL LANDSCAPE IN SPAIN: NIGHT</u>

Eight people on foot are moving cautiously towards the dilapidated building, out of which four are the same people who had disguised as shepherds. They are armed as they have pistol in their hands and two in their person. One man has a cat on his shoulder, which is quite. They have reached near the building wall. They move cautiously towards the basement staircase, where they can see a door and a window at the end. The door and window are open. They reach near the window and see two people sitting on the ground in candlelight. One cop shoots the two people at their temple with his silencer-equipped pistol from outside the window. Those two people die instantly. Four of the cops move inside the basement whereas the other four remain outside for vigil.

Cut to:

<u>59: INT: BASEMENT ROOMS: NIGHT</u>

Four cops cautiously move ahead to reach at the next door of the basement. The cop with a cat on his shoulder keeps the cat on the ground and takes out a remote control device from his pocket. This cat is actually a remotecontrolled toy cat but it appears as a real cat. He with the help of remote control sends the toy cat inside the other rooms of the basement. Another cop takes out a small LCD security TV from his pocket and switchs it on. He can now get the full view of the area inside the basement.

Cut to:

<u>60: INT; BASEMENT ROOMS ; NIGHT</u>

The cat moves and enters into a room where four people are sitting and two of them are sleeping on their chairs. A girl, whose hands and legs are tied and lips sealed with scotch tape, is lying on the ground on a rug. A candlelight is on. Seeing the cat inside the room one captor tries to catch her but the cat swiftly runs away from the room. The captor then goes back to his seat and he picks up a can of beer from the ground and drinks.

Cut to:

61 : INT: BASEMENT ROOMS: NIGHT

The cop holding the remote control device moves the cat from one room to another but can not see any person in any of the room except in the room where the girl is in captive condition.

They withdraw the cat, and keep the remote control and LCD security TV in their pockets. They become ready to move to the room, where four captors are sitting. There is extreme silence and they move forward very cautiously.

Cut to:

62: CAPTORS' ROOM IN BASEMENT: NIGHT

Four cops storm the room and stuns the four captors by aiming pistol on their temples.

One cop (on walkie-talkie)

"Come inside, mission accomplished. Take the girl away and also call the enforcement."

Two cops from outside rush there and untie the girl. Then they handcuff the captors.

Another eight cops rush inside the room within a minute and take away the four captors from the room.

Cop (on walkie-talkie to the girl)

"Are you Nina Goldsmith?"

Nina

Yes Sir, I am Nina Goldsmith."

Cop

"We are cops. Now you are free. Come with us."

All the cops and Nina Goldsmith go away from the basement room.

Cut to:

63: EXT : OPEN GRAZING FIELD, A BEAUTIFUL LANDSCAPE IN SPAIN: NIGHT

There are five police cars with red and white lights shining on the rooftop near the dilapidated building. The police chief comes near the building at that time the four captors are taken to the police car.

<u>Police Chief</u>
"Is there any death?"

<u>Cop (with walkie-talkie)</u>
"Yes Sir, two captors are dead inside the building."

<u>Police Chief</u>
"Collect the dead bodies."

The walkie-talkie with the Chief automatically gets on to receive message.

<u>Loud Voice (From walkie-talkie)</u>
"Hello, Chief Hunan. Report to Headquarters about the mission combing by night."

Chief answers through the walkie-talkie.

<u>Police Chief</u>
"Hello, Hunan speaking. Operation combing by night successful. Two captor dead and four captured. Total number six. Our side is fully safe and sound. Nina Goldsmith is also safe and sound. We are coming back."

<u>Loud Voice (from walkie-talkie)</u>
"Chief Hunan, Please send Nina Goldsmith to the airport immediately so that she can catch the flight for London, which has been delayed only for her at the airport. Kindly come to the airport to identify her before boarding. Keep this operation a top-secret basically away from the media."

<u>Police Chief</u>
" Yes, I am coming with Nina. Thanks."

He puts off his walkie-talkie. Police personnel are busy taking the dead bodies of the captor.

Cut to:
<u>64: INT: CONSULAR HALL, USA EMBASSY: MORNING</u>

<u>Second Day (On screen caption)</u>

All the visa applicants are tired. The gunmen also appear to be exhausted. Sharn woke up from sleep. He starts crying because he has defecated and urinated in his nappy and feeling uncomfortable. She is trying to comfort him but he is crying a lot. She gets up from the chair, opens his nappy pant and she removes it and after wiping his buttocks with the help of a paper napkin. She keeps him without nappy because she does not have additional nappies.

Lisa

"Sir, I would like to throw this nappy in the toiletbin."

Gunman

"Okay, go."

There is a toilet at the corner of the Consular Hall and a dustbin is kept just outside the toilet. Lisa leaves Sharn on her chair and goes to the toilet bin to throw the nappy and comes back to her chair. Sharn is still crying.

Lisa

"Sir, my son is hungry again. I need to feed him. Will you allow me to go to the kitchen."

Ronny, the gunman

" Yes, let us go."

Ronny and Lisa along with Sharn go away from the room.

Cut to:

65 : INT : KITCHEN OF THE EMBASSY OF FIRST FLOOR

Lisa enters into the kitchen along with Sharn and Ronny, the gunman. Ronny stands at the kitchen door. Lisa opens the wallmounted cupboards to take out the can of "Nido" milk.

Ronny

"Will you please make a cup of tea for me as well as for yourself, if you like."

Lisa

"Yes, Sir."

She puts water in the kettle. She plugs in the kettle for boiling. Exactly after a minute she puts off the electricity. She finds a packet of teabags.

Lisa

" Would you like your tea with milk or without milk and also tell me about the quantity of sugar."

Ronny

"Two-three cubes of sugar and without milk."

Lisa pours hot water in a cup and puts one teabag and three cubes of sugar. She gives the cup of tea with a spoon to Ronny. He accepts the cup of tea with a smile. She again pours hot water in a bowl and puts milk powder in it, then stirs with a spoon to make the milk for Sharn. After making the milk she sits on a kitchen stool and feeds Sharn with a tablespoon. He is happy after having his milk. When Lisa ends feeding her child, Ronny also finishes his tea. She keeps the utensils in the cupboard.

She exits the kitchen with Sharn, escorted by Ronny.

Cut to:

66 : INT: CORRIDOR OF THE FIRST FLOOR ADJACENT TO THE KITCHEN

Lisa is walking through the corridor of the first floor of the Embassy along with Sharn. They reach near the upper end of the stair case.

Another gunman (on first floor)
"Hello Ronny. It is boring. I really want to have tea."

Ronny (looks at him)
"I had it just now. Thanks to this lady and this little man."

Lisa becomes instrumental of a sudden fall of Sharn from the staircase when Ronny and the other gunman are busy among themselves. Lisa runs after him to stop him from falling further but by then Sharn has been hurt. Blood is oozing from his nose and forehead. He is crying uncontrollably.

Lisa (crying and weeping)
"Oh my god. Oh my god. Oh my god."

Ronny
"What happened?"

Lisa (weeping)
"He was trying to walk on his own but could not balance himself and fell down."

Ronny
" What to do now?"

Lisa
"I need a Doctor. Either I may be allowed to go out or a doctor should come from outside to treat my child. My husband is a doctor. He should be called."

Ronny (on his walkie-talkie)
"Boss, the infant boy has fallen from the staircase while trying to walk by himself. He is badly hurt. He requires medical help immediately."

<u>Loud Voice (from walkie-talkie)</u>
" Why was he on the staircase?"

<u>Ronny</u>
"He was hungry and I escorted him and his mother to the kitchen on firstfloor."

<u>Loud Voice (from walkie-talkie)</u>
"Okay, keep the child carefully. We will do something."

<u>Ronny</u>
"The child's father is a doctor, may be we can call him inside and I suppose it would not be counterproductive in anyway. We will be increasing the number of hostages and would not be leaking our information."

<u>Loud Voice (from walkie-talkie)</u>
"Okay, please keep the child carefully. We would take appropriate action."

Ronny and Lisa along with Sharn climb down from the staircase.

Cut to:
<u>67: ENT : CONSULAR HALL IN EMBASSY OF USA</u>

Ronny and Lisa along with unconscious Sharn come to the Consular Hall. Lisa sits on her chair and takes out her handkerchief. She tears it and ties it on Sharn's head to stop the oozing blood. She then secretly sends message through her micro-tip ring by touching the ground with her feet and micro-tip by finger.

Cut to:
<u>68: ENT ; DRAWING ROOM OF MRS JOHN FEIN ;DAY</u>

Mr Geoffrey Hunt is sitting on sofa and is in a gloomy mood. The TV is on but its volume is low. The TV repeats the same news of hostage taking of USA Embassy.

<u>Loud Voice from TV</u>
"Stand off is still continuing as Government is not able to negotiate as there is no communication. The government is trying to meet the demand of Mr Goldsmith and ensure the safety of the American diplomats."

Mrs John Fein brings a cup of tea for Geoffrey. Just then, the micro-receiver placed on TV beeps thrice. Geoffrey switches off the TV and listens to the message from the micro receiver.

Loud Voice (from micro receiver a mechanised sound is heard)
"Mom, I have purposely made Sharn fall from the staircase in order to go out for medical help or to call for medical help. They have agreed to call a doctor inside. Sharn will recover as the oozing blood from his head has stopped. I have told them that they should call my husband to treat Sharn, as he is a doctor. I lied in order to call Geoffrey inside as he can defuse bombs. I do not think that even after getting the ransom they will defuse the bombs until they have reached their hideouts. So Please ask Geoffrey to be ready in doctor's uniform with appropriate clinical kit as well as his tools for bomb disposal. He can inform this fact to his department or whatever he deems fit."

After this message the micro receiver goes blank.

Mrs John Fein
"Geoffrey, inform this fact to Mr David Lean. He should not send anyone else other than you or should not say that you are not a doctor but cop."

Mr Geoffrey Hunt picks up the phone and dials a number.

Mr Geoffrey Hunt
"Sir, I am sergeant Geoffrey Hunt speaking. I have received a message from my wife that she purposely made our son fall from the staircase in order to call for a medical help. She told them to call for her husband, who is a doctor, to treat the child. If they call you to send a doctor, then I will go inside the Embassy in a doctor's uniform with tool-kit. She says that my presence would be essential to defuse the bombs as and when they leave the building with ransom because she fears that they may not defuse these bombs until they have reached their hideouts."

After hearing from the other side, Geofrey answers back.

Mr Geoffrey Hunt
"Okay. Sir, I am coming to you right away."

He puts the phone down and gets up from the sofa without having the tea.

Mr Geoffrey Hunt
"Mom, I am going. Mr David Lean is asking me to be present in his office. He also says that Lisa's earlier message was true and Mr Goldsmith's daughter has been rescued from her captors in Spain and she is being brought here. I need to go immediately."

Mrs John Fein

"It is 6 O'clock. Will they call now because they have set a deadline of 8 O'clock today morning."

Mr Geoffrey Hunt

"If they have agreed to the request of Lisa then they will certainly call."

Cut to :

69 : INT ; MR DAVID LEAN'S OFFICE AT LONDON POLICE HEADQUARTERS : MORNING

Mr David Lean is sitting on his chair along with four other police personnel. Mr David Lean is talking on the phone.

Mr David Lean

"Okay, let her freshen up. Bring her to me at 7.45 a.m. sharp, when Mr Goldsmith is to call me."

Mr Geoffrey Hunt enters into his room and stands before him.

Mr Geoffrey Hunt

"Sir, did you receive any call from them."

Mr David Lean

"No, not yet. But I believe that there must be some introspection about making any decision at their end on this account. Let us wait and see."

The telephone bell rings and Mr David Lean picks up the phone and puts on the speakerphone so that every one present there could hear the conversation.

Mr David Lean

"Hello, I am David Lean speaking."

Loud Voice (from speaker phone)

"Mr David Lean. I am a close associate of Mr Jerald Goldsmith. We need medical help for an infant who is hurt. We understand that his father Mr Geoffrey Hunt is a doctor. We would like you to find Mr Geoffrey from 10 Grove Street near Macmillan Road, south of London and send him with his medical kit. I warn you against any possible smartness to be played by you or your cops. I hope you understand the gravity of the situation as there will be bloody consequences against your smartness."

Mr David Lean

"I understand. When should we send Mr Geoffrey Hunt?"

Loud Voice (from speaker phone)
"As soon as possible. Find him and send him."

Mr David Lean
"May I speak to Mr Goldsmith."

Loud Voice (from speaker phone)
" He would speak to you at 8 O'clock which is exactly after two hours."

It appears that the connection has been disconnected at the other end.

Mr David Lean
"Hello, Hello, Hello...."

He puts down the phone.

Mr David Lean (to Mr Geoffrey Hunt)
"Sergeant you would be going into the Embassy exactly after half an hour in a doctor's uniform with a medical kit including your own kit for bomb disposal concealed in the box."

Mr Geoffrey Hunt (in excitement)
"I would teach them a lesson."

Mr David Lean
"Sergeant, I know you are a daring cop. But you would have no mandate to do anything detrimental to the safety of the American diplomats. I make this point clear that our aim is to end the hostage drama peacefully with no casualty. So you will be a doctor inside and a mute spectator until they have left the building with the ransom and then you can defuse the bombs. The only mandate you have is to defuse the bombs as fast as possible and to let me know on your homely device, so that all the diplomats are taken out of the building immediately. Is that clear to you?"

Mr Geoffrey Hunt
"Yes, Sir."

Mr David Lean
"Now you can go and dress up yourself with a medical kit to leave for the Embassy exactly after half an hour."

Mr Geoffrey Hunt
"Okay, Sir. I will."

He leaves the room. Mr David Lean again puts on the speakerphone of his intercom device.

Mr David Lean

"Jenny, connect me to the Prime Minister."

Loud Voice(from Intercom)

"Yes Sir."

Mr David Lean is sitting and looks tense. After a while the intercom beeps.

Loud Voice (from Intercom)

"Sir, pick up the handset. The Prime Minister would be speaking to you."

Mr David Lean picks up the phone.

Mr David Lean

"Good morning Sir, I am David Lean speaking."

Hearing for a while, he again speaks.

Mr David Lean

"Sir, Miss Nina Goldsmith has been rescued. She would be talking to her father this morning. She would arrive in my office by 7.45 AM."

After a while, he again speaks.

Mr David Lean

"Despite of knowing the fact that Mr Goldsmith is not a criminal and that IRA men are behind this extortion, the situation has not changed. Now the IRA men would take the front seat and drive us. So we in any case have to fulfil their demand for the safety of the American diplomats."

He carefully listens..

Mr David Lean

"Yes, all arrangements have been made to fulfil their demands. The ransom amount and four military helicopters are ready for them. As soon as they contact at 8 O'clock, we will meet their demands."

Hearing for a while, he again speaks.

Mr David Lean

"I also hope that everything should end peacefully."

Hearing for a while, he again speaks.

Mr David Lean

"Okay, Sir. Thank you, Sir."

He keeps down the telephone handset.

Cut to:

<u>70 : EXT ; EMBASSY OF USA, LONDON ; MORNING</u>

Overview of the Embassy building and its adjacent road which has been cordoned off by police for their round the clock vigil. No journalist is seen at this hour. Mr Geoffrey Hunt is seen in front of the Embassy building in a doctor's uniform and with a kit box. He is ready to enter into the Embassy building after getting the signals from terrorists. One policeman announces his arrival on a handheld public address system to let the terrorists know that the doctor has come.

<u>Policeman (On PA system)</u>
" Hello. Doctor Geoffrey Hunt has come. He is ready to move into the Embassy. Please let him come inside the Embassy."

Seeing no response from the other side. He again repeats his message.

<u>Policeman (On PA system)</u>
" Hello. Doctor Geoffrey Hunt has come. He is ready to move into the Embassy. Please let him come inside the Embassy."

One Window of the first floor of the building is opened and a man signals in affirmation. After a few second one gunman appears near the Embassy gate to receive Mr Geoffrey Hunt.

Mr Geoffrey Hunt goes to him and enters inside the gate of the Embassy. The gunman is extremely alert. They both go inside the Embassy gate.

Cut to:

<u>71 : INT ; CONSULAR HALL OF THE EMBASSY: MORNING</u>

Mr Geoffrey Hunt enters the Consular Hall in a doctor's uniform and medical kit along with a gunman. Seeing Geoffrey in the consular hall, Lisa looks overwhelmed and happy. She gets up to receive him. Sharn, who was crying till now, stops crying and looks happy to find his father.

<u>Lisa</u>
"It is good that you are here. Sharn had a terrible fall."

<u>Mr Geoffrey Hunt</u>
"Do not worry. I will treat him now. Every thing would be allright."

Mr Geoffrey sits on a chair near Lisa and opens the kit to take out some ointment, cotton and bandage to dress the scull-wounds of Sharn.

Cut to:

72 : INT : OFFICE ROOM OF DAVID LEAN AT POLICE HEADQUARTERS ; MORNING

Mr David Lean, four police personnel and Ms Nina Goldsmith are sitting. The wall clock shows the time as 8 O'clock. They are looking at the telephone instrument in anticipation of a call at anytime. The telephone rings and Mr David Lean picks up the receiver and puts on the speakerphone.

Mr David Lean

"Hello. Good morning. This is David Lean speaking."

Loud Voice (Mr Goldsmith's sound from the speakerphone)

"Yes Mr David Lean. I would like to know whether my demands have been met by now."

Mr David Lean

"Yes Sir, everything has been arranged. Sir, as desired by you, the ransom amount and four helicopters are ready."

Loud Voice (Mr Goldsmith's sound from the speakerphone)

"That is great."

Mr David Lean

"Sir, you are our great politician and we are sure that you cannot be an extortionist."

Loud Voice (Mr Goldsmith's sound from the speakerphone)

"But for the cause of the integrated U.K., Mr David Lean!"

Mr David Lean

"Sir, your daughter would like to speak to you."

Loud Voice (Mr Goldsmith is surprised.)

" What? My daughter with you?"

Ms Nina Goldsmith

"Yes Dad. I am safe now. Do not follow any instructions from these bastards. The police have rescued me from my captors. Now you are free dad."

Loud Voice (Mr Goldsmith's sound from the speakerphone)

"Okay, honey. You saved me from any more sins. Now I am out of their clutches."

<u>Loud Voice (Another man's sound from the speakerphone)</u>

"Mr David Lean, I am Rudar Feinman. I was using Mr Goldsmith as my pawn. Despite exposing my game plan, you know that the situation has not changed drastically in your favour. The American diplomats including the Ambassador are our priceless hostages and some visa seekers too. If you play smart, these people would start dying immediately. Should I show a sample of dead body?"

<u>Mr David Lean</u>

"No Sir, that will not be necessary. I understand that you are in full command of the situation and nothing has changed so far. We have arranged your every demand."

<u>Loud Voice (Mr Rudar Feinman's sound from the speakerphone)</u>

"That is like a very wise and nice officer. Now Mr Lean I would like you to bring the four helicopters on the rooftop of the Embassy building with the ransom amount."

<u>Mr David Lean</u>

"As you desire, Sir."

<u>(Loud Voice (Mr Rudar Feinman's sound from the speakerphone)</u>

"It should be done immediately."

<u>Mr David Lean</u>

"I hope after receiving the ransom in full, all the hostages would be free including Mr Goldsmith."

<u>Loud Voice (Mr Rudar Feinman's sound from the speakerphone)</u>

"I know Mr Lean, you are much concerned about the American diplomats. Of course, they would be free but I would take Mr Goldsmith with me as a human shield to avoid any smartness from your side and ensure our safe journey to our hideouts."

<u>Mr David Lean</u>

"Sir, you are the smartest man."

<u>Loud Voice (Mr Rudar Feinman's sound from the speakerphone)</u>

"Thank you for the compliments. I would wait for the ransom and four helicopters for another ten minutes only."

<u>Mr David Lean</u>

"It would right away be available to you, Sir."

Suddenly Mr Rudar Feinman's sound is no more heard, it seems he has put off the telephone handset.

Mr David Lean
"Hello, Hello...Hello?"

Mr David Lean then disconnects the number and dials another number.

Mr David Lean
" Hello, Captain Dustan Hoff. These bastards would take Mr Goldsmith with them to use him as a shield. Captain you would follow these helicopters and execute our action plan in such a way that Mr Goldsmith is safe. Our action plan has to be changed a bit and executed before they cross the sea of England."

Mr David Lean ends the call and looks tense.

Cut to:
73: EXT: EMBASSY OF USA , LONDON :MORNING

It is an overview of the Embassy of USA building and their adjacent areas, where police personnel are still keeping the area cordoned off and are on high alert with their firearms. Four helicopters are seen descending on the roof of the Embassy building.

Cut to:
74: INT; AMBASSADOR'S ROOM : DAY

Mr Rudar Feinman, the conman of the operation and his five associates holding automatic guns are in the Ambassador's room. Mr Rudar Feinman is sitting on the chair of the Ambassador, whereas Mr Goldsmith is sitting on a couch. There is a TV in the Ambassador's room. Mr Rudar Feinman switches on the TV. BBC's live coverage is being telecast. BBC correspondence reports into the camera.

Loud Voice (from T.V)
"Today morning a startling revelation has been made by the London Police Headquarters, that Mr Jerald Goldsmith has not staged this hostagetaking episode to punish America for its favour to IRA cause but Mr Goldsmith had to do this under pressure from IRA terrorists. The IRA terrorists had kidnapped Ms Nina Goldsmith, the daughter of Mr Jerald Goldsmith, from her holiday resort in Spain and pressurised Mr Goldsmith to follow their instructions. Apparently to give this hostagetaking and extortion a different colour and escape from British Government's ire. The British detectives with the help of their counterpart in Spain have already rescued Ms Nina Goldsmith

from her captors in a Spanish hideout last night. Mr Rudar Feinman, a hardcore IRA terrorist, is the man behind this hostagetaking. Since the situation has not yet changed in favour of the Government, it has made all arrangements to meet the demands of Mr Rudar Feinman to ensure the safe release of American diplomats. Students' bloc in University of Cambridge has condemned the terrorist act of IRA men and has vowed to get even with thern. BBC will be present to cover the hours' top story as it unfolds today."

Mr Rudar Feinman picks up the remote control from the table and switches off the TV.

Mr Rudar Feinman (to two of his associates)
"Guider and Glenna go to the roof and let me know whether the four helicopters have arrived. In case, they have come, climb to the helicopters and see that all the ransom boxes are carrying money, gold and diamond."

Guider and Glenna
"Yes, Boss."

They leave the room.

Cut to:
75 : EXT; ROOF OF THE EMBASSY OF USA BUILDING; MORNING

Four helicopters have arrived on the roof of the building and are ready to fly at any moment. There is no one in these big military helicopters except the pilots. Guider and Glenna come to the roof and reach near the helicopters. They climb to each of the helicopters, where two big boxes are placed in each of the helicopters making a total of eight boxes containing money, gold and diamond. They open each and every box to check. Four boxes contain money whereas the other four boxes contain gold and diamond. After seeing the money, gold and diamond, they are very happy.

Guider (on his walkie-talkie)
"Boss, the helicopters have arrived with good money, gold and diamond. It looks very good. Now we can go. Come on up with every body."

Loud Voice (from walkie-talkie)
"You both wait there. We are coming."

Guider
"Yes, Boss."

Cut to:

76 : INT : AMBASSADOR'S ROOM : DAY

Mr Rudar Feinman gets up from his chair with a walkie-talkie. Three gunmen are sitting near him.

Mr Rudar Feinman (on walkie-talkie)

"Hello, everyone. The government has met our demands and four helicopters have arrived on the roof. We need to exit now. But before you exit, activate all the bombs on each of the wall. Do not forget to lock the door of the room from outside, where diplomats are putting on now. Hurry up and all of you reach the rooftop quickly."

Mr Rudar Feinman picks up the phone and dials a number.

Mr Rudar Feinman (in telephone)

" Hello, Mr David Lean. Thank you for meeting our demands. We are leaving the building and activating all the bombs, which I will be able to explode any minute by handheld remote controls in the event of slightest provocation from you enroute to my hideout in Northern Ireland. Secondly no one should try to cross the walls or get dropped on the roof or try to enter into the building in any way and create disturbances in the light rays of these live bombs. This would result in an automatic explosion of all the bombs. Beware of this fact and suitably advise your cops. I am taking Mr Goldsmith with me as I have told you earlier."

Mr Rudar Feinman disconnects the telephone. Mr Goldsmith is lying on the couch.

Mr Rudar Feinman

"Mr Goldsmith, you are coming with us."

Mr Goldsmith

" Why should I go with you? I will not."

Mr Rudar Feinman

"I will shoot you."

Mr Goldsmith

"I am ready to die but cannot follow your instruction anymore."

Mr Rudar Feinman (on walkie-talkie)

" Ten man report immediately in my room."

After a few second, ten of his associates arrive into the room.

<u>Mr Rudar Feinman (to all of them)</u>
"Mr Goldsmith is not cooperating. He is refusing to come with us but we need to take him as a deterrent for the police. Take him forcibly and put a tape on his mouth."

Before Mr Goldsmith could react, Rudar's ten associates surround him and put tape on his mouth. They also tie his hands and legs with a rope. Then they lift him and carry him away. Mr Rudar Feinman and his three gunmen follow them and exit from the Ambassador's room.

Cut to:
<u>77: INT: CONSULAR HALL OF USA- EMBASSY ; MORNING</u>

All visa and consular applicants are sitting on their chairs calmly including Ms Lisa, her husband Mr Geoffrey Hunt and son Sharn. The gunmen in the Consular hall are preparing to leave the hall. They have activated the bombs, two in this hall. A red ray emitting from each bombs merge with others making an aura of light.

<u>Ronny (to all the visa and Consular applicants)</u>
"Our demands have been met and we are leaving now. We have activated all the bombs on the Embassy walls including the wall of this hall. Our boss would deactivate these bombs with his remote controls after reaching our safe hideout in Northern Ireland. Till then none of you should try to go out of the building or even out of this hall. Disturbances or blockade in the emitting rays of these bombs would be a cause of vast explosion which would kill all the inmates of this building. Okay, Ladies and Gentlemen. It is our time to go. Thanks for cooperation."

Ronny along with his associate gunmen leave the Consular Hall. While leaving the Consular Hall they activate the bombs with the help of a remote control that are mounted on both ends of exit door, making it impossible for anyone to cross the rays emitted from the bombs and cross the exit door to go out of the hall.

Cut to:
<u>78 : EXT ; ROOF OF THE EMBASSY OF USA IN LONDON ;DAY</u>

This is an overview of the rooftop of the building of the Embassy of USA in London. Mr Rudar Feinman and his thirty associates including Mr Goldsmith get inside the helicopters. The British pilots get down from the helicopters and the IRA men takeover the seats of the pilots as per instruction of Mr Rudar Feinman. It is noisy on the rooftop because the whirring sound of lift fans of the four helicopters.

Ronny (to British pilots, while getting up to the helicopter)
"The staircase leading to the inside of the building has live bombs. If you cross the rays of the bombs, it will explode. So stay at the roof till we deactivate the bombs."

The British pilots are left behind on the roof and four helicopters, piloted by IRA men, ascend towards the sky carrying all the captors and Mr Goldsmith including the ransom.

Cut to:
79 : INT : DRAWING ROOM OF MRS JOHN FEIN: DAY

Mrs John Fein is sitting on the couch and is glued to the TV. The door bell rings. She gets up after switching off the TV and opens the door. She finds Mr David Lean along with three police personnel on the doorstep.

Mr David Lean
" Good morning, madam. I am David Lean, the police chief of London. Can we come in?"

Mrs John Fein
"Yes! Yes! I know you. Geoffrey, my son- in- law always talks about you and admires you."

Mr David Lean along with three police personnel enter into the room. They take out their overcoat. Mrs John Fein helps them to hang their overcoat from the coat hanger.

Mr David Lean
"Madam, our main purpose to visit your house was to see the one-way micro-communication device, which has been extremely helpful to track down the real culprit. Otherwise our beloved Member of Parliament Mr Goldsmith could have been branded as a hardcore terrorist."

Before Mrs John Fein could utter a word, the micro receiver on the top of the TV beeps thrice and a mechanised sound is heard. It catches everybody's attention. They are curious and move towards the micro-receiver.

Mrs John Fein
"This is the micro-receiver. My daughter Lisa is sending some message."

Loud Voice (mechanised sound from receiver)
"Mom. These IRA men have left the building but have activated all the bombs. We can not get out of the consular hall until the bombs mounted on the wall emanating red rays are defused. Geoffrey has opened a bomb device and finds the inner structure confusing. He is impressed of the masterly crafting of the bomb device. There are many wires and all confusing. He is still trying to think as to which wire is vital and should be cut for its diffusion."

After hearing the message, everyone present in the drawing room look grim.

Cut to:
80 : INT : CONSULAR HALL OF THE EMBASSY OF USA IN LONDON: DAY

Mr Geoffrey Hunt is standing and trying to defuse a bomb mounted on the wall. Lisa is also standing nearby. Sharn is sleeping in the lap of an old lady, who is amongst the visa applicants. A few men are also standing nearby and looking curiously.

One man
" Are you sure Mister that you can defuse this bomb? Are you an amateur trying to save us? I understand you are a doctor."

Lisa
" He is an amateur Doctor and a chief specialist of bomb disposal squad of London Police. His name is Detective Geoffrey Hunt."

Same man
" Is he your husband?"

Lisa
"Yes. He is my husband."

Same man
"Is that child yours?"

Lisa
"Yes."

Mr Geoffrey Hunt (angrily)
"Keep quiet. Do not talk and distract my attention, otherwise every one of us will die."

Lisa (to that person)
"Now everybody go and sit on your respective chairs. There should be no murmuring at all."

Cut to:

81 : EXT ; FOUR HELICOPTERS FYING IN THE SKY: DAY

Four helicopters, carrying the captors and Mr Goldsmith, are flying in the sky of the city of London. All of a sudden sixteen helicopters appear in the sky and each helicopter is carrying military personnel on aboard. Soon four military helicopters surrounds each enemy helicopter. One military helicopter speeds ahead and comes parallel to the enemy helicopter carrying Mr Rudar Feinman and Mr Goldsmith on aboard. Mr Rudar Feinman and his associates are stunned to see the military helicopters chasing them. Mr Rudar Feinman looks excited and angry.

Military Captain (on aboard the helicopter flying parallel speaks in his walkie-talkie)

"I am the military captain Dustan Hoff speaking. Sir."

Mr Rudar Feinman's walkie-talkie automatically turns on and Dustan Hoff's words are heard.

Mr Rudar Feinman (in his walkie-talkie)

" Why are you chasing us? Are you not aware that I have the remote controls and can explode the Embassy at once."

Military Captain (on aboard the helicopter flying parallel speaks on his walkie-talkie)

" Yes. Sir, I know this fact. We have information that students' extremist bloc in the University of Cambridge are planning to blow your helicopter with the help of paid Afghan mercenaries. We have come to your rescue, Sir, to ensure your safe passage to your hideout and consequently the safe release of American diplomats. We also request you to release Mr Goldsmith enroute to your hide out, Sir."

Mr Rudar Feinman (in his walkie-talkie)

"Captain if you are trying to fool me by telling a concocted story then I assure you that you would find the American diplomats dead any time. So do not try to outsmart me."

Military Captain (on aboard the helicopter flying parallel speaks in his walkie-talkie)

" No Sir, we can not dare to do that. We do not have such mandate except to ensure your safe passage and safe release of the American diplomats including Mr Goldsmith."

Mr Rudar Feinman (in his walkie-talkie)
"The American diplomats would be released when we reach our safe hideout. But you must not try to cross the sea of England and enter into our territory. If you do so, you would lose your helicopters and would be returning to London on foot."

Military Captain (on aboard the helicopter flying parallel speaks in his walkie-talkie)
"Sir, we will follow your instruction. But kindly release Mr Goldsmith."

Mr Rudar Feinman (in his walkie-talkie)
"(Laughs) Captain, he is our big catch. He has been our stern enemy, advocating against our cause. He has to sacrifice himself for the IRA cause."

Military Captain (on aboard the helicopter flying parallel speaks in his walkie-talkie)
"No Sir, you would be making a mistake if you harm him or kill him. Most of Europe is a democratic and every body has a right of expression and so too Mr Goldsmith. Sir, if you violate the democratic norms, you would be isolated in the International community, which largely appreciate democratic norms and behaviour."

Mr Rudar Feinman
"I do not want to talk to you anymore."

Mr Rudar Feinman switches off the walkie-talkie.

Pilot (of the enemy helicopter carrying Mr Rudar Feinman)
"Is he trying to fool us by chatting?"

Mr Rudar Feinman
"He cannot befool us as long as this remote device is in my hand.(showing remote device)"

Pilot (of the enemy helicopter carrying Mr Rudar Feinman)
" We will kill this bastard Goldsmith. If you allow, I will release him by throwing him out of our flying helicopter."

Mr Rudar Feinman
"He will be suitably punished in our hideout. So do not worry."

Captain Dustan Hoff, inside the military helicopter that is flying parallel to the enemy helicopter, dials a number on a cellular mobile phone.

Captain Dustan Hoff (in mobile phone)
" Hello Sir, this is Dustan Hoff speaking."

Cut to:

82: INT: DRAWING ROOM OF MRS JOHN FEIN ; DAY

Mr David Lean and his three junior colleagues are still at the residence of Mrs John Fein. They are sitting on the couch. Mr David Lean is talking on his Cellular phone. Mrs John Fein brings tea for them.

Mr David Lean (In his mobile phone)
" Yes, Captain Hoff. Please go on. I am listening."

After hearing for a while, he again speaks into the phone.

Mr David Lean (in his mobile phone)
"Captain, you continue to follow them. As and when I confirm the completion of the bomb disposal, you fulfil your mandate. Till then you keep talking to them."

Mr David Lean turns off his phone. He appears to be tense. He picks up his tea-cup.

Mr David Lean (to his other colleagues)
"They have heinous design. They would kill Mr Goldsmith, if they reach to their hideouts to avenge their cause. They are not ready to release him at all."

Micro-receiver at the top of the TV beeps thrice and every body present in the room become attentive and silent.

Loud Voice (a mechanised sound is heard)
"Mom. Geoffrey defused two bombs in the consular hall; the structures of each bomb was different from the other. That is why it took half an hour. We are out of the consular hall and have seen that all the exit door leading to outside of the building is covered by the bomb-rays. There appears to be more than twenty-five bombs. The task to defuse all of them is enormous, in case the structures are very different from each other. Kindly speak to Mr David Lean and tell this fact and ask him to gather a group of bomb disposal unit to enter into the building if Geoffrey is able to clear a passage for them. We are to find an easy passage, which Geoffrey can clear for them. Okay, Mom."

Mr David Lean immediately dials a number on his phone.

Mr David Lean (speaks into the mobile phone)
" Hello, Sergeant Cavin Blair. I am David Lean speaking. Thirty personnel of your bomb disposal unit may arrive right now outside

the USA Embassy to enter into the building for bomb disposal as and when I signal to you."

Cut to:

83 : INT : EMBASSY OF USA , LONDON : DAY

Lisa and Geoffrey Hunt (carrying his toolkit) are walking through the hallway of the Embassy.

Lisa

"They have closed all the exit routes."

Mr Geoffrey Hunt

"They have mounted more bombs on the exit side from where they came inside the building and left the building. May be the back door is spared."

Lisa

"Let us see."

Lisa and Geoffrey Hunt walk through the passage and reach the back door, where they can see that two bombs are mounted on both side of the door.

Mr Geoffrey Hunt

"I believe, if I clear this door then there may not be more hurdles and our men can come in from the back."

Lisa

"I also think so. Helicopters can drop our men in the backyard lawn."

Mr Geoffrey Hunt

"Okay. Let me work then..."

Mr Geoffrey Hunt opens his tool kit and takes out a knife and a screwdriver to open the bomb.

Cut to:

84 : EXT : TWENTY HELICOPTERS FYING IN THE SKY : DAY

Twenty helicopters are flying in the sky far away from London. Mustard grown farm field is seen from above the sky. Four military helicopters cover each enemy helicopter. Mr Rudar Feinman turns back and can see the helicopter of Captain Dustan Hoff, which is chasing them. Mr Rudar Feinman turns his walkie-talkie on and speaks into it.

Mr Rudar Feinman (into his walkie-talkie)
"Hello Captain."

Walkie-talkie of Mr Dustan Hoff in other helicopter automatically turns on and Mr Rudar Feinman's voice is heard.

Military Captain (on aboard the helicopter flying parallel speaks in his walkie-talkie)
"Yes, Sir."

Mr Rudar Feinman (into his walkie-talkie)
"Now you need not escort us. We are far away from London and I do not find a threat."

Military Captain (on aboard the helicopter flying parallel speaks in his walkie-talkie)
"But, Sir, I have mandate to escort you up to the border of your territory to ensure proper safety of American Diplomats. I cannot withdraw until I reach up to your territory, Sir."

Mr Rudar Feinman (into his walkie-talkie)
"I do not see a threat and I am telling you to go back."

Military Captain (on aboard the helicopter flying parallel speaks in his walkie-talkie)
"I can only withdraw if you deactivate the bombs and throw away the remote controls and I also need to receive a confirmation from my boss that the Embassy building has been secured and the diplomats are safe."

Mr Rudar Feinman (into his walkie-talkie)
"I am not a fool. The remote is the actual deterrent for you. It ensures our safety from you. The military! The butchers!"

Military Captain (on aboard the helicopter flying parallel speaks in his walkie-talkie)
"Sir, you must trust us."

Mr Rudar Feinman (into his walkie-talkie)
"I do not trust you and I will not trust you."

Military Captain (on aboard the helicopter flying parallel speaks in his walkie-talkie)
"Then let me do my duty to escort you and ensure your safety as well as the safety of American diplomats. As all the twenty helicopters flying in the sky are of the same colour and size, assailant, however smart he may be, would keep guessing as to where to fire his missile."

Cut to:

85: INT: DRAWING ROOM OF MRS JOHN FEIN ; DAY

Mr David Lean and his three junior colleagues are still at the residence of Mrs John Fein. They are sitting on the couch and looking through magazines to pass their time. Micro receiver on the top of the TV beeps thrice and catches the attention of everyone present in the room.

Loud Voice (mechanised sound from receiver)
"Mom, Geoffrey has cleared an exit door towards the backyard of the Embassy. You may speak to Mr David Lean to drop about thirty personnel of bomb disposal unit in the backyard by helicopters to come inside the Embassy building to secure it. Let the helicopter not touch the ground. Keeping in view the bomb structure, Geoffrey says that the extreme vibration may cause an automatic blast. Now I am taking out all the visa applicants to the backyard."

Mr David Lean, his three colleagues and Mrs John Fein are happy and smiling. Mr David Lean turns his Cellular phone on and dials a number.

Mr David Lean (speaks into the phone)
"Hello, Sergeant Cavin Blair. I am David Lean speaking. You may drop thirty personnel of your bomb disposal unit at the backyard of the USA Embassy using the helicopters. Instruct the helicopter pilots that they do not touch down the ground. Ask your personnel to finish the job fast. You be in touch with me on walkie-talkie and report me every minute."

Mr David Lean turns his phone off. He gets up from the couch and so does his three colleagues, apparently to leave the place.

Mr David Lean (to Mrs John Fein)
"Your daughter and son-in-law have done a great job to the nation and I am proud of them. I am proud of the micro-device, a fantastic innovation of your daughter, which has done a great service to this nation. I will recommend for a royal medal for them from her majesty's government. Now Madam, I would take your leave and see further course of action."

Mrs John Fein
"Thank you for praising Lisa and Geoffrey. I would also like to go with you to meet them as and when they are out of the building."

Mr David Lean

"That is good. Let us go."

They move towards the exit door.

Cut to:

86 : EXT : BACKYARD OF THE EMBASSY OF USA, LONDON: DAY

A military helicopter is seen descending towards the ground and after a few seconds stables itself in the air. The lateral door of the helicopter is opened and military personnel, equipped with their toolbox on their back, jumps from the helicopter on the ground. When thirty personnel have jumped from the helicopter, the helicopter flies away from there. They are silent. Mr Geoffrey Hunt is seen in the backyard welcoming all of them by waving his hands. He takes all of them towards the exit door of the building in the backyard. Every one of them enters into the building.

Cut to:

87 : EXT : TWENTY HELICOPTERS FYING IN THE SKY : DAY

Twenty helicopters are flying in the sky far away from London and above the sea of England. Blue water surface of the sea of England is seen all over from the sky. Four military helicopters cover each enemy helicopter. Mr Rudar Feinman turns back and can see the helicopter of Captain Dustan Hoff, which is chasing them. Mr Dustan Hoff turns his mobile phone, dials a number and speaks into it.

Mr Dustan Hoff (into the mobile phone)

"Sir, we are flying above the sea of England and are shortly reaching the territory of the Northern Ireland. I am afraid; we may have to abort our mission if you do not signal before the end of the sea of England. I would need your confirmation while we are above the sea of England, Sir, otherwise everything would go futile."

After hearing for a while, he turns his phone off. He looks very tense and so does the pilot of the helicopter.

Pilot of the helicopter (to Mr Dustan Hoff)

" What he says?"

Mr Dustan Hoff

"He says that it would take ten more minutes. He asks us to wait."

Pilot of the helicopter (to Mr Dustan Hoff)
"But I am afraid, we would cross the sea within ten-eleven minutes."

Mr Dustan Hoff
"This bastard Feinman has the remote. What to do except to wait for confirmation of the bomb disposal group."

Pilot does not speak further. Mr Rudar Feinman is on his helicopter and turns his walkie-talkie on and speaks into it.

Mr Rudar Feinman (into his walkie-talkie)
"Hello Captain".

Walkie-talkie of Mr Dustan Hoff in other helicopter automatically turns on and Mr Rudar Feinman's voice is heard.

Military Captain (on aboard the helicopter flying parallel speaks in his walkie-talkie)

" Yes, Sir."

Mr Rudar Feinman (into his walkie-talkie)
" Now we are above the sea of England and just near our territory. I think, there is no need for you to escort us further. Anyway I am thankful to you for facilitating us the safe passage."

Military Captain (on aboard the helicopter flying parallel speaks in his walkie-talkie)
"Sir, I assure you that we will not cross over the sea and enter into your territory. But we will ensure your safety above the sea from any attack from sea-bandits."

Mr Rudar Feinman
"I think, there is no need to do that."

Military Captain (on aboard the helicopter flying parallel speaks in his walkie-talkie)

"Sir, let me do my duty."

Cut to:
88 : EXT : EMBASSY OF USA, LONDON: DAY

It is a frontal view of the Embassy of USA building and their adjacent areas, where police personnel are still keeping the area cordoned off and are on high alert with their firearms. A jeep comes to this place and stops. Mr David Lean, his three junior colleagues and Mrs John Fein get down from the jeep. Mr David Lean is holding a walkie-talkie in his hand. One police captain comes to him.

<u>Police Captain</u>
"Good day, Sir."

<u>Mr David Lean</u>
"How is everything here?"

<u>Police Captain</u>
"The bomb disposal is yet to be confirmed Sir, before we could enter into the building for a thorough check."

Mr David Lean turns his walkie-talkie on and speaks into it.

<u>Mr David Lean (into his walkie-talkie)</u>
"Hello, Sergeant Cavin Blair. You need to get things done fast. Time is running out. We may have to abort our mission unless you confirm within five minutes. Report the situation."

<u>Loud Voice (Cavin Blair's voice is heard from the walkie-talkie)</u>
"Sir, we have accomplished almost ninety per cent of work. The room, where the diplomats are locked and the exit door leading to the front side of the building is to be secured. I hope it would be possible within five minutes. Sir."

<u>Mr David Lean (sees his watch and speaks into his walkie-talkie.)</u>
"Okay, do it fast and confirm."

Cut to:
<u>89 : EXT : TWENTY HELICOPTERS FYING IN THE SKY : DAY</u>

Twenty helicopters are flying in the sky far away from London and above the sea of England. The sea of England is about to end. Four military helicopters cover each enemy helicopter. Mr Dustan Hoff and the pilot are extremely tense. They are looking into their watches and eagerly awaiting a call on their phone.

Cut to:
<u>90 : INT : EMBASSY OF USA, LONDON: HALLWAYS : DAY</u>

The two police personnel complete the bomb disposal on the door of the locked room and Mr Cavin Blair opens the door. He enters into the room.

Cut to:
<u>91 : INT : EMBASSY OF USA, LONDON: ROOM:DAY</u>

Mr Cavin Blair enters into the room, where all the diplomats are either sitting on chairs or lying on the ground. They look questioningly at Mr Cavin Blair.

Mr Cavin Blair

"I am Sergeant Cavin Blair. You have been rescued. Come quickly out of the building. Follow me and hurry up."

Mr Cavin Blair exits from the room and so do the diplomats. They empty the room immediately.

Cut to:

92 : INT : EMBASSY OF USA, LONDON: EXIT DOOR LEADING TO OUTSIDE:DAY

Police personnel open the exit door leading to the outside of the building after the bomb disposal. All the diplomats move out of the building through the exit door.

Mr Cavin Blair (speaks into his walkie-talkie)

"Sir, our mission is complete. Diplomats and others are moving out. We may, however, do a thorough check of the building."

Loud Voice (Mr David Lean's voice is heard from the walkie-talkie) "Thanks sergeant. Do as you deem fit."

Cut to:

93 : EXT : EMBASSY OF USA, LONDON: DAY

It is a frontal view of the Embassy of USA building in London. Mr David Lean, Mrs John Fein and other police personnel are eagerly waiting. Mr David Lean dials a number on his mobile phone and speaks into it.

Mr David Lean (speaks into his phone)

"Captain Dustan Hoff."

After hearing from Mr Dustan Hoff, he again speaks into the phone.

Mr David Lean (speaks into his mobile phone)

"Captain, the threat is over and everybody secured. Now accomplish your mission. God bless you."

Mr David Lean disconnects his phone. Embassy's frontal gate is opened and diplomats as well as visa applicants come out of the building. Lisa along with Sharn and Geoffrey Hunt come to Mrs John Fein and they hug each other. The Ambassador of USA comes to Mr David Lean and he moves forward to welcome him.

Ambassador
"Thank you, David."

Mr David Lean hugs the Ambassador.

Cut to:
94 : EXT : TWENTY HELICOPTERS FYING IN THE SKY : DAY

Twenty helicopters are flying in the sky far away from London and above the sea of England. Four military helicopters cover each enemy helicopter. Buildings on the seashore are seen not very far away from their position. Mr Rudar Feinman and his associates are happy to find that they are to reach the seashore of their territory. Mr Dustan Hoff and his pilot are very tense. Mr Dustan Hoff has received the message on his phone. The pilot of his helicopter positions his mouthpiece of wireless.

Pilot
"All sea-hawks! Be ready to strike at once. Operation Gold haul begins. One...two....three."

Each of the sixteen military helicopters shoots an arrow, the tail of which is tied with a strong nylon rope and in control at their end. Arrow is pointed towards the bottom hold of enemy helicopter and therefore a group of four helicopters are in control of one enemy helicopter due to nylon rope's metallic end tied with the bottom hold of it. Suddenly military helicopters dive towards sea surface very fast making each enemy helicopter imbalanced and making them to fall into the sea. In this course of action all sixteen helicopters are flying just above the sea surface, whereas enemy helicopters are drowned into the sea with everybody on aboard. Drowning into the sea does not allow the enemy helicopters to burst into flames. The armed military divers jump from their helicopters into the sea to save Mr Goldsmith and the box containing ransom amount.

Cut to:
95 : INT: UNDERWATER OF THE SEA OF ENGLAND :DAY

Enemy helicopters are seen completely drowned into the water. Military divers are equipped with oxygen cylinders on their back and are searching for Mr Goldsmith. They find that Mr Goldsmith is in the cabin of Mr Rudar Feinman. Mr Rudar Feinman is trying to come out of the cabin and so too Mr Goldsmith but Mr Rudar Feinman is trying to lock him inside the cabin after coming out of the cabin. A military diver shoots Mr Rudar Feinman into his head and pulls Mr Goldsmith out of the cabin. Mr Rudar Feinman's dead body is floating in the sea.

A bloody fight between the military divers and the IRA men is seen below the water. IRA men are frantically trying to come out to the sea surface in order to inhale and breathe whereas military divers are trying to keep them inside the water to suffocate them. Because the military divers are almost four times more in number than IRA men, each IRA men are handled by four military divers and are being assaulted by them with knife and pistols. The IRA men are bleeding helplessly and are destined to die in the sea.

Cut to:

96 : EXT : OVERVIEW OF THE WATER SURFACE OF SEA OF ENGLAND : DAY

Sixteen helicopters are flying above the water surface of the sea of England and a ladder made of rope from each helicopter are hanging above the sea surface to enable the military divers to aboard the helicopters. Blue water surface of the sea of England is seen all over from the above.

One by one military divers are appearing above the sea surface after killing all the IRA men. Two divers are seen with the box of ransom, whereas four divers are trying to comfort Mr Goldsmith. After a while, when Mr Goldsmith is at ease, they help him aboard the helicopter of Captain Dustan Hoff, who is trying to give a moral support from the above to help him climb the ladder and to aboard the helicopter.

Captain Dustan Hoff (to Mr Goldsmith)

"Come on Sir, we are victorious now. You are safe. Come on..."

Mr Goldsmith is able to aboard the helicopter. He sits beside Captain Dustan Hoff. Four military divers bring the ransom box into the helicopter. All divers come back and sit in the helicopter.

Captain Dustan Hoff

"Sir, I am Captain Dustan Hoff, leading the contingent of 'Operation Gold haul'.

Mr Goldsmith

"Thank you Captain. I am extremely grateful to you. You have saved me from dying."

Captain Dustan Hoff (into his walkie-talkie)

" All sea-hawks report back to the headquarters. Mr Goldsmith is on board and I am taking him to the Headquarters including the ransom."

The pilot carrying Mr Dustan Hoff and Mr Goldsmith navigates his helicopter to ascend towards the sky and makes a U-turn to come to London.

Captain Dustan Hoff (dials a number in his phone and speaks into the phone)

"Sir, Captain Dustan Hoff reporting. Operation Gold haul successful. Mr Goldsmith is on board and so are the ransom boxes. The enemy is dead. No casualty on our side."

The pilot carrying Mr Dustan Hoff and Mr Goldsmith speeds and navigates the helicopter above the sea to reach London. All the other helicopters are also following the same course of action. After a few seconds all the sixteen helicopters are flying above the sea of England. All military personnel aboard the sixteen helicopters are jubilant. The blue water surface of the sea of England is seen from above the sky. The sun is shining in the sky. It also appears to be jubilant with the victory of good over evil.

Fade out:

The End